No Grid Survival Projects Bible

Discover the Key to Thriving Off the Grid with an All-In-One Resource for 2500 Days, DIY Projects, Home Security, Sustainable Living for a Thriving Homestead

Max Maverick

Table of Content

MODULE A: OFF-GRID ESSENTIAL

Chapter 1: Introduction to Off-Grid Living

The Essence of Living Off-Grid

Living off-grid means choosing a life less dependent or entirely independent from conventional urban networks such as electricity, water, and heating. This choice is often driven by a desire for greater control over one's life, an intent to reduce one's ecological footprint, and a pursuit of a more harmonious existence with nature.

The Benefits of Choosing This Lifestyle

Autonomy: Managing your own energy, food, and water resources independently.
Economic Savings: Reduced utility bills and lesser dependence on public services.
*Lower Environmental Impact***:** Adoption of sustainable technologies and reduction of waste.
Improved Quality of Life: A deeper connection with nature and often a less stressful living rhythm.

Challenges of Off-Grid Living

Despite numerous benefits, transitioning to an off-grid lifestyle also presents significant challenges:
Initial Investment: Setting up renewable energy systems and infrastructures can require a substantial financial outlay.
*Technical Skills***:** A certain level of technical expertise is necessary to manage and maintain off-grid systems.
Isolation: In some areas, living off-grid can also mean less proximity to medical, educational, and entertainment services.

Content Overview

This book guides the reader through various aspects of off-grid life, from generating energy to water collection, from self-produced food to emergency self-sufficiency and security. Each book in the bundle delves into a specific theme, offering detailed and practical guidance for anyone wishing to embark on this lifestyle path.

Basic Survival Skills Everyone Should Know

Survival skills are essential for anyone, particularly those choosing to live off-grid. These skills not only prepare you for emergencies but also enhance daily life by fostering a deep connection with the environment and increasing self-reliance.

Essential Skills for Off-Grid Living

Emergency Preparedness: Understanding how to prepare and respond to emergencies is crucial. This includes creating an emergency plan and having a well-stocked survival kit.
Navigation: Skills in using a compass, reading maps, and understanding natural navigational cues are vital, especially in remote areas.
Food Foraging and Hunting: Knowing how to identify edible plants, track and hunt animals, and fish responsibly can be invaluable.
Water Procurement and Purification: Finding and purifying water is a life-saving skill. Techniques include boiling, chemical purification, and filtration.
First Aid: Basic first aid knowledge is necessary for dealing with common injuries and health issues. This includes learning how to treat wounds, manage fractures, and recognize symptoms of major health conditions.
Shelter Building: Being able to construct a temporary shelter using natural or improvised materials can protect you from adverse weather conditions.

Integrating Skills into Daily Life

Incorporating these survival skills into daily routines not only prepares one for potential emergencies but also enriches the off-grid living experience. It cultivates a lifestyle of preparedness, awareness, and respect for nature.
Mastering these basic survival skills is not just about ensuring safety and survival. It's about enhancing independence and confidence, making you better equipped to handle the challenges of off-grid living and enjoying the freedom it brings.

Chapter 2: The Empowering Journey of Self-Sufficiency: Reasons to Embrace This Lifestyle

Complete Control Over Your Life

The decision to become self-sufficient is rooted, in large part, in the desire for autonomy and control over one's life. It's not about restrictive control, but rather about freedom from reliance on external systems that can often prove unpredictable or unreliable.

Freedom from Market Volatility

One of the realities of our modern world is the volatility of markets. Prices for goods and services fluctuate based on various factors beyond our control. Whether it's an increase in fuel prices affecting the cost of heating your home or a spike in food prices due to poor harvests or increased transportation costs, these changes can significantly impact our daily lives and financial stability. In contrast, self-sufficiency provides a more predictable cost of living. Growing your own food, generating your own energy, and sourcing your own water can insulate you from market volatility. You have a direct hand in producing what you need, reducing costs, and eliminating uncertainty associated with market fluctuations.

Protection Against Supply Chain Disruptions

Our modern economy relies on complex and interconnected supply chains spanning countries and continents. Despite the advantages of this interconnection, changes in one region of the world might affect the availability and cost of goods in other regions. Self-sufficiency offers a buffer against these disruptions. If your food comes from your garden, a drought halfway across the world won't make your grocery bills skyrocket. If your power comes from solar panels on your roof, a disruption in the supply of natural gas won't leave you in the cold.

Confidence in Quality and Safety

When we rely on external sources for our needs, we also have to trust in the quality and safety of the products we consume. Unfortunately, this trust is sometimes misplaced, as stories of contaminated food, dangerous products, and unethical business practices are all too common. On the other hand, self-sufficiency gives you the confidence of knowing exactly where your resources come from and how they were produced. You know that the food you grow is free from harmful pesticides, the water you drink is properly filtered, and the energy you use doesn't contribute to pollution. In addition to providing tangible resources, self-sufficiency also delivers an intangible sense of security, control, and tranquility of mind. It's about taking back your autonomy and molding your life to fit your wants and values. It's about taking control of your fate rather than just being a bystander.

Re-establishing a Connection with Nature

In today's digitally-driven and urbanized world, it's easy to lose touch with nature. We spend our days surrounded by concrete and screens, often disconnected from the natural world and its cycles. Embracing self-sufficiency offers a way to mend this disconnection, inviting nature back into our lives in a meaningful and symbiotic manner.

Understanding and Appreciating Natural Cycles

One of the most profound ways in which self-sufficiency reconnects us with nature is through understanding and appreciating natural cycles. When you grow your own food, you become intimately aware of the changing seasons and how they impact growth cycles. You learn to work with nature, planting in sync with the seasons, and understanding the important role that weather, sunlight, and pollinators play in the growth of your crops. Similarly, when you generate your own energy—whether through solar, wind, or hydropower—you become more attuned to natural patterns. You understand the power of the sun, the force of the wind, or the flow of water in a personal and immediate way. This deepened understanding can foster a sense of awe and appreciation for nature's rhythms and complexities. It can also lead to a more sustainable lifestyle as you learn to work with, rather than against, these natural cycles.

Living More Sustainably and Responsibly

Becoming self-sufficient encourages a more sustainable and responsible way of living. When we source our own food, water, and energy, we become more mindful of our consumption. We value these resources more, waste less, and become more committed to conserving them. Furthermore, many aspects of self-sufficiency—such as growing organic food, using renewable energy, or recycling water—directly contribute to environmental sustainability. By living more sustainably, we can reduce our ecological footprint and live in harmony with the environment, rather than at its expense.

Promoting Mental and Emotional Well-being
Finally, re-establishing a connection with nature through self-sufficiency can have significant benefits for our mental and emotional well-being. Numerous studies have shown that exposure to nature can reduce stress, boost mood, and improve mental health. When we engage with nature in a direct, hands-on manner—such as gardening, installing solar panels, or setting up a water collection system—we not only benefit from these positive effects but also actively participate in the natural world. This can lead to feelings of relaxation, satisfaction, and fulfillment that are hard to find in the hustle and bustle of modern urban life. Re-establishing a connection with nature is one of the most profound and rewarding aspects of the self-sufficiency journey. It's about understanding and appreciating natural cycles, living more sustainably, and promoting mental and emotional well-being. It's about reconnecting with the natural world and rediscovering our place within it.

Enjoying the Benefits of Homegrown Food
One of the most tangible and gratifying benefits of a self-sufficient lifestyle is the ability to produce your own food. This goes beyond reducing grocery bills or avoiding the logistics of supermarket shopping. Growing your own food comes with numerous benefits that significantly enhance your health, sense of fulfillment, and connection to the food you consume.

Boosting Nutritional Value
Homegrown food is often more nutritious than store-bought produce. Fruits and vegetables start to lose their nutritional value as soon as they're harvested, and it can be days or even weeks before they end up on supermarket shelves. By contrast, when you grow your own food, you can harvest it at peak ripeness and consume it when its nutrient content is highest. Furthermore, when you grow your own food, you have control over how it's grown. You can avoid harmful pesticides, use organic fertilizers, and cultivate varieties that are bred for flavor and nutrients rather than transportability and shelf life. This can result in food that's not only more nutritious but also tastier and more varied.

Promoting Food Security
Having a garden also helps ensure food security. If you own a small cattle operation, orchard, or garden, you have a consistent supply of food that is not reliant on supply networks or retailers. Whether you're experiencing a personal financial crisis or a more significant upheaval, this can be a reassuring reassurance during difficult times.

Encouraging Mindful Eating and Living
Homegrown food can change our relationship with food for the better. When you've planted, nurtured, and harvested your own food, you develop a deeper appreciation for it. This can lead to more mindful eating habits, where you savor your meals rather than eating mindlessly. Additionally, it might raise your awareness of the resources used in food production, encouraging more sustainable and considerate eating habits.

Fostering a Sense of Achievement
Finally, growing your own food can bring a profound sense of achievement. There's something uniquely satisfying about eating food you've grown yourself, knowing that your hard work and dedication have resulted in something delicious and nutritious. This sense of achievement can boost your self-confidence and provide a tangible reward for your efforts towards self-sufficiency. The benefits of homegrown food extend far beyond the practicalities of providing sustenance. It's about enhancing nutritional value, promoting food security, encouraging mindful eating, and fostering a sense of achievement. It's an essential component of self-sufficiency that improves our mental and emotional health in addition to our physical health.

Chapter 3: Tracing the Roots: The History of Self-Sufficiency

Self-sufficiency, at its core, is not a new concept. It is deeply rooted in our history and evolution, tracing back to the very dawn of humanity. However, our understanding and approach to self-sufficiency have changed over time, influenced by societal changes, technological advancements, and shifts in values and ideologies.

The Dawn of Self-Sufficiency: Hunter-Gatherer Societies

The first human societies were inherently self-sufficient. Our hunter-gatherer ancestors relied on their skills and knowledge to source food, build shelter, and meet their basic needs. They hunted wild animals, foraged for edible plants, and used natural materials to construct their dwellings and tools. While these societies lacked many of the comforts and conveniences we enjoy today, they exemplified self-sufficiency in its purest form. They were intimately connected with their environment and relied on their own efforts and communal cooperation for survival.

The Shift to Agriculture and Settlements

The development of agriculture around 10,000 years ago brought about a significant change in human societies. People started domesticating animals and growing crops in place of only hunting and gathering. Due to this change, people were able to settle down in one area, which facilitated the development of villages and ultimately cities.

While agriculture still involved a degree of self-sufficiency, it also led to increased specialization. Some individuals became farmers, while others pursued crafts, trade, or warfare. This division of labor allowed societies to become more efficient and prosperous, but it also meant that individuals were no longer self-sufficient in the way their hunter-gatherer ancestors had been.

The Industrial Revolution and the Decline of Self-Sufficiency

Significant social transformations were brought about by the Industrial Revolution in the 18th and 19th centuries. Mechanized production and the construction of factories made items more affordable and widely available.
People increasingly moved to cities to work in factories, further distancing themselves from the self-sufficient lifestyle of their ancestors.
During this period, self-sufficiency was often associated with rural, backward lifestyles, while urbanization and consumption were seen as symbols of progress and modernity.

The Self-Sufficiency Movement in the 20th Century

In the mid-20th century, amid growing concerns about industrialization, environmental degradation, and the homogenization of culture, a new interest in self-sufficiency emerged.
Pioneers like Scott and Helen Nearing, who left city life to build a self-sufficient homestead in rural Vermont in the 1930s, and later authors like John Seymour and Carla Emery, who wrote extensively about self-sufficient living, inspired a new generation to explore self-sufficiency. This trend was further fueled by the counterculture movement of the 1960s and 70s, which often emphasized self-sufficiency as a way of rejecting consumerism and reconnecting with nature.

Self-Sufficiency in the 21st Century

These days, worries about climate change, resource depletion, and the need for a more robust and sustainable lifestyle are fueling a renewed interest in self-sufficiency. With advances in technology, it is now possible to combine the benefits of modern living with a high degree of self-sufficiency. For example, renewable energy systems, permaculture practices, and digital communication tools allow us to live more independently without completely withdrawing from society.
As we navigate the nuances of self-sufficiency, understanding its history offers valuable insights. It inspires us to integrate these time-tested principles into our lives, enabling us to redefine what modern self-sufficiency can mean. It serves as a reminder of our capability and resilience, a testament to the innate human potential for adaptation and growth as we shape our own paths towards a more sustainable and self-reliant future.
Self-sufficiency, at its core, is not a new concept. It's deeply rooted in our history and evolution, tracing back to the very dawn of humanity. However, the way we understand and approach self-sufficiency has changed over time, influenced by societal changes, technological advancements, and shifts in values and ideologies.

Chapter 4: Facing Challenges Along the Path of Self-Sufficiency

Strategies for an Effective Transition

Although self-sufficiency has many advantages, it's vital to understand that there may occasionally be difficulties and roadblocks. This section will examine some typical obstacles that could appear on the way to self-sufficiency and talk about how to overcome them.

Managing Limited Resources

One of the key challenges of self-sufficiency is managing limited resources. When relying on our own resources to meet basic needs such as food, water, and energy, it becomes essential to use these resources wisely and sustainably. We will discuss methods to optimize resource usage, such as water conservation, energy efficiency, and material recycling.

Getting used to the change in climate

The challenge of climate change to self-sufficiency is substantial. The capacity to cultivate crops, gather water, or produce energy can be impacted by extreme weather events such as heatwaves, floods, or droughts.

We will explore strategies to address these changes, such as crop diversification, rainwater harvesting systems, and the adoption of climate-resilient technologies.

Balancing Self-Sufficiency with Modern Society Engagement

Self-sufficiency does not necessarily mean complete isolation from modern society. Many individuals who embrace the self-sufficient lifestyle also desire to participate in the community and enjoy the benefits of modern life. However, balancing self-sufficiency with societal engagement can be a challenge. We will explore ways to find a balance, such as sharing skills with the community, accessing external services when needed, and using digital tools to connect with like-minded individuals.

Addressing Emotional and Psychological Challenges

Self-sufficiency can bring about emotional and psychological challenges. Managing daily responsibilities, the weight of important decisions, and the possibility of setbacks can create stress and frustration. We will discuss strategies to address these challenges, such as creating a support network, practicing mindfulness, and promoting effective self-care.

Managing challenges along the path of self-sufficiency requires awareness, flexibility, and adaptability. Recognizing common challenges and having strategies in place to address them can contribute to a smoother transition to a self-sufficient lifestyle. Self-sufficiency is a journey of continuous learning, and each challenge overcome represents an opportunity to grow and refine skills.

MODULE B: SOLAR ENERGY
Chapter 1: Solar Energy Basics

Solar energy is a sustainable and environmentally friendly type of energy that is quickly gaining popularity as a viable option for a growing number of business and household uses. It is crucial that you comprehend the basic concepts and technical terms associated with solar power if you are interested in this technology. We'll look at some of the most important ideas surrounding solar energy in this part.

Photovoltaic (PV) Cell: A type of solar cell that uses sunlight to generate electricity, a photovoltaic cell is sometimes referred to as a PV cell. PV cells are used in the creation of solar panels and are usually built from semiconducting materials like silicon.

A solar panel is made up of several photovoltaic cells connected to one another in order to generate a useful amount of power. Solar panels are frequently erected on top of buildings or put directly on the ground in locations with enough sunlight.

Solar Array: A solar array is a cluster of solar panels that are connected to one another to generate a greater quantity of power. Solar arrays are often utilized in solar projects that are of a commercial or utility scale.

The direct current (DC) energy generated by solar panels is converted into alternating current (AC) electricity by a solar power inverter, which is subsequently utilized by various home appliances and other gadgets.

Net Metering: Under a "net metering" billing arrangement, excess electricity produced by a solar system is returned to the grid and the homeowner is credited for the additional energy produced by the system on their utility bill. This can assist in offsetting the expense of the electricity that must be obtained from the grid during those periods when the solar system is not producing enough energy to fulfill the needs of the home.

Solar Energy Storage: The term "solar energy storage" refers to the act of storing extra solar energy via the utilization of batteries or other forms of energy storage devices so that it may be used at a later time. When the sun isn't shining, this can assist in guaranteeing that a house or company still has a stable supply of electricity.

Solar Energy System

That Is Not Linked To the Electrical Grid: An off-grid solar system is a solar energy system that is not connected to the electrical grid. Off-grid solutions use a battery bank or another type of energy storage technology to ensure that electricity is available even when the sun isn't shining.

Solar Energy System Linked to the Electrical Grid: A solar energy system that is linked to the electrical grid is referred to as a grid-tied solar system. The practice of "net metering" is frequently utilized by grid-connected systems to compensate for the cost of power that is purchased from the grid with the extra electricity that is generated by the solar system.

Solar Efficiency: The quantity of sunlight that is captured by a solar panel and transformed into useful power is referred to as the solar panel's solar efficiency. Solar efficiency is commonly stated as a percentage, with higher percentages indicating that solar panels have a better level of efficiency.

Insolation from the Sun: The amount of solar energy that reaches a particular location on Earth's surface is referred to as insolation from the sun. Latitude, climate, and season are some of the variables that affect how much solar insolation reaches the Earth's surface.

Peak Sun Hours: The number of hours of the day when the solar insolation is strong enough to create a considerable quantity of power is referred to as the peak sun hours. In most cases, the number of hours of peak sunlight is determined by taking into account the angle of the sun, the season, and a few other parameters.

Solar Tracking System: A solar tracking system is an apparatus that rotates solar panels in order to track the sun's path throughout the day. A solar tracking system is used to mount solar panels. This could lead to an increase in the total power output of the solar panels.

Concentrated Solar Power (CSP): CSP is a method that uses mirrors or lenses to focus sunlight into a tiny area. This heat is then produced, which may be used to generate electricity. We call this process "concentrating the sun."

Thin-Film Solar Cell: Solar cells created from extremely thin layers of semiconductor materials are known as thin-film solar cells. While thin-film solar cells are less expensive to produce than regular photovoltaic cells, the former usually have higher efficiency.

Solar Thermal Energy: This sustainable energy source can be used to heat buildings, produce electricity, or power various industrial processes. It gets its heat from the sun.

This is often accomplished by concentrating sunlight into a tiny area, where it is then utilized to create heat. This may be done through the use of mirrors or lenses.

Solar Reflectance: Solar reflectance is the capacity of a substance to reflect sunlight. When it comes to cool roofing applications, materials that have a high solar reflectance are typically selected because of their ability to assist in minimizing the amount of heat that is collected by a structure.

Solar Heat Gain Coefficient (SHGC): The solar heat gain coefficient, also known as the SHGC, is a measurement that determines how much solar radiation is transmitted through a window or another type of glazing system. A lower solar heat gain coefficient, or SHGC value, indicates that less solar radiation is allowed to pass through the window. This can assist in lowering the amount spent on air conditioning during the warm summer months.

Solar Carport: A solar carport is a structure that not only offers protection from the sun for vehicles that are parked underneath it but also generates power from the sun itself. Solar carports are becoming increasingly popular in the commercial and industrial sectors.

Solar-Powered Water Pumps: Solar-powered water pumps are devices that draw water from a well or other water source using sun energy rather than traditional electrical power. Solar-powered water pumps are frequently utilized in isolated places that have limited access to conventional sources of electrical power.

Solar-Powered Ventilation Systems: Solar-powered ventilation systems generate electricity from the sun to run fans or other ventilation equipment that helps move air around a building. This can help minimize the demand for air conditioning during the warmer months of the year.

Solar-Powered Lighting Systems: Solar-powered lighting systems use light from the sun to power LED lights, which can be used for normal outdoor lighting or as an emergency light in the event of a power loss. Solar-powered lighting systems are becoming increasingly popular.

Solar-Powered Air Conditioning: Solar-powered air conditioning systems make use of solar energy to power air conditioning units, which can assist in lowering the expense of cooling a building during the warm summer months. Solar-powered air conditioning systems are available today.

Solar-Powered Pool Heating: Heating a swimming pool with solar energy, solar-powered pool heating systems heat swimming pools using solar energy, which may help lengthen the swimming season and lower the expense of heating a pool.

Solar-Powered Charging Stations for Electric Vehicles: Charging stations that use solar energy to power themselves are referred to as solar-powered charging stations for electric vehicles. This has the potential to lower the costs associated with charging electric cars while also lowering emissions of greenhouse gases.

Solar energy is an industry that is expanding at a quick rate and has many terminologies and ideas that it is essential to comprehend. Understanding these basic terminologies and ideas is a fantastic place to start whether you are interested in putting a solar energy system in your home or business or if you just want to learn more about this technology. If you do so, you will be better prepared to make educated judgments on solar energy and its ability to assist in meeting our energy demands in a manner that is both clean and sustainable.

Off-Grid Solar Power System Components

Those solar power systems that function off the utility grid are called "off-grid" systems. In order to be used in places that are not connected to the utility grid, these devices produce and store electricity.

These systems are made up of several different components that, when combined, create and distribute electricity to power a wide variety of appliances and electronic gadgets. It is crucial for anyone interested in adopting this technology to power their home or business to have a solid understanding of the components that make up an off-grid solar power system.

Solar Panels:

In a solar power system that is not connected to the grid, the solar panels are the most crucial component. Typically, they are composed of a number of solar cells, which are responsible for transforming sunlight into direct current (DC) power. Solar panels are often positioned either on the ground or on the top of buildings so that they may get the greatest amount of sunlight possible. Both the size and quantity of solar panels needed will depend on how much electricity is needed to run the house or business. This could vary depending on several aspects, such as the size of the structure, the quantity of appliances and devices that require power, and the amount of sunlight present in the surrounding area.

Charge Regulator or Charger:

In a solar power system that is not connected to the grid, a charge controller is an essential component. It does this by controlling the amount of power that is sent from the solar panels to the batteries. This prevents the batteries from being either overcharged or undercharged. This is significant because overcharging the batteries can cause harm to them, while undercharging them will lessen the amount of time they will last.

In accordance with the dimensions of the solar power installation, charge controllers are available in a variety of forms and dimensions. PWM, which stands for "Pulse Width Modulation," and MPPT, which stands for "Maximum Power Point Tracking," are the two most popular forms of charge controllers.

Batteries:

When power is generated by the solar panels, it can be stored in batteries for later use. Because deep cycle batteries can be repeatedly discharged and then recharged, they are frequently used in off-grid solar power systems.

The amount of electricity necessary to power the house or company, as well as the duration of time that the batteries are expected to supply power, are the two primary factors that will determine the size and quantity of batteries that are required. This could depend on a number of factors, including the building's size, the number of devices and appliances that need to be powered, and the availability of sunlight in the area.

Inverter:

An inverter is needed to convert the direct current (DC) electricity produced by the solar panels and stored in the batteries into alternating current (AC). This makes it possible to use DC electricity to power a variety of devices and appliances. Most residential and commercial buildings use AC power as their energy source.

There is a wide range of sizes and types of inverters available; choosing the right one will depend on the size of the solar power system and the amount of electricity that will be needed. Inverters that produce pure sine waves and inverters that produce modified sine waves are the most prevalent types of inverters. Pure sine wave inverters are more expensive but create a type of alternating current (AC) power that is cleaner and more stable than modified sine wave inverters, which are cheaper but have the potential to produce a less stable form of alternating current (AC).

Generator:

Even though off-grid solar power systems are developed to supply electricity without the need for a generator, it is often a good idea to include a backup generator as part of the system. When there is insufficient sunshine or when the batteries are all used up, one can turn to the usage of generators to generate the necessary electricity.

The type and size of generator that must be utilized depend on the size of the solar power system and the quantity of energy that the generator must produce. Generators powered by gasoline or diesel are the most widely used kind. Generators that run on diesel are widely used. While gasoline generators are more portable and require less maintenance, diesel generators are generally made to last longer and burn fuel more efficiently.

Monitoring System: A monitoring system is used to monitor the solar power system's performance. This involves keeping track of the energy produced, the quantity of electricity stored in the batteries, and the amount of electricity used by different devices and appliances. This data can be used to identify any potential flaws or issues that may develop as well as to enhance the system's general performance.

Depending on the size of the solar power system and the quantity of information that is necessary, monitoring systems are available in a wide variety of configurations, sizes, and kinds. Some monitoring systems are straightforward and just supply the most fundamental of data, but others are more complex and are able to supply extensive information on the operation of each component of the system.

Mounting System:

The mounting system is what is utilized to affix solar panels to the ground or to the surface of a rooftop. The mounting system needs to be sturdy enough to withstand the effects of wind, rain, and other types of precipitation, and it also needs to be able to hold the solar panels at the appropriate angle to ensure that they get the most possible sunshine exposure.

The size and weight of the solar panels, as well as the type of roof or ground surface on which they will be put, determine the appropriate mounting method to use. Mounting systems are available in a variety of sizes and types. Roof mounts, ground mounts, and pole mounts are the three types of mounting systems that are used the most frequently.

Wiring and Connectors:

In order to link all of the individual components of the solar power system to one another, wiring and connectors are utilized. Part of this process involves connecting the batteries to the inverter, the charge controller to the solar panels, the inverter to the appliances and devices, and so on.

Wiring and connections for the solar power system need to be able to withstand the system's voltage and current, and they also need to be of the appropriate size to prevent any power from escaping or being wasted. In addition, they need to have correct installations and connections in order to avoid any potential electrical risks.

13

Load Center:

The inverter is responsible for generating alternating current (AC), which is then distributed through the load center, which is a distribution panel, to the numerous appliances and gadgets located in the house or company. In order to prevent electrical harm to the various home appliances and equipment, the load center often has circuit breakers or fuses installed in it.

In order to prevent any potential electrical risks, the load center needs to have the right dimensions so that it can manage the quantity of electricity that is generated by the solar power system. Additionally, it needs to be placed and linked in the right way.

People who want to become less dependent on the utility grid and more self-sufficient are turning to off-grid solar power systems in increasing numbers. This trend is expected to continue. It is crucial for anybody who is interested in adopting this technology to power their house or company to have a solid understanding of the components that make up an off-grid solar power system.

An off-grid solar power system must include several key components, including solar panels, charge controllers, batteries, inverters, generators, monitoring systems, mounting systems, cabling and connections, and load centers. To guarantee that the system operates securely and effectively, each component must have the appropriate dimensions, be placed correctly, and have the appropriate connections made.

If installed appropriately and with all the essential parts, off-grid solar power systems can offer a consistent source of electricity for remote homes and businesses, as well as for individuals looking to reduce their environmental impact and increase their level of self-sufficiency.

Adding New Technological Advances in Solar Energy

The efficiency and sustainability of solar power systems can be further improved by keeping up with the latest developments, which is imperative given the speed at which solar energy technologies are developing. A number of cutting-edge technologies have surfaced recently that have the potential to drastically alter the solar energy market.

Bifacial Solar Panels: Due to their ability to absorb sunlight from both directions, bicluster solar panels can provide more energy overall. These panels work especially well in sandy or snowy conditions because they can capture reflected sunlight from the ground or other surfaces.

Perovskite Solar Cells: In comparison to conventional silicon-based cells, perovskite solar cells are a potential new technology that offer great efficiency at a reduced cost.

They are lightweight and flexible, allowing for a wider range of applications, including portable solar devices and building-integrated photovoltaics (BIPV).

Floating Solar Farms: Also known as floatovoltaics, floating solar farms are installed on bodies of water such as lakes, reservoirs, and even oceans. These systems reduce land use, improve solar panel efficiency due to the cooling effect of water, and can help reduce water evaporation from reservoirs.

Solar Windows: Solar windows integrate transparent solar cells into window glass, allowing buildings to generate electricity without the need for traditional solar panels. This technology can transform windows into energy-generating surfaces, contributing to the building's overall energy efficiency.

Energy Storage Solutions: The capacity and efficiency of solar energy storage systems are increasing because to developments in battery technology, such as solid-state and flow batteries.

These innovations enable longer-lasting and more reliable energy storage, which is essential for off-grid solar systems and enhancing grid stability.

Smart Inverters: Smart inverters can optimize energy production, improve grid stability, and enable better integration with other renewable energy sources. They can also provide real-time data on system performance, making it easier to manage and maintain solar power systems.

Building-Integrated Photovoltaics (BIPV): BIPV involves integrating solar panels into building materials, such as roofing tiles, facades, and windows. This approach not only generates electricity but also enhances the aesthetic appeal and functionality of buildings.

Solar Desalination: Solar desalination uses solar energy to convert seawater into fresh water. This technology can provide a sustainable solution for water-scarce regions, addressing both energy and water needs simultaneously.

Agrivoltaics: Agrivoltaics involves the simultaneous use of land for both solar energy production and agriculture. Solar panels are installed above crops, providing shade and reducing water evaporation while generating electricity. This approach can increase land use efficiency and provide additional income for farmers.

Chapter 2 - The Evolution of Solar Energy

In the early 20th century, significant advancements in solar energy technology began to take place. One notable breakthrough was the invention of the first solar thermal collector by William J. Bailey in 1908. This collector was capable of heating water by utilizing the sun's energy.

The 1950s marked another milestone in the history of solar power energy with the development of the first modern solar cell. Scientists at Bell Laboratories, including Daryl Chapin, Calvin Fuller, and Gerald Pearson, invented the silicon photovoltaic (PV) cell, which was more efficient and practical for generating electricity from sunlight. This invention paved the way for the utilization of solar energy on a larger scale.

During the space race between the United States and the Soviet Union in the 1960s, solar power technology found its way into space applications. The first successful use of solar panels on a satellite was achieved by the Vanguard 1 satellite, launched by the U.S. in 1958. Solar power became an essential source of energy for space missions due to its reliability and ability to generate electricity in the absence of an atmosphere.

The development of solar cell technology persisted in the ensuing decades. New materials like gallium arsenide and thin-film solar cells have been developed, which has increased solar panel efficiency and reduced their cost. Globally, governments and institutions started allocating funds for solar energy research and development as a sustainable and renewable substitute for fossil fuels.

The oil crisis in the 1970s further spurred interest in solar energy as a means to reduce dependence on fossil fuels. In response, various government incentives and subsidies were introduced to promote the adoption of solar power systems.

In recent years, solar energy has experienced exponential growth and widespread adoption. The declining costs of solar panels, coupled with increased efficiency and technological advancements, have made solar power more affordable and accessible to a larger population. Solar farms, rooftop installations, and off-grid systems have become increasingly common, contributing to the transition to a cleaner and more sustainable energy future.

Today, solar power is recognized as a crucial component of the global renewable energy mix. In order to achieve energy independence, lower greenhouse gas emissions, and fight climate change, it is essential.

Governments, businesses, and individuals worldwide are embracing solar energy as a reliable and environmentally friendly source of electricity.

Initial Developments in Solar Technology

The first modern solar cell was invented in 1954 and is credited to American scientist and engineer Dr. Calvin Fuller of Bell Laboratories. The solar cell was constructed using silicon, the most common type of material used in the creation of solar cells.

In the 1960s and 1970s, NASA started equipping its satellites and spacecraft with solar panels in order to generate power. This constituted a significant step forward in the evolution of solar power as it provided conclusive evidence that solar energy could be effectively utilized as a dependable source of electricity in outer space.

Solar energy began to gain popularity as an alternative source of electricity on Earth in the 1970s, particularly in isolated places where it was difficult or impossible to connect to the power grid. This was in part caused by the energy crisis that hit the United States in the 1970s, which sparked a fresh interest in renewable energy sources.

During the 1980s and 1990s, advancements in solar technology allowed for the creation of solar cells that were both more effective and more reasonably priced. This resulted in a surge in the use of solar power in a range of applications, including residential and commercial structures, as well as distant power systems for telecommunications and other sectors. In addition, the price of solar energy has decreased significantly in recent years.

Recent Steps Forward in Technological Developments

Significant advancements in solar technology in recent years have increased the efficiency, affordability, and accessibility of solar power. These developments are directly responsible for these modifications.

The invention of thin-film solar cells is one of the most significant steps forward in technical innovation that has taken place in recent years. Traditional solar cells are constructed of silicon; these cells, which are manufactured from materials such as copper, indium, gallium, and selenide, are far thinner and lighter than their silicon counterparts. Because of this, they are more adaptable and easier to install, which opens up the possibility of employing them in a broader variety of contexts.

The creation of solar concentrators, which employ lenses or mirrors to focus sunlight into a smaller area, increasing the amount of energy that can be captured from each solar cell, is yet another significant step forward in technical progress. Furthermore, new developments in energy storage technology allow for the storage of extra solar energy in batteries for usage even in the absence of the sun.

This has helped to overcome one of the most significant constraints of solar power, which is that it can only be used when the sun is up and shining.

The Current Situation Regarding Solar Power

Solar energy is now one of the renewable energy sources that is expanding at one of the highest rates in the globe. In 2006, solar energy accounted for only 0.1% of the world's total power output. By the year 2020, however, this percentage had increased to 4.4%.

In the United States of America alone, there are already over 700,000 solar power installations, with a total capacity of 97.2 gigawatts (GW) of energy. When compared to the mere 1 GW of solar capacity that was installed in 2008, this represents a significant increase.

Solar panels may now be installed at a cost that is more affordable for homes and businesses thanks to a steady decline in the cost of solar electricity over the past few years. According to the Solar Energy Industries Association, the price of installing a household solar panel system has decreased by more than 70% since 2010.

The use of solar electricity has also been encouraged by governments all over the world via the implementation of a variety of policies and financial incentives. For example, several countries offer financial incentives like tax credits, rebates, and other reductions to encourage the installation of solar panels.

In addition, several nations have established goals for the proportion of their energy that must come from non-conventional, environmentally friendly sources such as solar power.

The Obstacles That Solar Energy Must Overcome

In spite of the fact that solar power has witnessed substantial growth and development in recent years, the sector is still faced with a number of obstacles.

The unpredictable nature of solar electricity is one of the most difficult obstacles to overcome. To guarantee a continuous supply of electricity, energy storage devices are required, as solar panels are only able to produce power while the sun is shining.

The technology that stores energy in batteries has undergone considerable advancements in recent years; yet, it is still rather pricey, and its deployment on a broad scale is not yet economically viable in many situations.

The restricted supply of land that is appropriate for solar farms is another obstacle that must be overcome by solar power. Solar panels may be mounted on roofs and other surfaces, but in order to construct large-scale solar farms, extensive tracts of land are required. This type of property might be challenging to acquire in places with a high population density.

In addition, the production of solar panels needs substantial quantities of energy and resources, both of which can contribute to the deterioration of the environment. Even if it is obvious that solar electricity is better for the environment, it is very vital to guarantee that the production of solar panels and their disposal are carried out in an environmentally conscious and responsible way.

The history of solar power energy dates back thousands of years, during which time people have been using various techniques to harness the power of the sun. In spite of the fact that the development of solar energy as a viable source of power is a phenomenon that took place much more recently, tremendous growth and development has taken place in this field in recent years.

Solar power has become more practical, economical, and available in recent years as a direct result of technological advancements; as a result, governments all over the world are actively working to increase its use via the implementation of a variety of incentives and regulations. However, the industry is still faced with a number of obstacles, the most significant of which are the intermittent nature of solar power and the limited availability of land that is suitable for solar farms.

In spite of these obstacles, solar power is well positioned to play an increasingly significant part in the global energy mix in the coming years. This will be the case as the world strives to lessen its dependency on fossil fuels and move toward a more sustainable and renewable energy future.

Chapter 3: The Science Behind Solar Energy

How Solar Panels Work

Solar panels are machines that use light from the sun to create electricity. They are made up of several interconnected solar cells. Typically, silicon or other semiconducting materials are used to make these solar cells. An electric current is produced when sunlight strikes the solar cells because it pushes electrons out of their locations within the atoms.

The Process of Electricity Generation Using Solar Panels

The functioning of solar panels is based on the photoelectric effect, first explained by Albert Einstein in 1905. The photoelectric effect occurs when photons, particles of light, collide with a material, causing electrons to be ejected from the atoms of that material. When a sufficient number of electrons are liberated, they can be used as an electric current.

Solar panels consist of individual solar cells. Each cell has a layer of silicon or another semiconducting material in the middle, with two conductive layers on either side. The silicon layer is doped with other atoms to create a p-n junction, which acts as an electron valve, allowing the flow of electrons in one direction. When sunlight reaches the silicon layer, it prompts the electrons to move across the p-n junction into the conductive layer, where they can be collected and used to generate an electric current.

While solar panels primarily produce direct current (DC) power, this type of electricity is not suitable for most residential and commercial applications. An inverter, typically installed alongside the solar panels, converts DC power into alternating current (AC), which is used in homes and businesses.

Components of Solar Panel Systems

In addition to the solar panels themselves, a typical solar panel system comprises various supporting components, including:

- *Mounting hardware*: Solar panels are often installed on rooftops or the ground. Mounting equipment secures the panels and ensures they are positioned to receive maximum sunlight.
- *Inverter*: The solar panels' DC power is transformed into AC electricity by the inverter, which is then used in both household and commercial settings.
- *Batteries:* Some solar panel systems include batteries that store surplus power generated by the panels for use during periods of low sunlight.
- *Charge controller:* Charge controllers are used in systems with batteries to prevent overcharging or rapid discharge of the batteries.
- *Monitoring system*: The majority of solar panel systems come with a monitoring system that lets users keep tabs on how much power is produced and used.

Various Solar Panel Types

There exist multiple varieties of solar panels, each possessing unique benefits and drawbacks. The most typical kinds consist of:

- *Monocrystalline solar panels:* Made from a single crystal of silicon, monocrystalline panels are highly efficient but come at a higher price.
- *Polycrystalline solar panels*: Polycrystalline solar panels are more affordable than monocrystalline solar panels, however they are less efficient due to their numerous silicon crystal construction.
- *Thin-film solar panels:* Materials including copper indium gallium selenide, cadmium telluride, and amorphous silicon are used to make thin-film solar panels.
- They have lower efficiency but are more affordable compared to crystalline panels.
- *Concentrated solar panels*: These panels use lenses or mirrors to concentrate sunlight onto a smaller area of solar cells, increasing their efficiency. However, they are more expensive than other types of solar panels.

Recent Innovations in Solar Technology

Recent developments in solar technology have increased the effectiveness, affordability, and accessibility of solar energy. Among them are:

- *Bifacial solar panels*: The effectiveness of these panels is increased by their ability to capture sunlight from both sides.
- *Perovskite solar cells*: a more recent variety of solar cell that, when compared to conventional silicon-based cells, claims to have higher efficiency and cheaper production costs.
- *Building-integrated photovoltaics (BIPV):* These are solar panels integrated directly into building materials, such as windows or roof tiles, providing a seamless and aesthetically pleasing way to incorporate solar power into structures.
- *Solar skins:* Customizable solar panel skins that blend with the aesthetics of a building's architecture, making solar installations more visually appealing.

Understanding the science behind solar energy and the functioning of solar panels is essential for harnessing this renewable energy source effectively. Solar power has the potential to contribute significantly to a sustainable and clean energy future.

Benefits of Solar Panel Use

There are various benefits to using solar panels to generate electricity.

- *Renewable:* As long as the sun shines, solar energy is a renewable resource that will never run out. It is thus among the most environmentally friendly sources of electricity.
- *Non-polluting:* Solar energy does not release any harmful byproducts into the atmosphere or contribute to pollution, unlike the burning of fossil fuels. It is a clean and environmentally friendly source of power.
- *Economically viable*: Although the upfront cost of installing solar panels can be high, they can result in significant cost savings over their lifetime. Once installed, the electricity generated by solar panels is essentially free, leading to long-term cost reductions.
- *Dependable*: Solar panels are relatively reliable and require minimal maintenance once installed. They can continue producing electricity even during power disruptions or emergencies, providing a reliable source of energy.
- *Adaptable applications*: Solar panels can be used in a wide range of settings, from modest residential setups to expansive commercial installations. They are adaptable to various energy requirements and can be included into the current infrastructure.
- *Increased property value:* A home or business's worth may rise with the installation of solar panels. Potential purchasers are frequently prepared to pay more for a home that has solar panels installed.
-

Challenges to Consider with Solar Panels

While solar panels offer numerous advantages, there are also some challenges to be aware of:

- *High initial cost:* The upfront cost of installing solar panels can be a significant barrier for individuals and businesses, making it challenging for some to justify the investment. However, the long-term cost savings can offset this initial expense.
- *Weather dependence*: Solar panels rely on sunlight to generate power, which means their energy production is affected by factors such as cloud cover, precipitation, and snowfall. The amount of energy generated may fluctuate depending on the weather conditions.
- *Space requirements*: Solar panels require ample space for installation, which may not be feasible for all households or businesses. Adequate roof or ground space is necessary to accommodate the panels.
- *Maintenance:* Even while solar panels usually require little upkeep, routine cleaning and inspection are nevertheless required to guarantee optimal performance.
- This maintenance helps to ensure that the panels are operating effectively and efficiently.
- *Disposal:* In order to prevent harm to the environment, hazardous elements found in solar panels must be disposed of appropriately. Recycling programs, however, are in place to lessen their adverse effects and encourage appropriate disposal techniques.

An innovative and promising method for producing clean, sustainable electricity is solar paneling. Through the utilization of solar energy, they offer dependable, reasonably priced, and ecologically sustainable power. Even while installing solar panels has certain disadvantages, like the initial cost and space requirements, these are usually outweighed by the advantages. It is anticipated that more homes and businesses will use solar energy to meet their electricity demands while lessening their environmental impact as a result of continuous technical breakthroughs and cost reductions.

Solar Radiation

Solar radiation is the term used to describe the energy that is released by the sun and then travels through space to arrive at Earth. Because it is a form of electromagnetic radiation, which means that it is made up of waves whose frequency and wavelength can be determined, it can be measured. Solar radiation is the source of all life on Earth, as well as the light and heat that sustain it. It is also responsible for keeping the surface of the planet at a comfortable temperature.

Solar radiation is almost entirely produced by the sun itself. It releases energy in the form of electromagnetic waves, which travel across space and arrive at the Earth. Solar radiation includes various forms of electromagnetic waves, such as visible light, ultraviolet light, and infrared radiation.

- *Visible light:* This portion of solar energy can be seen by the human eye and is composed of various colors, each with a distinct wavelength and frequency. The visible light portion of the electromagnetic spectrum is where the sun emits the greatest amount of energy relative to the other parts of the spectrum.
- *Ultraviolet (UV) radiation*: This portion of the sun's energy has a frequency greater than that of visible light. It is responsible for sunburns and other forms of skin damage, but it also plays a crucial role in maintaining human health by assisting the body in the production of vitamin D. A deficit in vitamin D can be caused by insufficient exposure to UV light, which can be detrimental in both excess and inadequate amounts.
- *Infrared (IR) radiation*: This portion of the sun's energy has a frequency lower than that of visible light. It is the source of the heat that warms both the surface of the Earth and the atmosphere. IR radiation is essential to the process of preserving the temperature and climate of the Earth. However, an excessive amount of IR radiation can raise the temperature of the Earth and contribute to the phenomenon of global warming.

Radiation from the sun may be evaluated based on both its strength and its spectrum. The quantity of energy that is emitted from the sun and travels all the way to the surface of the Earth is referred to as the intensity of solar radiation. The distribution of energy over a variety of wavelengths and frequencies is what we refer to as the spectrum of solar radiation. The quantity of solar radiation that makes it to the surface of the Earth is influenced by a number of different elements. These factors include the distance that the Earth is from the sun, the tilt that the Earth maintains on its axis, and the presence of atmospheric gases such as water vapor, carbon dioxide, and ozone.

The Earth's orbital distance from the sun is one of the most important parameters that determine the amount of energy received from the sun's rays. Because the orbit of the Earth around the sun is not perfectly circular, the distance between the Earth and the sun changes throughout the course of a year. January is the month when the Earth is closest to the sun, and July is the month when it is furthest away from the sun. This indicates that the level of solar radiation that is present in January is greater than the level that is present in July. The angle at which the axis of the Earth is tilted relative to the sun is another element that influences the quantity of solar radiation. There is an inclination of 23.5 degrees on the axis of the Earth with respect to the plane that it follows around the sun. This indicates that the angle at which solar radiation impacts the surface of the Earth shifts during the course of a year. Since the Northern Hemisphere is tilted toward the sun during the summer months, it takes in a greater amount of solar radiation than the Southern Hemisphere does during this time of year. The scenario is quite different throughout the winter.

The amount of solar radiation that reaches the surface of the Earth may also be influenced by atmospheric gases such as water vapor, carbon dioxide, and ozone, amongst other things. These gases have the ability to absorb and scatter solar radiation, which can have an effect on the intensity and spectrum of the radiation that is received at the surface of the earth. Ozone, for instance, is responsible for absorbing the majority of the UV light that is present in the atmosphere; as a result, this serves to shield the Earth from potentially damaging UV radiation.

Solar radiation is an essential source of energy for a wide variety of applications, including but not limited to solar power generation, agricultural modeling, and climate simulation. The process of generating energy from solar power involves the use of solar panels to convert solar radiation into electricity. Agriculture is dependent on solar radiation for the process of photosynthesis, which is the way that plants transform the energy from sunlight into usable form. Data gathered from solar radiation is incorporated into climate models in order to better comprehend and forecast Earth's weather.

When designing buildings and urban environments, it is essential to take solar radiation into consideration as one of the important factors. The amount of solar radiation that enters a structure may have an effect not just on its energy efficiency but also on the climate inside and the level of comfort that it provides. Solar radiation statistics are used by urban planners and architects to create cities and structures that take advantage of natural illumination to the greatest extent possible while reducing the need for artificial lighting and heating.

Instruments such as pyranometers and spectrometers are utilized by scientists in the process of measuring the radiation emitted by the sun. Pyranometers measure the overall quantity of solar radiation that impacts a surface, whereas spectrometers detect the spectrum of solar radiation that is emitted by the sun.

Chapter 4 - The Benefits of Solar Power

Environmental

The environment refers to the natural world and all its living and nonliving components. Environmental issues arise as a result of human actions that impact the natural environment, and these issues have become a major concern due to the growing awareness of their detrimental effects.

Three primary categories of environmental problems exist: pollution of the air, water, and land. The atmospheric emission of pollutants including carbon dioxide, sulfur dioxide, and nitrogen oxides results in air pollution. Contaminants that find their way into bodies of water, such as lakes, rivers, and seas, cause pollution. The buildup of waste products on the ground, Particularly non-biodegradable elements like plastic, is know as land pollution.

One of the most pressing environmental challenges of our time is climate change, which is mostly caused by the combustion of fossil fuels, which releases greenhouse gases into the atmosphere. These gases trap heat, which leads to climate change and other adverse consequences on the environment such as increasing sea levels, more frequent and stronger heatwaves, droughts, and floods.

Deforestation is another major environmental issue that arises from the removal of trees for human uses such as logging, agriculture, and urbanization. Deforestation causes many species to lose their habitat and releases carbon stored in trees into the atmosphere, which contributes to climate change.

A serious environmental problem is water scarcity, especially in arid and semi-arid areas. Due to changes in rainfall patterns and an increase in the frequency of droughts, climate change makes water shortages worse. Animal and human health are also at risk due to industrial and agricultural practices that frequently contaminate freshwater supplies.

Biodiversity loss is a major concern as it threatens numerous organisms and ecosystems. Human activities such as habitat degradation, climate change, and pollution contribute to the decline in biodiversity.

Environmental issues have significant repercussions for society and the economy. Air pollution is linked to respiratory and other health problems, while water pollution can cause waterborne diseases. Climate change can disrupt food production, water availability, and energy sources, leading to social and economic disruptions.

To address environmental problems, various approaches can be taken, including conservation, restoration, and sustainable development. Restoration involves repairing damaged ecosystems, while conservation aims to protect natural areas and species from harm. Sustainable development involves meeting human needs while preserving the natural environment for future generations.

Fighting environmental issues requires making extensive use of renewable energy sources such as hydropower, wind, and solar electricity. These sources are essential in the fight against climate change since they can be renewed endlessly and do not release greenhouse gases.

Mitigating environmental problems can also be achieved by the implementation of environmentally responsible agricultural techniques, such as crop rotation and organic farming. These methods lessen the usage of synthetic fertilizers and pesticides, which can damage aquatic resources and endanger wildlife.

Enforcing environmental regulations and policies is essential for effective environmental management. For example, laws can limit pollutant emissions from industrial and transportation sources. Policies can also incentivize the use of renewable energy sources and environmentally responsible agricultural practices.

Individual actions play a significant role in addressing environmental problems. Simple steps like reducing energy consumption, increasing recycling rates, and relying more on public transportation can have a significant impact.

Recent Technological Developments:

The environmental advantages of solar electricity have been amplified by the introduction of new technology. Bifacial solar panels, for instance, can increase energy efficiency by capturing sunlight from both sides. Modern recycling techniques make it possible to dispose of and reuse solar panels in a safe and effective manner, cutting waste and lessening the negative effects on the environment. Solar energy is now even more environmentally benign because to advancements in solar panel manufacture, which have also decreased the carbon footprint of production processes.

All things considered, resolving environmental issues is difficult and calls for cooperation from businesses, governments, and private citizens. Together, we can protect the environment and ensure a sustainable future for future generations as well as for ourselves.

Economic

Solar energy offers numerous financial benefits, which is contributing to its increasing popularity as an energy source. Factors such as the desire for cleaner energy, technological advancements, and falling solar panel prices are driving the demand for solar energy. Below are the financial advantages of using solar energy:

Reduced expenses: Solar energy can significantly lower your monthly electricity bills. After installing solar panels, you can generate your own electricity at no additional cost. With a 25-year lifespan, solar panels will continue to generate electricity and lower your monthly electricity costs for a considerable amount of time.

A robust return on investment: A solar power system installation is a long-term investment with potential for significant returns. almost the previous ten years, the price of solar panels has dropped by almost 70%, making them more affordable. Another benefit of installing a solar power system on your house is that it can raise its value.

Energy independence: Solar energy enables individuals, businesses, and communities to achieve energy independence. By generating their own power, they become less reliant on the grid and fossil fuels, enhancing their energy self-sufficiency.

Job creation: The solar industry is a rapidly growing sector that creates employment opportunities. Currently, over 250,000 people are employed in the solar industry in the United States, and this number is expected to continue increasing. The installation of solar panels requires skilled labor, generating jobs in the industry.

Lower electricity rates: The utilization of solar energy helps reduce the overall cost of electricity. As more people adopt solar energy, the demand for grid-supplied power decreases, leading to lower electricity costs.

Government incentives: Many governments worldwide provide financial incentives to incentivize the installation of solar panels. These incentives, which can lower the initial installation costs and increase the financial viability of solar energy for homes and businesses, may take the form of tax credits, rebates, and grants.

Reduced carbon dioxide emissions: Solar power is a clean source of energy that does not emit carbon dioxide into the atmosphere. By utilizing solar energy, the severity of climate change effects can be mitigated, and the demand for fossil fuels can be reduced.

Energy security: By lowering a country's dependency on foreign energy sources, solar energy improves energy security. Communities, organizations, and individuals may experience higher energy security as a result of this increased energy independence.

Improved competitiveness: Solar energy has been shown to improve the competitiveness of businesses in their respective markets. By lowering manufacturing costs, solar energy can help companies compete more effectively.

Sustainable development: Using solar energy is one step toward sustainable development. It's a clean, eco-friendly energy source that meets current needs without jeopardizing the ability of future generations to meet their own.

Recent Technological Developments:
The efficiency and cost-effectiveness of solar electricity have considerably increased thanks to recent developments in solar technology, such as the creation of perovskite solar cells. Compared to conventional silicon-based cells, these cells can attain better efficiencies and are less expensive to build. The economic advantages of solar energy systems have also increased due to advancements in energy storage technology, such as lithium-iron phosphate batteries, which have made it more practical to store extra solar electricity for use during cloudy periods.

Solar energy offers numerous financial advantages. It helps save money on electricity bills, provides energy independence, creates employment opportunities, reduces carbon emissions, lowers power costs, improves competitiveness, ensures energy security, and promotes environmentally sustainable growth.

Energy Independence
Energy independence refers to the ability of a nation, community, or individual to generate their own power without relying on external sources or importing energy. Utilizing renewable energy sources, such solar, wind, and hydropower, is one way to achieve energy independence. Now let's examine the advantages of attaining energy independence:

Energy security: By lowering reliance on foreign energy sources, energy independence increases energy security. This reduces vulnerability to geopolitical risks, supply disruptions, price volatility, and conflicts related to energy resources.

Cost savings: Energy independence can result in cost savings for individuals, communities, and nations. The price of renewable energy has significantly decreased in recent years, making it more competitive with conventional fossil fuels. Furthermore, free and renewable energy is produced by renewable energy systems, which lowers costs over time.

Environmental sustainability: Encouraging ecologically sustainable practices requires energy independence. The absence of greenhouse gas emissions from renewable energy sources contributes to climate change and global warming. By switching to renewable energy, carbon footprints are drastically reduced, tackling the pressing issue of climate change.

Employment creation: Renewable energy projects generate jobs through their installation, upkeep, and operation. Renewable energy-related businesses have grown significantly; in the US, the solar industry alone has created over 250,000 employment, and the wind industry employs over 100,000 people.

Economic growth: Energy independence can drive economic development. By reducing dependence on imported energy and utilizing renewable energy sources, communities and nations can save foreign exchange and promote the growth of domestic industries. This contributes to job creation and overall economic expansion.

Energy independence makes it possible for communities living in isolated or off-grid locations to have consistent access to energy. In order to reduce poverty and promote economic progress, access to electricity is essential. Households, educational institutions, and medical facilities can get the energy they require from renewable energy technology.

Energy efficiency: When compared to conventional fossil fuel systems, renewable energy sources like solar and wind have higher energy efficiency. Energy losses during transmission and distribution can be minimized by producing renewable energy near to its point of use.

Resilience: Energy independence enhances community and national resilience during crises. By generating their own energy through renewable energy systems, communities and countries ensure access to electricity during natural disasters, power outages, and emergencies.

National security and well-being: Reducing reliance on external energy supplies enhances a nation's safety and well-being. Energy independence reduces the potential for energy-related conflicts and geopolitical threats.

Empowerment: The ability to control one's own energy production is a benefit of energy independence for both people and communities. It gives individuals the option to select the energy they use, lessening their reliance on outside resources and encouraging the creation of energy locally.

Recent Technological Advancements

Innovations such as microgrids and advanced battery storage systems have greatly enhanced the potential for energy independence. Microgrids allow communities to generate, store, and manage their own energy locally, which can operate independently from the traditional grid. This is particularly beneficial for remote or disaster-prone areas. Furthermore, improvements in smart grid technology allow for improved management and integration of renewable energy sources, enhancing the overall dependability and efficiency of energy systems. Long-term economic, social, and environmental well-being depend on energy independence. With advantages including energy security, cost savings, environmental sustainability, job development, economic growth, energy accessibility, energy efficiency, resilience, national security, and empowerment, renewable energy sources offer a route to energy independence. Energy independence will remain a key objective as countries and communities shift to renewable energy sources.

Chapter 5 - How Do Solar Panels Work?

The sun is the most powerful example of fusion in our solar system, and its effects are visible just by looking out a window. As far back as 1839, scientists discovered its potential as a powerful energy source on Earth. A French scientist, Edmund Becquerel, found that some materials produced energy when exposed to light (Knier, 2008).

Although this was a significant scientific breakthrough, it wasn't initially viewed as a practical energy source. It wasn't until 1905 that Albert Einstein developed a theory for photovoltaic energy: the ability to generate a current when two materials are exposed to light.

As science progressed, so did solar technology. In 1954, Bell Labs created the first practical photovoltaic cell, and soon after, NASA began to recognize the utility of solar panels. They were considered for the first space missions as an easy and accessible alternative to traditional fossil fuels, converting energy from the sun without the need for additional fuels in space. This was a major scientific milestone.

Today, solar panels are refined and available to anyone. The reason for this significant development lies in the miniaturization and increased efficiency of solar cells. Modern solar panels are more efficient in transmitting the current they produce due to advancements in semiconductor technology.

The Process of Electricity Generation Using Solar Panels

Albert Einstein discovered the photoelectric effect in 1905, which is how solar panels turn sunlight into electric current. When photons, or light particles, collide with a substance, electrons are forced out of the material's atoms, producing the photoelectric effect. An electric current can be produced when enough electrons are liberated. Multiple solar cells make up each solar panel. Every cell consists of two conducting layers encased in a layer of silicon or another semiconductor material. To produce a p-n junction, which functions as an electron valve and only permits one direction of electron flow, the silicon layer is doped with additional atoms. Electrons are prompted to travel across the p-n junction and into the conductive layer when sunlight reaches the silicon layer.

The main energy produced by solar panels is direct current (DC). But since alternating current (AC) is needed for the majority of home and commercial uses, an inverter—which is usually put next to the solar panels—converts DC power into AC.

Components of Solar Panel Systems

In addition to the solar panels themselves, a typical solar panel system includes various supporting components:
- *Mounting hardware*: Secures the panels on rooftops or the ground, ensuring they are positioned to receive maximum sunlight.
- *Inverter:* Converts the DC power produced by the solar panels into AC electricity for use in residential and commercial settings.
- *Batteries:* Store surplus power generated by the panels for use during periods of low sunlight.
- *Charge controller*: Prevents overcharging or rapid discharge of the batteries.
- *Monitoring system*: Gives users the ability to see how much power is produced and used.

Various Solar Panel Types

Solar panels come in a variety of forms, each with pros and cons of their own:
- *Monocrystalline solar panels*: Constructed from a solitary silicon crystal, they exhibit exceptional efficiency at a higher cost.
- *Polycrystalline solar panels*: Composed of multiple silicon crystals, they are less efficient than monocrystalline panels but more cost-effective.
- *Thin-film solar panels:* They are less effective but more reasonably priced since they are made of materials like amorphous silicon, cadmium telluride, and copper indium gallium selenide.
- *Concentrated solar panels*: Use lenses or mirrors to concentrate sunlight onto a smaller area of solar cells, increasing their efficiency but at a higher cost.

Solar Inverters

For homes and businesses to use AC electricity instead of DC electricity produced by solar panels, inverters are essential. Inverters come in two primary varieties:

- *Central inverters*: Convert DC energy from all the solar panels in a system into AC energy. They are cost-effective for small systems but less efficient for larger ones due to the high volume of DC energy conversion required.
- *Micro-inverters*: installed on every solar panel, providing panel-level DC to AC conversion. For larger systems, they are more effective since they divide the conversion duty equally.

Racking

Proper mounting of solar panels is essential for optimal performance. Solar panels are often tilted to maximize direct sunlight exposure. This is particularly important outside the equatorial regions, where the sun's angle varies throughout the year. Rotating mounts can ensure more direct sunlight throughout the day, increasing energy generation. Additionally, racking protects the wiring and electronics from weather damage, ensuring longevity and efficiency.

Charge Controllers

Charge controllers regulate the energy received from solar panels, preventing overloads in batteries. They ensure a consistent current, protecting batteries and improving overall system stability. Without a charge controller, fluctuations in solar energy could lead to inconsistent power supply and potential damage to batteries.

Batteries

Batteries are used to store the energy produced by solar panels so it may be used when there isn't any sunshine. They are a crucial component of all solar power systems, but off-grid systems more than any other.
To guarantee optimum performance and longevity, regular maintenance and periodic replacement are required.

Determining the Number of Solar Panels Needed

The number of solar panels required depends on several factors, including space, energy consumption, and the number of people using the power. To calculate your needs:

1. *Analyze your power bill:* Look at the kilowatts used in a year to find the average consumption.
2. *Consider your environment:* Sunny days, latitude, and local weather patterns significantly impact solar panel efficiency.
3. *Consult professionals*: Get multiple opinions from solar companies to determine the optimal number of panels for your specific situation.

Maintenance and Monitoring

Maintenance is crucial for the longevity and efficiency of a solar power system. Key components require regular checks:

- *Solar Panels*: Clean every six months or as needed to remove dirt and debris.
- *Batteries:* Regularly check electrolyte levels (for lead-acid batteries) and monitor for signs of wear.
- *Inverter:* Keep clean and ensure cooling systems are functioning.
- *Charge Controller:* Ensure it regulates energy consistently to protect batteries.

Real-time data on system performance can be obtained from monitoring systems, which makes it easier to spot and fix problems early. Options for both automated and manual monitoring are provided.

Innovations in Solar Technology

Recent advancements have significantly improved solar technology:

- *Bifacial Panels:* Capture sunlight from both sides, increasing efficiency.
- *PERC Technology*: Enhances cell efficiency by adding a reflective layer to capture more sunlight.
- *Improved Batteries*: New battery technologies, like lithium iron phosphate (LiFePO4), offer longer life and greater efficiency.

Understanding how solar panels work and maintaining them properly is essential for harnessing solar energy effectively. Technological advancements continue to improve solar panel efficiency and accessibility, making solar power a viable and sustainable energy source for the future.

Chapter 6: Harnessing the Sun: Building Your Own Solar Panel System

One of the best methods to become energy independent and lessen your environmental impact is to use solar energy. Solar power is a renewable and sustainable energy source that is produced when sunlight is captured and transformed into electrical current. This chapter explores the definition of solar panel systems, the parts that make them up, and a comprehensive installation instructions.

What is a Solar Panel System?

Photovoltaic (PV) cells are used in solar panel systems to convert sunlight into electrical power. Semiconductive materials, such as silicon, are used to make these cells; these materials absorb sunlight and produce an electric field. Depending on how your system is configured, the generated electricity can either be utilized right away, stored in batteries for use at a later time, or even transmitted back to the electric grid.

Materials for a Solar Panel System

- *Solar Panels:* These come in various sizes and efficiencies. The number you need will depend on your energy needs and the amount of sunlight your location receives.
- *Inverter:* Converts the DC power generated by the solar panels into AC power for use in your home.
- *Charge Controller:* Manages the flow of electricity to the batteries and prevents overcharging.
- *Batteries:* Store energy for when the sun isn't shining. The size and number of batteries depend on your power usage and sunlight availability.
- *Mounting Hardware*: Includes racking to mount the panels onto your roof or a ground-based structure.
- *Wiring and Connectors*: Connect the solar panels to the charge controller, the charge controller to the batteries, and the batteries to the inverter.
- *Disconnect Switches*: Necessary to safely disconnect various parts of the system for maintenance or emergencies.
- *Meter and Fuse Box Connections*: Needed if you plan to connect your system to the grid or need to fuse the solar panel system.
- *Tools:* Basic tools include a drill, wire strippers, a crimping tool, wrenches, and a multimeter to test voltages.
- *Safety Equipment:* Personal Protective Equipment (PPE) such as safety glasses, gloves, and possibly a hard hat, depending on the installation location.

Recent Technological Advancements

- *Bifacial Solar Panels*: These panels can capture sunlight on both sides, increasing efficiency.
- *Solar Tracking Systems*: Devices that adjust the angle of solar panels throughout the day to maximize sunlight exposure.
- *Improved Energy Storage Solutions*: New battery technologies like lithium-iron-phosphate (LiFePO4) offer better performance and longevity.

Building a Solar Panel System

From initial planning to final testing, there are various phases involved in building a solar panel system. When handling electricity, exercise caution and get advice from an expert if you have any doubts about any part of the procedure.

Step-by-Step Guide

Step 1: Evaluate Your Solar Potential
- Check your location for its solar potential. The best orientation for solar panels in the Northern Hemisphere is true south. Ensure your selected location receives plenty of sunlight and is free from shading throughout the day.

Step 2: Determine Your Energy Needs
• To better understand your consumption, do an energy audit. This will assist you in figuring out how big of a solar panel system you require.

Step 3: Acquire Necessary Components
- Based on your energy needs and budget, purchase the necessary components: solar panels, inverter, charge controller, batteries, mounting equipment, disconnect switches, wiring and connectors, meter, fuse box connections, and safety equipment.

Step 4: Obtain Necessary Permits
- Check with your local government and utility company about any necessary permits or regulations for installing solar panel systems.

Step 5: Install Mounting Equipment
- Install your mounting hardware in the selected location, ensuring it's sturdy and secure. If you're mounting on a roof, make sure the roof's structure can support the weight of the panels.

Step 6: Install Solar Panels
- Attach the solar panels to the mounting hardware, making sure they're secure and angled correctly for optimal sun exposure. Connect the panels together using the appropriate wiring and connectors.

Step 7: Install Electrical Components
- Using the proper wire, attach the solar panels to the charge controller. Next, attach the charge controller to the batteries. Connect the batteries to the inverter. Install any necessary disconnect switches, fuses, or meter connections.

Step 8: Test the System
- Once all the components are connected, test the system to ensure it's generating and storing power correctly. A multimeter can be useful for checking voltages and ensuring connections are correct.

Step 9: Finalize Installation
- Once you've confirmed everything is working correctly, finalize the installation. This might involve sealing around mounts, tidying up wiring, or setting up monitoring systems to keep track of your system's performance.

Step 10: Maintenance
- Regularly check your system to ensure it's working optimally. This includes cleaning panels, checking connections, and testing system output.

Cost Considerations and Financial Incentives

- *Upfront Costs:* Consider the initial investment for components and installation.
- *Long-term Savings*: Savings on electricity bills over time can offset initial costs.
- *Financial Incentives*: Many governments offer tax credits, rebates, and other incentives to reduce the cost of installing solar panels.

Building a solar panel system can be complex. While it's possible to do it yourself, especially for smaller systems, larger installations will often benefit from professional expertise. Always prioritize safety and seek professional help if needed.

Chapter 7: PROJECT: Building a Solar Power System

Building your own solar power system can be a rewarding and cost-effective way to harness renewable energy. This project will guide you step-by-step through the process, ensuring you understand each component and its function within the system. By the end of this chapter, you will have a comprehensive understanding of how to design, install, and maintain a solar power system for your home or business.

Project Objective and Expected Outcomes
Objective:
The objective of this project is to build a fully functional solar power system that generates and stores electricity for use in your home or business. The system will be designed to maximize efficiency and sustainability while minimizing reliance on traditional power grids.

Expected Outcomes:
- A fully operational solar power system that reduces or eliminates electricity bills.
- Increased energy independence and a lower carbon footprint.
- Enhanced understanding of solar technology and its practical applications.

Step-by-Step Guide to Building a Solar Power System
Step 1: Gathering Necessary Materials and Tools
Materials:
- **Solar Panels:** Choose based on your energy needs and budget. Monocrystalline panels offer high efficiency, while polycrystalline panels are more cost-effective.
- **Mounting Hardware:** Includes racks, brackets, and any necessary supports for roof or ground installation.
- **Charge Controller:** Manages the flow of electricity to the batteries and prevents overcharging.
- **Deep Cycle Batteries:** For energy storage. Select batteries that are reliable and designed for solar systems.
- **Inverter:** Transforms solar panel and battery DC power into AC power suitable for domestic usage.
- **Wiring and Connectors:** To connect solar panels, charge controller, batteries, and inverter.
- **Disconnect Switches:** For safely disconnecting parts of the system during maintenance or emergencies.
- **Fuse Box Connections:** Necessary if connecting the system to the grid or if fuses are needed for safety.
- **Monitoring System (Optional):** To track system performance and energy production.

Tools:
- Drill and drill bits
- Screwdrivers
- Wrenches and pliers
- Wire strippers and crimping tools
- Multimeter (for testing electrical connections)
- Safety gear (gloves, safety glasses, hard hat)
- Ladder or scaffolding (for roof installations)

Step 2: Designing Your Solar Power System
1. **Evaluate Your Energy Needs:**
   - Conduct an energy audit to determine your average electricity consumption. Review your electricity bills to find your average daily usage in kilowatt-hours (kWh).
2. **Assess Your Solar Potential:**
   - Determine the optimal location for your solar panels. The ideal spot should receive maximum sunlight throughout the day and be free from obstructions. Use tools like solar pathfinders or online solar calculators to assess your site's solar potential.
3. **Choose the Right Components:**
   - Select solar panels, charge controller, batteries, and an inverter based on your energy needs and budget.

Step 3: Installing Solar Panels: Step-by-Step Guide

1. **Install Mounting Hardware:**
   - Secure the mounting brackets or racks to your roof or chosen location, ensuring they are tilted at the optimal angle for maximum sun exposure. Use a level to ensure the mounts are properly aligned.
2. **Attach Solar Panels:**
   - Carefully lift and place the solar panels onto the mounting hardware. Secure the panels using bolts and brackets, ensuring they are firmly in place.
3. **Connect Solar Panels:**
   - Use appropriate wiring to connect the solar panels in series or parallel, depending on your system design. Ensure all connections are secure and weather proofed.

Step 4: Setting Up Solar Batteries and Storage
1. **Select a Safe Place:**
   - Place batteries in a dry, well-ventilated room away from intense heat or light.
2. **Connect Batteries**:
   - To obtain the required voltage and capacity, connect batteries in series or parallel using sturdy wires. Make sure that everything is properly insulated and tighten all connections.

Step 5: Connecting Solar Panels to Batteries: A Technical Guide
1. **Install the Charge Controller:**
   - For convenient access, place the charge controller close to the batteries. As directed by the manufacturer, connect the charge controller's input to the solar panel's output.
2. **Connect Batteries to Charge Controller:**
   - Attach the battery bank to the charge controller, ensuring proper polarity (positive to positive, negative to negative).
3. **Safety Checks:**
   - Double-check all connections for proper insulation and secure fastening. Use a multimeter to verify voltage and current levels.

Step 6: Setting Up a Charge Controller and Inverter
1. **Install the Inverter:**
   - Mount the inverter in a cool, dry place close to the batteries. Connect the battery bank to the inverter input, following the manufacturer's guidelines.
2. **Connect Inverter to Electrical System:**
   - Use appropriate wiring to connect the inverter output to your home's electrical panel or specific circuits. Install disconnect switches and fuses as needed for safety and compliance with local regulations.

Step 7: Testing Your Solar Power System
1. **Initial Power-Up:**
   - Turn on the charge controller and inverter, following the manufacturer's startup procedures. Verify that the system is generating and storing power correctly using a multimeter and monitoring system.
2. **Load Testing:**
   - Connect various appliances and devices to the system to ensure it can handle the expected load. Monitor performance and check for any issues or irregularities.

Step 8: Maintenance and Monitoring: Ensuring Long-Term Success
1. **Regular Inspections:**
   - Perform visual inspections of all components at least twice a year. Look for signs of wear, corrosion, or damage. Clean solar panels with water and a soft brush to remove dust and debris.
2. **System Monitoring:**
   - Use a monitoring system to track energy production and consumption. This can help you identify and address issues promptly. Keep a log of maintenance activities and performance metrics.
3. **Battery Maintenance:**
   - If the battery is flooded, check the electrolyte levels and add distilled water as necessary. Make that there are no corrosion or loose connections on any of the batteries.

These comprehensive instructions will help you construct a dependable and effective solar power system. This project will improve your knowledge of renewable energy technologies in addition to giving you a sustainable source of electricity. Accept the sun's power and get the rewards of renewable energy!

MODULE C: WIND ENERGY

Chapter 1: Embracing the Wind: Creating Your Own Wind Turbine System

Wind power is an excellent resource for generating renewable energy, particularly in areas with consistent and strong winds. Like solar power, wind energy can help you achieve energy self-sufficiency and reduce reliance on traditional power grids. This chapter provides an overview of wind energy, the materials needed for a wind turbine system, and a step-by-step guide on how to build and install your own wind turbine.

Understanding Wind Energy

Utilizing the wind's inherent power, wind energy produces electricity. A wind turbine's blades spin when the wind blows, spinning a shaft that powers a generator. Electrical power is produced by this mechanical motion. Depending on the exact configuration, the generated energy can be consumed right away, stored in batteries for later use, or sent back into the power grid.

Components of a Wind Turbine System

Building a wind turbine system requires several key components:

- **Wind Turbine**: This device captures the wind's energy and consists of blades that turn a shaft connected to a generator.
- **Tower**: The turbine is mounted on a tower, which raises it above obstructions to capture the most wind.
- **Batteries**: To store energy for periods of low wind, a battery system is essential.
- **Charge Controller**: This manages the electricity going into the battery, preventing overcharging.
- **Inverter**: Converts the DC power produced by the turbine into AC power for home use.

Step-by-Step Guide to Building a Wind Turbine System

1. **Evaluate Your Site's Wind Potential**
   - Use tools like an anemometer to measure wind speed and direction over time.
   - Check online wind maps and consult local data to understand the wind patterns in your area.
   - Consider potential obstacles such as buildings or trees that may affect wind flow.

2. **Determine Your Energy Needs**
   - Conduct an energy audit to determine how much electricity you consume. This will help size your wind turbine appropriately.
   - Evaluate your daily, monthly, and annual energy usage to understand your peak and average power needs.

3. **Acquire Necessary Components**
   - Purchase the wind turbine, tower, batteries, charge controller, and inverter based on your energy needs and budget.
   - Research different types of turbines and inverters to find those best suited for your specific conditions.

4. **Obtain Necessary Permits**
   - Check with local authorities and utility companies for permits and regulations regarding wind turbine installations.
   - Ensure compliance with zoning laws, building codes, and environmental regulations.

5. **Install the Tower**
   - Securely install the tower in an open area free from obstructions. Ensure it is anchored properly to withstand high winds.
   - Consider using a tilt-up tower for easier maintenance and access to the turbine.

6. **Mount the Wind Turbine**
   - Attach the turbine to the tower, ensuring it is oriented correctly to maximize wind capture.
   - Use a crane or other lifting device if necessary to safely place the turbine on the tower.

7. **Install Electrical Components**
   - Connect the turbine to the charge controller, then to the batteries, and finally to the inverter. Ensure all wiring is secured and weatherproof.

- Use high-quality, weather-resistant wiring and connectors to ensure long-term durability and safety.

8. **Test the System**
   - Use a multimeter to check voltages and ensure the system is generating and storing power correctly.
   - Conduct a series of tests to monitor performance under different wind conditions and loads.

9. **Regular Maintenance**
   - To guarantee optimum performance, check and maintain the electrical, tower, and turbine components on a regular basis. This include examining the components for wear and tear, cleaning them, and making sure the connections are tight.
   - Schedule periodic professional inspections to ensure all components are functioning correctly and safely.

Integration with Other Renewable Systems

Think about combining your wind turbine system with solar panels or other renewable energy sources. By utilizing both solar and wind energy, this hybrid technique can produce electricity more consistently.

For instance, solar panels can produce energy during sunny days when the wind might be low, and wind turbines can generate power during cloudy, windy days. This complementary system can enhance overall energy reliability and efficiency.

Environmental and Economic Benefits

Wind energy offers numerous benefits, including reducing carbon emissions, lowering electricity bills, and contributing to energy independence. By harnessing wind power, you can significantly cut down on the use of fossil fuels, thus helping to mitigate climate change. Government incentives and tax credits can also offset installation costs, making wind energy a viable option for many. Moreover, using wind energy can lead to substantial savings on electricity bills over time, as the wind is a free resource once the initial setup is complete.

Examples and Case Studies

Incorporating real-world examples and case studies can offer significant perspectives on the actual implementations of wind turbine systems. For instance, highlighting successful DIY wind turbine projects can demonstrate the feasibility and benefits of such systems. Examples of small communities or individual households that have achieved energy independence through wind power can be particularly inspiring and informative.

Building a wind turbine system is a significant but rewarding project that can provide clean, renewable energy for your home. You may successfully harness the wind's power to attain energy self-sufficiency and contribute to a sustainable future by knowing the parts and procedures involved. For your wind turbine system to be successful and efficient over the long run, regular maintenance and careful planning are essential. Your energy independence and environmental effect can be further improved by combining wind power with other renewable energy sources. You can take advantage of all the benefits that wind energy has to offer with the appropriate strategy.

Chapter 2: Expanding Horizons with Wind Energy

Basics of Wind Energy: Harnessing Natural Forces

Wind energy is one of the oldest forms of harnessing natural forces to generate power. Its basic idea is to harness wind energy's kinetic energy and turn it into mechanical energy, which can subsequently be changed into electrical power. The sun's uneven heating of the Earth's surface, which creates wind and air movement, is the first step in this process. Through the smart placement of wind turbines in regions with reliable wind patterns, we can harness this boundless energy source.

Harnessing wind energy involves more than just placing turbines in a windy spot. Understanding wind patterns, speed, and direction over time is crucial. Tools like anemometers measure these factors, while wind maps provide valuable data on local wind conditions. This comprehensive understanding ensures the optimal placement and efficiency of wind turbines.

Advantages and Limitations of Wind Energy

The many benefits of wind energy are what make it so appealing. Wind energy provides a sustainable answer to our expanding energy needs because it is a renewable resource. Once installed, wind turbines have low operational costs, requiring minimal maintenance compared to fossil fuel-based energy systems. Furthermore, wind energy is environmentally friendly, producing no greenhouse gases or pollutants during operation, significantly reducing our carbon footprint.

However, wind energy is not without its limitations. Because wind energy is intermittent, its production can be unexpected. Consequently, in order to guarantee a steady supply of power, dependable storage solutions or hybrid systems are required. Installing a wind turbine can have high upfront costs since it requires a large infrastructure and technological investment. Additionally, wind turbines require considerable space, often best suited to open areas or high towers, and can be considered noisy or visually intrusive by some.

Wind Energy in Off-Grid Living: A Sustainable Choice

Wind energy offers a dependable and sustainable power source for people who want to live off the grid. A hybrid system that maximizes energy production and guarantees a consistent power supply is created when wind turbines are combined with other renewable energy sources, including solar panels. This strategy encourages a more robust and self-sufficient manner of life in addition to improving energy security.

Modern Innovations in Wind Energy Technology

Advancements in wind energy technology have revolutionized how we harness and utilize this resource. Modern turbines are designed to be more aerodynamic and efficient, capturing a greater amount of energy from the wind. Innovations such as smart grid integration allow wind turbines to seamlessly blend into existing energy infrastructures, improving distribution and management.

Energy storage solutions have also seen significant advancements. New battery technologies enable better storage of wind-generated electricity, ensuring a stable power supply even during periods of low wind. Additionally, vertical axis wind turbines offer a versatile alternative, capable of capturing wind from any direction and suitable for urban environments with variable wind patterns.

Understanding Wind Turbines: Types and Functionality

Wind turbines come in various designs, each suited to different environments and energy needs. Horizontal axis wind turbines (HAWTs) are the most common, featuring blades that rotate around a horizontal axis. These turbines are highly efficient and often used in large-scale wind farms. However, they require significant space and are typically installed on tall towers. On the other hand, the blades of vertical axis wind turbines, or VAWTs, revolve around a vertical axis. Because they can gather wind from any direction, these turbines are perfect for residential and urban settings.

Chapter 3: Implementing and Maintaining Wind Energy Systems

Installation and Maintenance of Wind Turbines

Installing a wind turbine involves several critical steps, beginning with a thorough site assessment. Evaluating the wind potential of a location is essential, using tools like anemometers and wind maps to gather data on wind patterns. Once a suitable site is identified, obtaining necessary permits and complying with local regulations is crucial.

The installation process starts with constructing a solid foundation to anchor the turbine tower securely. Erecting the tower and ensuring its stability is the next step, followed by assembling the turbine components and attaching them to the tower. Electrical connections must be carefully made, linking the turbine to the system's inverter and batteries.

Regular maintenance is vital to ensure the long-term efficiency of wind turbines. Routine inspections should be conducted to check for wear and tear, especially on the blades and moving parts. Lubricating these parts ensures smooth operation, while inspecting the electrical connections and components helps prevent potential issues. Keeping the turbine and blades clean is also crucial for maintaining optimal performance.

Wind Energy Storage: Options and Efficiency

Achieving the greatest possible advantage from wind energy systems requires efficient storage options. The variable nature of wind power requires batteries intended for wind energy storage to be able to store excess energy during periods of high production and supply it during periods of low wind. Lead-acid, lithium-ion, and flow batteries are among the storage battery types that are appropriate for wind energy systems. Because they are affordable and dependable, lead-acid batteries are frequently utilized, despite having a lower energy density and a shorter lifespan than other options. Lithium-ion batteries are more expensive, but they last longer and have a higher energy density.

A more recent technology, flow batteries, offer deep discharge capabilities and a long cycle life, making them scalable storage options. In order to achieve effective energy transfer and storage, there are technological issues when connecting wind turbines to storage batteries. A system needs sufficient wiring, voltage regulation, and safety precautions to function correctly. It is also helpful to set up a charge controller and system monitoring tools to ensure that the storage batteries last as long as possible and to prevent overcharging.

Monitoring and Managing Your Wind Power System

Maintaining the efficiency of your wind power system and quickly resolving any possible problems require constant management and monitoring. You may monitor energy production, storage levels, and general performance by putting in place a monitoring system. With the help of sophisticated monitoring technologies, you can optimize your energy use and make well-informed decisions by receiving real-time data and warnings.

Your wind power system's long-term performance also depends on routine maintenance. This covers regular maintenance such as cleaning, lubrication, electrical connection inspections, and inspections. You can extend the life of your system and keep it operating efficiently by taking care of small problems before they grow into larger ones.

Safety Precautions and Regular Maintenance

Prioritizing safety above all else is imperative when utilizing wind energy technologies. Wind turbine installation and maintenance require handling electrical components and working at heights, both of which can be dangerous if safety precautions aren't taken. To avoid mishaps, always wear the proper safety equipment, such as gloves, harnesses, and helmets, and abide by safety regulations.

Regular maintenance is not only essential for system efficiency but also for safety. Ensuring that all components are in good working condition and securely installed reduces the risk of accidents. Keeping the area around the wind turbine clear of debris and obstructions also enhances safety.

Project Objective and Expected Outcomes

This project aims to offer a thorough manual for installing and maintaining a wind power system that satisfies your energy requirements and encourages sustainable living.

Gathering Necessary Materials and Tools

Before starting your wind power project, gather all the necessary materials and tools. This includes wind turbines, towers, storage batteries, charge controllers, inverters, wiring, and safety equipment. Having all the required components on hand will streamline the installation process and ensure that you have everything needed to complete the project successfully.

Designing Your Wind Turbine System

Designing a wind turbine system involves assessing your energy needs, evaluating the wind potential of your location, and selecting the appropriate components. Consider factors such as wind speed, direction, and consistency, as well as the space available for installation. You can ensure that you have a dependable source of renewable energy and increase efficiency by designing a system that precisely matches your needs.

Installing the Wind Turbine: Step-by-Step Guide

Installing a wind turbine involves several steps, from preparing the site to connecting the electrical components. Follow this step-by-step guide to ensure a successful installation:
Site Assessment: Evaluate the wind potential of your location using tools like anemometers and wind maps.
Permits and Regulations: Obtain necessary permits and comply with local regulations.
Foundation Construction: Build a solid foundation to anchor the turbine tower.
Tower Installation: Erect the tower and ensure it is stable and secure.
Turbine Assembly: Assemble the turbine components and attach them to the tower.
Electrical Connections: Connect the turbine to the system's inverter and batteries, ensuring all connections are secure and weatherproof.

Setting Up Storage Batteries and Connections

An essential part of a wind power system are storage batteries, which offer a consistent energy source when the wind isn't as strong. Choosing the right battery type, connecting the batteries to the wind turbine system, and making sure that the safety features and voltage regulation are in place are all part of setting up storage batteries.

Connecting the Wind Turbine to Batteries: A Technical Guide

Connecting the wind turbine to storage batteries requires careful consideration of wiring, voltage regulation, and safety protocols. Efficient energy transfer is ensured by appropriately sized wire and connectors, and the system is safeguarded against overcharging and other potential problems by voltage regulators and safety systems. You can securely and effectively make the required connections by adhering to a technical guide.

Setting Up a Charge Controller and System Monitoring

Controlling the amount of electricity that goes from the wind turbine to the storage batteries requires a charge controller. It guarantees that the batteries are charged effectively and avoids overcharging. Connecting a charge controller to the wind turbine and batteries, adjusting its settings, and keeping an eye on the system's operation are all part of the setup process.

Testing Your Wind Turbine System

It is essential to verify the wind turbine system after installation to make sure everything is operating as it should. Check energy generation, storage capacity, and general performance with monitoring tools. During testing, take care of any problems that crop up to maximize the effectiveness of the system.

Troubleshooting Typical Problems

Wind power systems might have problems even with meticulous design and installation. Mechanical deterioration, electrical malfunctions, and irregular energy output are common issues. Finding the source of the issue, carrying out any required fixes or modifications, and guaranteeing that the system operates at peak efficiency are all part of troubleshooting.

Maintenance and Monitoring: Ensuring Long-Term Efficiency

For your wind power system to operate efficiently over the long run, regular maintenance and observation are necessary. Regularly inspect the system, clean the parts, lubricate the moving parts, and inspect the electrical connections.
Implement a monitoring system to track performance and address any issues promptly. You can guarantee a dependable and sustainable energy supply for many years to come by keeping up with system maintenance.
You may successfully harness wind energy, become energy independent, and contribute to a clean future by using this thorough instructions. When used and managed correctly, wind energy is a flexible and potent resource that can supply your home with a dependable and environmentally responsible source of electricity.

Chapter 4: Project: Building Your Own Wind Power System

Project Objective and Expected Outcomes

The objective of this project is to provide a detailed, step-by-step guide to building and maintaining a wind power system. By following this guide, you will achieve energy independence, reduce your carbon footprint, and gain a sustainable source of renewable energy for your home. This project aims to empower you with the knowledge and skills needed to harness wind energy effectively.

Step 1: Evaluating Your Wind Potential

Before diving into the construction of your wind power system, it is crucial to evaluate the wind potential at your location. Follow these steps:

1. **Site Assessment:**
    *   Use an anemometer to measure wind speed and direction over a period of several weeks to gather accurate data.
    *   Consult local wind maps and meteorological data to understand long-term wind patterns in your area.
2. **Optimal Site Selection:**
    *   Choose a site that is elevated and free from obstructions like buildings and trees.
    *   Ensure the location has consistent wind flow, ideally with an average wind speed of at least 10 mph.

Step 2: Designing Your Wind Turbine System

Designing an efficient wind turbine system involves careful planning and consideration of various components. Here's how to get started:

1. **Determine Your Energy Needs:**
    *   Conduct an energy audit to estimate your household's electricity consumption.
    *   Calculate the total wattage required to meet your energy demands.
2. **Choosing the Right Turbine:**
    *   Select a wind turbine that matches your energy needs and wind conditions. Horizontal axis wind turbines (HAWTs) are suitable for higher wind speeds, while vertical axis wind turbines (VAWTs) are better for variable wind directions.
3. **System Components:**
    *   Wind Turbine: Choose a model based on your energy requirements and wind speed.
    *   Tower: Select a tower height that places the turbine in optimal wind conditions.
    *   Batteries: Determine the type and number of batteries needed for energy storage.
    *   Charge Controller: Prevents overcharging and manages the flow of electricity.
    *   Inverter: Converts DC power from the turbine to AC power for home use.

Step 3: Gathering Necessary Materials and Tools

Having all the necessary materials and tools before starting the installation will streamline the process:

1. **Materials:**
    *   Wind turbine and blades
    *   Tower and mounting hardware
    *   Deep-cycle batteries
    *   Charge controller
    *   Inverter
    *   Electrical wiring and connectors
    *   Concrete for foundation
2. **Tools:**
    *   Wrenches and screwdrivers
    *   Drill and bits
    *   Multimeter
    *   Anemometer
    *   Safety gear (gloves, helmet, safety glasses)

Step 4: Installing the Wind Turbine: Step-by-Step Guide

1. **Foundation and Tower Setup:**
    *   Dig a hole for the tower foundation and pour concrete to create a stable base.
    *   Assemble the tower sections and securely attach the wind turbine at the top.
    *   Erect the tower and anchor it firmly to the foundation.
2. **Mounting the Wind Turbine:**

- Follow the manufacturer's instructions to mount the turbine blades and nacelle.
- Ensure the turbine is oriented to capture the maximum wind flow.

Step 5: Setting Up Storage Batteries and Connections

1. **Battery Bank Installation:**
   - Choose a well-ventilated and dry location for the battery bank.
   - Connect the batteries in series or parallel, depending on your system's voltage requirements.
2. **Wiring and Connections:**
   - Use appropriate gauge wiring to connect the wind turbine to the charge controller.
   - Connect the charge controller to the battery bank.
   - Wire the inverter to the battery bank and the household electrical system.

Step 6: Connecting the Wind Turbine to Batteries: A Technical Guide

1. **Connecting the Turbine to the Charge Controller:**
   - Use heavy-duty wiring to connect the wind turbine to the charge controller. Ensure the connections are secure and weatherproof.
2. **Connecting the Charge Controller to Batteries:**
   - When connecting the charge controller to the battery bank, according to the manufacturer's instructions. To avoid any voltage drops, make sure all of the connections are secure.
3. **Connecting the Batteries to the Inverter:**
   - Align the positive and negative terminals of the battery bank so that they are properly connected to the inverter.

Step 7: Setting Up a Charge Controller and System Monitoring

1. **Charge Controller Installation:**
   - Install the charge controller close to the battery bank for efficient monitoring.
   - Configure the settings based on your battery type and system requirements.
2. **Monitoring System:**
   - Set up a monitoring system to track energy production, battery levels, and overall performance.
   - Use digital displays or online monitoring tools for real-time data.

Step 8: Testing Your Wind Turbine System

1. **Initial Testing:**
   - Use a multimeter to check the voltage output from the wind turbine.
   - Ensure the charge controller and inverter are functioning correctly.
2. **System Performance Check:**
   - Monitor the system over a few days to ensure it is operating efficiently and meeting your energy needs.

Step 9: Troubleshooting Common Issues

1. **Identifying Problems:**
   - Check for loose connections or wiring faults if the system isn't producing power.
   - Inspect the turbine blades and tower for any physical damage.
2. **Resolving Issues:**
   - Re-tighten any loose connections.
   - Replace damaged components as necessary to ensure the system operates smoothly.

Step 10: Maintenance and Monitoring: Ensuring Long-Term Efficiency

1. **Regular Inspections:**
   - Perform routine inspections of the turbine blades, tower, and electrical connections.
   - Clean the turbine blades to prevent debris buildup.
2. **Battery Maintenance:**
   - Check battery electrolyte levels and top up with distilled water if necessary.
   - Ensure terminals are clean and free from corrosion.
3. **System Monitoring:**
   - Continuously monitor the system's performance using the installed monitoring tools.
   - Address any performance issues promptly to maintain efficiency.

MODULE D: ALTERNATIVE ENERGY

Chapter 1: Harnessing Energy: The Comprehensive Guide to Propane Generators

Propane generators are a popular choice among individuals aiming for self-sufficiency. They offer many advantages, such as being a clean-burning fuel, having a longer shelf life compared to gasoline, and being relatively easy to store and use.

Understanding Propane Generators

A propane generator functions similarly to other types of generators but uses propane as its fuel source. Propane, or liquefied petroleum gas (LPG), is stored under pressure and is delivered to the generator via a regulator and a hose. Upon combustion, the propane powers the generator, creating electricity. Propane generators are highly versatile and can be used in various settings, from residential backup power to off-grid applications.

Benefits of Propane Generators

Propane generators offer several benefits that make them an attractive choice for self-sufficiency:
- **Long Shelf Life:** Propane doesn't degrade over time, making it an excellent choice for long-term storage.
- **Clean Burning:** Propane is more environmentally friendly than gasoline or diesel because it burns cleanly and produces less harmful pollutants.
- **Availability:** Propane is widely available, even when other types of fuel may be scarce.
- **Safe Storage:** Propane can be safely stored in tanks of various sizes, from small portable cylinders to large underground tanks.

These benefits make propane generators particularly useful for those who prioritize long-term sustainability and environmental impact.

Drawbacks of Propane Generators

Despite the many benefits of propane generators, there are a few disadvantages to take into account:
- Lower Efficiency: Propane generators often have lower efficiency levels than diesel or gasoline generators, which could lead to increased fuel usage.
- Higher Cost: Running a propane generator can be more expensive over time because propane is generally more expensive than other fuels.
- Cold Weather Considerations: To guarantee optimal operation, propane may need extra precautions in cold weather, such as a tank warmer.

Understanding these drawbacks is necessary in order to decide if a propane generator is the best choice for your requirements.

Selecting a Generator for Propane

It's crucial to take the following aspects into account when choosing a propane generator:
- **Power Output:** Determine the generator's power output to ensure it meets your energy needs. Calculate your total wattage requirements by adding the wattages of all the devices you plan to power simultaneously.
- **Size and Portability:** Consider the generator's size and portability, depending on whether you need a stationary or portable unit. Portable generators are ideal for camping and temporary setups, while stationary units are better for long-term installations.
- **Propane Tank Storage:** Assess the available space for storing a propane tank and choose a generator that accommodates your storage options. Ensure the tank size matches the generator's fuel consumption rate.
- **Runtime:** Evaluate the generator's runtime, which indicates how long it can operate on a single tank of propane. Longer runtimes are beneficial for extended power outages.

You can select a generator that meets your unique needs and limitations by keeping these things in mind.

Maintaining Your Propane Generator

To ensure your propane generator operates effectively, regular maintenance is necessary. Follow these maintenance tasks:

- **Oil Check and Replacement:** Regularly check the oil levels and replace it as recommended by the manufacturer. Clean oil ensures the engine runs smoothly and reduces wear and tear.
- **Spark Plug Inspection:** Inspect the spark plugs and clean or replace them if necessary. Clean spark plugs improve engine efficiency and prevent misfires.
- **Air Filter Maintenance:** Regularly check and clean or replace the air filter to ensure optimal air flow and combustion.
- **Fuel System Inspection:** Inspect the propane hose, regulator, and connections for leaks or damage. Replace any worn or damaged parts promptly.
- **Regular Testing:** Test the generator regularly to ensure it's functioning correctly and ready for use. Running the generator periodically helps keep the engine components lubricated and prevents corrosion.
- Maintaining your generator on a regular basis will increase its lifespan and guarantee that it will function dependably when essential.

Environmental Aspects to Take into Account

When compared to gasoline and diesel, propane is thought to burn cleaner and produce less emissions and contaminants. For people who are worried about lowering their carbon footprint, this makes it a more environmentally responsible option. Furthermore, propane generators can facilitate the switch to more sustainable energy practices and lessen dependency on fossil fuels.

Safety Advice

It's crucial to abide by safety regulations when utilizing propane generators in order to avoid mishaps and guarantee safe operation:

- **Proper Ventilation:** To avoid carbon monoxide buildup, run the generator in a well-ventilated area at all times. Never operate a generator inside or in a small area.
- **Leak Detection:** Regularly check for propane leaks using a soap and water solution. If bubbles form around a connection, it indicates a leak that needs to be fixed.
- Propane tanks must to be securely kept out of direct sunlight and heat sources in a cold, dry place. Make sure the tanks are securely attached and upright to prevent tipping.
- **Emergency Shutdown:** Be prepared to turn off the generator promptly in the event of an emergency. Learn where the emergency stop switch is located and how to use it.

You may use your propane generator safely and effectively by following these safety guidelines.

For people looking for a dependable backup power supply or off-grid life, propane generators can be a great option. They are a good choice for a lot of people because of their availability, extended shelf life, and clean burning quality. Like any power sources, though, they have their own set of drawbacks and things to think about. You can choose if a propane generator is the appropriate choice for you by being aware of these aspects and adhering to safety and maintenance regulations. For your house or off-grid location, a propane generator can offer a steady and sustainable energy supply with the correct configuration.

Chapter 2: A New Energy Frontier: DIY Biogas at Home

The notion of producing your own energy at home is a fundamental principle of self-sufficiency. One intriguing method of achieving this goal is through the creation of biogas, a type of biofuel naturally generated from the decomposition of organic waste. This chapter explores the world of DIY biogas production, its benefits, potential drawbacks, and how to create your own biogas generator at home.

Understanding Biogas

Anaerobic digestion or fermentation of organic materials, such as manure, sewage, municipal trash, green waste, plant material, and crops, results in the production of biogas, a kind of sustainable energy. Methane and carbon dioxide make up the majority of biogas, which can be used as fuel for cars or to heat buildings and produce power. In addition to being environmentally beneficial, this renewable energy source effectively manages organic waste.

Benefits of DIY Biogas Production

- **Waste Management:** A DIY biogas generator turns kitchen scraps and garden waste into valuable fuel, thereby contributing to efficient waste management.
- **Renewable and Eco-friendly:** Biogas is a renewable source of energy and is considered carbon-neutral. Its usage helps reduce greenhouse gas emissions.
- **Cost-Efficient:** Once set up, a biogas plant can help save on energy costs, as it reduces the need for purchasing cooking gas or electricity.

These benefits make biogas an attractive option for those seeking to live more sustainably and reduce their environmental impact.

Drawbacks of DIY Biogas Production

While biogas production is beneficial, it does come with some drawbacks:

- **Consistent Supply of Organic Waste:** It requires a consistent supply of organic waste to generate biogas, which might be challenging to maintain.
- **Trial and Error:** It may take some trial and error to get the system running smoothly.
- **Initial Setup Costs:** The initial setup costs can be high, although these can be offset by long-term energy savings.

Understanding these drawbacks helps in preparing adequately for the challenges of biogas production.

Creating Your Own Biogas Generator

Building a biogas generator at home is a relatively straightforward process, but it requires careful planning and execution. Here's a simplified step-by-step guide:

1. **Select a Suitable Location:** Find a place in your yard that is flat, sunny, and easily accessible. The area should be safe from flooding.
2. **Acquire a Digester Tank:** The digester is where the organic waste will decompose and produce gas. A large, sturdy plastic or metal tank will serve as your digester.
3. **Set Up the Input and Output:** The input is where you'll put the organic waste. The output allows the digested sludge to exit the tank. Both should be well-sealed to prevent leaks.
4. **Install a Gas Collector:** The biogas produced will rise to the top of the tank and should be collected. This can be done using a floating drum or a gas bag.
5. **Feed the Digester:** Start adding your organic waste. This can include food scraps, grass clippings, and animal waste. Avoid adding non-biodegradable materials.
6. **Use Your Biogas:** The biogas can be used similarly to propane for cooking, heating, or generating electricity. Be sure to use a pressure regulator and clean the biogas to remove impurities.

These steps provide a clear path to setting up a functional biogas generator at home.

Maintenance of the Biogas Generator

Regular maintenance of your biogas generator is essential. This includes periodically checking for leaks, ensuring the digester is working correctly, and routinely feeding the digester with organic waste. Proper maintenance ensures the longevity and efficiency of your biogas system.

The DIY Guide to Building Your Own Biogas Generator at Home

Building a biogas generator at home is a project that's both challenging and rewarding. This guide will outline the necessary materials and provide step-by-step instructions to create your own biogas generator.

Materials Needed:

- **Anaerobic Digester:** A large water tank or barrel (around 55 gallons) that's sturdy, airtight, and resistant to corrosion.
- **Inlet Pipe:** A large PVC pipe and cap for introducing the organic waste into the digester.
- **Outlet Pipe:** A large PVC pipe for the removal of digested waste.
- **Gas Outlet:** A small, flexible pipe to collect the biogas from the digester.
- **Gas Storage:** A gas bag or inflatable bladder for storing the produced biogas. Ensure this is durable and leak-proof.
- **Valves:** To control the flow of biogas from the storage to its point of use.
- **Sealants:** High-quality waterproof sealants to ensure all connections are airtight.
- **Building Materials:** Basic building tools and materials, such as a drill, saw, wrenches, nuts, bolts, and screws.

Step-by-step Guide:

1. **Prepare Your Tank:** Thoroughly clean your tank and allow it to dry. This tank will serve as your anaerobic digester.
2. **Install the Inlet Pipe:** Drill a hole in the top of the tank and install your large PVC pipe. This will be the feedstock entry point. Seal around the hole with a waterproof sealant to prevent gas leaks.
3. **Install the Outlet Pipe:** Drill another hole near the bottom of the tank on the side and install the second PVC pipe. This will allow digested material to be removed. Again, seal around the hole to maintain an airtight system.
4. **Install the Gas Outlet:** Drill a third hole in the top of the tank, opposite the inlet pipe, and install your small, flexible pipe. This is where the gas will be collected. Secure and seal this pipe as you did with the others.
5. **Set Up the Gas Storage:** Connect your gas bag or inflatable bladder to the gas outlet pipe. Ensure it is securely fastened and sealed to prevent gas leaks.
6. **Initial Feedstock Addition:** Add a mixture of organic waste and water (in a 1:1 ratio) into the digester through the inlet pipe. Cow manure is an excellent starter due to the microbes it contains.
7. **Wait for Gas Production:** Seal the tank and allow the bacteria to begin producing biogas. This may take a few weeks. Once gas production starts, it will push the digested waste out of the outlet pipe.
8. **Regular Feeding:** Once your digester starts producing biogas, continue feeding it regularly with organic waste to maintain production.
9. **Maintenance:** Check regularly for leaks and blockages. If the biogas production slows down, it may be necessary to clean out the digester and start the process again.

Building your own biogas generator can be an exciting project that allows you to contribute to a greener planet while producing your own renewable energy. It's a perfect example of a practical application of self-sufficiency. This guide serves as a starting point for your DIY biogas generator project, but remember, every project can be unique, and modifications might be necessary based on your specific circumstances and availability of materials. Stay flexible, keep safety as your priority, and enjoy the process of becoming more self-reliant.

Chapter 3: Embracing the Power of Biodiesel: Your Guide to DIY Biodiesel Generators at Home

Interest in alternative energy sources has surged due to the global shift towards sustainable living, with biodiesel emerging as one of the most viable options. Generators that run on biodiesel are an effective way to power your house while lowering your carbon footprint. The purpose of this chapter is to provide you a thorough overview of biodiesel generators, including their advantages, possible disadvantages, and how to put one up at home.

What is Biodiesel?
A renewable energy source, biodiesel can be made from a range of organic materials, including used cooking oil, animal fats, and some kinds of algae. It may be used in the majority of diesel engines without modification and is frequently utilized as a substitute for petroleum-based diesel. In comparison to petroleum diesel, biodiesel is non-toxic, biodegradable, and produces a great deal fewer pollutants.

Why Choose a Biodiesel Generator?
- **Eco-Friendly:** Biodiesel is a renewable energy source, making it an environmentally-friendly option. It burns cleaner than fossil fuels, reducing greenhouse gas emissions.
- **Energy-Efficient:** Biodiesel has a high energy output, which makes it an excellent choice for powering generators.
- **Versatile:** If you want to increase your energy independence, biodiesel may be used in a regular diesel generator with no changes. This makes the switch easy.
- **Financial Gains:** Creating biodiesel at home from leftover cooking oil or other waste can be economical, especially over time.

These advantages make biodiesel a compelling choice for those seeking sustainable energy solutions.

Considerations When Using Biodiesel Generators
While there are numerous benefits to using biodiesel generators, there are a few factors to consider:
- **Availability of Raw Materials:** The production of biodiesel at home relies on the availability of raw materials. If you're planning on making biodiesel from used cooking oil, consider how often you'll have enough oil to produce a substantial amount of fuel.
- **Storage:** Biodiesel needs to be stored properly to maintain its efficiency. It can degrade over time if not stored in suitable conditions, leading to potential problems in your generator.
- **Maintenance:** Biodiesel can be a bit more maintenance-intensive than regular diesel. It's important to clean the generator regularly and check for any build-up of residue that could potentially harm the engine.

Understanding these considerations ensures that you are well-prepared for the maintenance and operational aspects of using biodiesel.

Building Your Biodiesel Generator
There are easier methods to incorporate biodiesel into your home energy setup, even though installing a biodiesel generator at home might be a complicated procedure requiring a solid grasp of the underlying science. Acquiring a conventional diesel generator and using homemade or commercially available biodiesel as fuel is one of the simplest approaches.

While a comprehensive guide to producing biodiesel at home would require a separate chapter due to its complexity, it's possible to convert waste cooking oil into biodiesel using a process called transesterification. This process involves mixing the oil with an alcohol (usually methanol) and a catalyst (such as lye), which results in biodiesel and a byproduct called glycerin that can be used to make soap.

DIY Biodiesel Production: A Step-by-Step Guide
Making biodiesel at home is a rather involved procedure that calls for cautious handling of potentially dangerous materials and a solid understanding of chemistry. It's critical to emphasize that when producing biodiesel, safety precautions must be followed extremely seriously. Wear safety gear at all times, such as gloves and goggles, and work in an area with good ventilation far from sparks or open flames. Having said that, you can make your own biodiesel fuel if you have the necessary

skills and understanding.

Supplies Needed
Before you begin, make sure you have all the necessary materials and tools:
- **Used Cooking Oil:** This will be your main ingredient. You'll need about 5 gallons for a small batch.
- **Methanol (Wood alcohol):** Methanol acts as the catalyst for the reaction. For every gallon of oil, you'll need roughly one fifth of a gallon of methanol.
- **Lye (Sodium Hydroxide):** You'll need lye to react with the methanol and create the necessary chemical reaction.
- **Thermometer:** Needed to monitor the temperature of the oil.
- **Stirring Tool:** A motorized stirring tool is best for this process, but manual options can work as well.
- **Scale:** Used for measuring your ingredients accurately.
- **Containers:** You'll need a variety of containers for the different stages of the process, including a main processing container, a settling container, and additional containers for storage.
- **Funnel and Filters:** For filtering out any impurities and for transferring biodiesel between containers.
- **Safety Gear:** Gloves, goggles, and a good apron are necessary to protect yourself from chemical splashes.

Biodiesel Production Process
Now, let's discuss the step-by-step process:
1. **Prepare Your Materials:** First, gather all your ingredients and tools. Ensure your work area is clean and well-ventilated. Wear your safety gear at all times.
2. **Heat the Oil:** The oil needs to be heated to help stimulate the reaction. Pour your used cooking oil into the main processing container and heat it to around 130-135 degrees Fahrenheit (55-57 degrees Celsius). Use your thermometer to monitor the temperature.
3. **Prepare the Methoxide:** While your oil is heating, carefully mix your methanol with the lye to form methoxide. For every gallon of oil, you'll need about 0.2 gallons of methanol and approximately 3.5 grams of lye. Be very careful when handling these chemicals, particularly the lye, as it can cause chemical burns. Slowly add the lye to the methanol while stirring until it dissolves completely.
4. **Combine the Oil and Methoxide:** Once your oil has reached the correct temperature and your methoxide is fully dissolved, slowly add the methoxide to the oil while stirring. Continue stirring for about 20 minutes to ensure the reaction takes place.
5. **Let It Settle:** After you've stirred the mixture for the appropriate amount of time, let it sit for at least 24 hours. The biodiesel will rise to the top, and the glycerin, a byproduct of the process, will settle at the bottom.
6. **Remove the Glycerin:** After the mixture has settled, you can remove the glycerin at the bottom. This can be saved for making soap or disposed of safely.
7. **Neutralize the Methoxide:** In this step, we have to neutralize the excess methoxide left in our newly created biodiesel. This is done by slowly adding a mixture of warm water and vinegar (1:4 ratio) into the processor while stirring. Add the mixture until the pH of the biodiesel is neutral, which is 7. Remember to do this process slowly and carefully. Over-acidifying the biodiesel can lead to soap formation and decrease the quality of the fuel.
8. **Test the pH:** Test the pH of the biodiesel using litmus paper or a digital pH meter. Simply take a small sample of biodiesel, let it cool, and then apply the litmus paper or digital pH meter. If the pH is still high (above 7), slowly add more vinegar and water mixture until a neutral pH is achieved.
9. **Final Settling:** Once you've reached a neutral pH, stop the processor and let the biodiesel sit for at least 8 hours. During this time, any remaining glycerin will settle at the bottom of the processor, separating from the biodiesel. This glycerin can be safely drained from the bottom of the processor and saved for other uses, like making soap.

And there you have it! The resulting product is your own homemade biodiesel, ready to be used in your generator. Please bear in mind that safety is paramount in these operations, so always take the necessary precautions. Wear the proper safety equipment and conduct these procedures in a well-ventilated location away from sparks or open flames at all times.

Chapter 4: Ethanol Fuel: A Bioenergy Powerhouse

Ethanol fuel, also known as ethyl alcohol, grain alcohol, or simply ethanol, is an alternative fuel derived from plant materials such as corn, sugarcane, and even agricultural and forest residue. It is an eco-friendly biofuel that offers a renewable way to power your vehicle, heat your home, or run a variety of appliances and machines. This chapter will delve into the topic of ethanol fuel, its production, benefits, and potential drawbacks.

What is Ethanol Fuel?

Similar to the fermentation process used to make wine or beer, ethanol is a form of alcohol that is further distilled to increase its alcohol level. Ethanol is usually combined with gasoline to form a mixture known as E10, which is 10% ethanol and 90% gasoline, or E85, which is 85% ethanol and 15% gasoline, when used as fuel. The majority of contemporary cars can run on these ethanol-gasoline mixtures without the need for any changes.

Why Choose Ethanol Fuel?

There are several reasons to consider using ethanol fuel:
- **Renewable and Sustainable:** Unlike fossil fuels, which are limited and cause damage to the environment when extracted, ethanol is made from renewable plant materials. As long as we manage our crop resources effectively, we can continue producing ethanol without depleting our planet's natural resources.
- **Reduced Greenhouse Gas Emissions:** Ethanol burns cleaner than gasoline, resulting in fewer greenhouse gas emissions. This helps combat climate change and improves air quality.
- **Energy Independence:** By producing and using ethanol, countries can decrease their reliance on foreign oil, thereby bolstering their energy security and creating local jobs.
- **Versatile:** Ethanol can be used in a variety of applications, including powering vehicles, heating homes, and running appliances. Some engines can run entirely on ethanol, while others may require a blend of gasoline and ethanol.

These benefits highlight the potential of ethanol as a sustainable energy source.

Potential Drawbacks of Ethanol Fuel

While ethanol fuel presents many benefits, it's also essential to understand the potential downsides:
- **Energy Content:** Ethanol has less energy per volume than gasoline. This means that a vehicle running on pure ethanol or a high ethanol blend will typically have a lower fuel economy than one running on gasoline alone.
- **Production Concerns:** The production of ethanol, especially from corn, can compete with food production. This competition can potentially lead to increased food prices.
- **Infrastructure:** While the infrastructure for ethanol use is growing, it is not as readily available as traditional gasoline. This means that finding a fueling station that offers high ethanol blend fuels can sometimes be a challenge, depending on where you live.

Understanding these drawbacks helps in making an informed decision about using ethanol fuel.

DIY Ethanol Production: Your Step-By-Step Guide

Making your own ethanol fuel at home can be a fascinating project, but it's essential to remember that it involves handling potentially dangerous materials and should be undertaken with caution. The fermentation of sugars produces ethanol, but to make it usable as a fuel, you'll need to distill it, which involves heating the ethanol to its boiling point. Please note that this is a general guide and does not replace specific instructions provided by a professional kit or guidebook.

Materials Required

- **Sugar:** You'll need a source of sugar to feed the yeast during fermentation. Common sources include corn, sugarcane, or even regular table sugar.
- **Yeast:** This will ferment the sugar, turning it into ethanol. Turbo yeast is commonly used due to its high alcohol tolerance and fast fermentation rate.
- **Water:** Required to dissolve the sugar and facilitate fermentation.
- **Fermentation Vessel:** A large, clean container for the fermentation process.
- **Airlock:** This allows carbon dioxide to escape from the fermentation vessel without letting air in.
- **Stove or Heat Source:** Required for distillation.

- **Distillation Apparatus:** This could be a professionally made still or a homemade one. It should have a pot for heating the fermented mixture, a condenser for cooling the vapor, and a collector for catching the distilled ethanol.

Step-By-Step Instructions

1. **Mixing and Fermentation:** Dissolve the sugar in warm water within your fermentation vessel. Once the sugar is completely dissolved, allow the mixture to cool before adding the yeast. Attach the airlock to your fermentation vessel and let the mixture sit in a warm place. Fermentation times can vary, but expect this process to take at least a week.
2. **Distillation:** Once fermentation is complete, the liquid (now a type of alcohol) is ready to be distilled. Pour the fermented liquid into your distillation apparatus. Apply heat gradually. Ethanol boils at 173.1 degrees Fahrenheit (78.37 Celsius), which is lower than water, so the ethanol will vaporize first.
3. **Condensation and Collection:** As the ethanol vapor rises through the distillation apparatus, it will enter a condenser, where it's cooled and returned to a liquid state. The liquid ethanol is then collected in a separate container.
4. **Purification:** The collected ethanol might still contain traces of water. To remove the remaining water, you can add a drying agent such as a type of molecular sieve designed to absorb water. Once the drying agent is added, shake the mixture and let it sit.
5. **Storage:** Once the ethanol has been dried and filtered, it can be stored in a clean, airtight container. Be sure to label the container clearly.

Producing ethanol at home requires adherence to safety guidelines and awareness of local and federal laws. Always prioritize safety and ensure your working space is well-ventilated, free from open flames, and that you're using the correct protective gear. By following these steps, you can create your own ethanol fuel, contributing to a more sustainable and self-sufficient lifestyle.

Maintenance and Usage Tips for Ethanol Fuel

Once you have successfully produced ethanol, it's important to understand how to maintain and use it effectively:

- **Storage:** Ethanol should be stored in tightly sealed containers to prevent contamination and evaporation. Store in a cool, dry place away from direct sunlight and sources of ignition.
- **Blending:** If you plan to use ethanol as a fuel blend (like E10 or E85), ensure proper mixing with gasoline. Use clean containers and mix thoroughly before use.
- **Engine Compatibility:** Most modern engines can run on ethanol blends, but always check the manufacturer's guidelines. High ethanol content fuels might require engine modifications.
- **Fuel System Checks:** Regularly inspect your fuel system for any signs of wear or damage, especially if using high ethanol content fuels. Ethanol can be corrosive to certain materials.

Environmental Impact and Benefits

Ethanol fuel offers several environmental benefits:

- **Carbon Neutrality:** Ethanol is considered carbon-neutral because the CO_2 released during combustion is offset by the CO_2 absorbed by the plants during their growth.
- **Reduction in Pollutants:** Ethanol combustion produces fewer harmful pollutants compared to gasoline, improving air quality.
- **Renewable Resource:** Unlike fossil fuels, ethanol is made from renewable plant materials, reducing the depletion of finite resources.

You may help promote sustainable energy practices and lower greenhouse gas emissions by including ethanol fuel in your energy mix. Ethanol fuel is a promising replacement for traditional fossil fuels. Its renewable nature, lower greenhouse gas emissions, and potential for energy independence make it a tempting option for anyone looking to live a more independent and ecologically conscious lifestyle.

While there are several obstacles in the way of ethanol's future viability as an energy source, bioenergy research and development are persistently striving to get over these problems. Gaining knowledge about the advantages, disadvantages, and manufacturing process of ethanol fuel enables you to make wise choices and move toward a future with more sustainable energy.

Chapter 5: Harnessing Energy from Wood: An Introduction to Wood Gas

Wood gas, also known as syngas, is a form of renewable energy that has been used for many years but is not as well known as other forms of alternative energy. Wood gasification, the process used to create wood gas, was widely utilized during World War II when gasoline was in short supply. Today, with increasing interest in sustainable and renewable sources of energy, wood gasification is regaining attention.

What is Wood Gas?

Wood gas is a combustible mixture primarily composed of carbon monoxide, hydrogen, and methane. This gaseous mixture is produced by heating wood or other biomass in an environment with controlled oxygen. The process, called gasification, involves four stages: drying, pyrolysis, combustion, and reduction.

How Does Wood Gasification Work?

The process of wood gasification produces carbon dioxide, hydrogen, and carbon monoxide from organic or fossil-based carbonaceous materials. This is accomplished by reacting the material with a controlled quantity of oxygen and/or steam at high temperatures (>700°C) without causing combustion.

The wood gasification process occurs in four stages:

1. **Drying:** As the wood is heated, it releases moisture. This is a crucial stage as dry wood burns more efficiently.
2. **Pyrolysis:** As the temperature increases, the wood starts to chemically decompose and releases volatile gases. Charcoal remains as a byproduct.
3. **Combustion:** The volatile gases released during pyrolysis burn in the presence of oxygen, creating heat. This stage produces carbon dioxide and water vapor.
4. **Reduction:** In the final stage, the charcoal reacts with carbon dioxide and steam, producing carbon monoxide and hydrogen. This mixture of carbon monoxide, hydrogen, and other gases is known as wood gas.

Applications of Wood Gas

Wood gas can be used in various applications, similar to other types of combustible gases. It can power internal combustion engines, which can be used to run generators, pumps, or vehicles. It can also be used for heating purposes. However, because of the low energy density compared to other fuels, wood gas is not typically used in applications requiring high energy efficiency or high power.

Benefits of Wood Gas

The primary benefit of wood gas is that it is a renewable source of energy, as it can be produced from any biological material, not just wood. This includes agricultural waste, such as corn cobs or husks, and other biomass like grass clippings or leaves. Additionally, gasification is an efficient way to convert these types of biomass into a usable form of energy.

- **Renewable Resource:** Wood gas can be produced from various biomass sources, making it a sustainable and renewable energy option.
- **Waste Utilization:** Agricultural and forestry waste can be efficiently converted into energy, reducing waste and promoting resourcefulness.
- **Carbon Neutral:** It is a carbon-neutral energy source because the carbon dioxide collected by plants during their growth balances the carbon dioxide generated during the combustion of wood gas.
-

Considerations and Drawbacks

Even though wood gas is a green energy source, there are a few crucial things to remember. Although the gas produced by the gasification process is less energy-dense than other fuels, it still requires a significant quantity of heat. Before being used, the wood gas also needs to be thoroughly cleaned and filtered to get rid of dangerous materials like ash and tar.

- **Energy Density:** Wood gas's efficiency in high-power applications may be impacted by its lower energy density when compared to other fuels.
- **Heat Requirement:** The gasification process requires high temperatures, which necessitates proper insulation and heat management.

- **Filtration:** The gas produced needs to be thoroughly cleaned to remove impurities like tar and ash to prevent damage to engines and other equipment.

DIY Wood Gas Generator: Step-by-Step Guide

Although building a wood gas generator at home can be difficult, it is possible to create a green energy source with proper preparation. Please be aware that there are risks involved in building and using a wood gas generator before you begin. Use the proper personal protective equipment (PPE), work in a well-ventilated location, and put safety first at all times.

Materials You Will Need:

- Two steel drums (one large for the gasifier unit and one smaller for the filter)
- Insulating material, such as perlite or vermiculite
- Metal pipes for the gas outlet and air inlet
- A small electric fan or blower
- Basic tools: Welder, drills, saws, and metal cutters
- Sealant that can withstand high temperatures

Steps to Build a Wood Gas Generator:

1. **Preparation of the Drums:** The large drum will act as the gasifier unit where the wood will be burned, and the smaller drum will act as the filter. Make sure the drums are clean and free of any residual materials.
2. **Constructing the Gasifier:** Cut a hole at the top of the larger drum. This will serve as the fuel inlet where you will insert the wood. Next, cut another hole on the side towards the bottom. This will be where the gas exits the drum.
3. **Insulation:** Fill the space between the inner wall and outer wall of the gasifier with insulating material such as perlite or vermiculite. This will help to retain heat within the gasifier.
4. **Air Inlet and Outlet:** You will need to attach pipes to the holes you cut for the gas outlet and air inlet. The size of these pipes will depend on the volume of gas you plan to produce. The air inlet pipe should also be connected to an electric fan or blower. This will ensure that there is a steady supply of oxygen to support the gasification process.
5. **Building the Filter:** Cut a hole in the smaller drum that aligns with the gas outlet of the gasifier. Connect these two holes with a pipe – this will carry the raw wood gas into the filter drum. Inside this drum, you'll need to create layers of filtering material (such as straw, wood chips, or small stones) to remove impurities from the gas.
6. **Sealing the System:** After you have everything assembled, make sure to seal all the joints and connections using a high-temperature resistant sealant. This will prevent gas leaks.
7. **Testing:** Before running the system with wood, perform a smoke test to check for leaks. You can do this by burning a small piece of paper inside the gasifier and observing where the smoke exits. If smoke escapes from anywhere but the designated outlet, you'll need to seal the leak.

Operating Your Wood Gas Generator

After building your wood gas generator, you may start experimenting with various biomass kinds to determine which ones perform the best for you. The following advice will help you run and maintain your generator:

- **Selecting the Appropriate Biomass**: To determine which kind of biomass will work best for your generator, experiment with sawdust, wood chips, and agricultural waste.
- **Feeding the Gasifier:** Ensure a steady and consistent feed of biomass to maintain the gasification process. Avoid overloading the gasifier, which can lead to incomplete combustion.
- **Monitoring the System:** Regularly check the gasifier, filter, and pipes for any signs of blockages, leaks, or wear. Clean and replace filters as needed to maintain optimal performance.
- **Safety First:** Always operate the generator in a well-ventilated space, and never leave it unattended while it's running. Have fire extinguishing equipment nearby in case of emergencies.

An interesting and environmentally friendly energy source that can offer a renewable and carbon-neutral substitute for conventional fuels is wood gas generation. You can lessen your carbon impact and help create a more sustainable future by using wood gas. This manual can be used as a starting point for your do-it-yourself wood gas generator project, but don't forget to put safety first and have fun learning about this intriguing new energy source.

Chapter 6: Biomass and Biogas

Biomass and biogas are becoming as essential elements of the renewable energy landscape as the globe progresses toward sustainable energy solutions. This chapter explores the fundamentals of biomass and biogas, their advantages and challenges, and the modern technologies enhancing their efficiency, with a particular focus on their role in off-grid living.

Understanding Biomass: A Renewable Resource

Organic material derived from plants and animals is called biomass. It is a flexible and sustainable energy source that may be utilized to provide gasoline for vehicles, heat, and power. Animal dung, wood, food waste, and agricultural residues are common sources of biomass. Numerous processes, including pyrolysis, gasification, anaerobic digestion, and combustion, can turn biomass into energy.

Types of Biomass:
1. _Wood and Wood Residues_: Forest residues, sawdust, and wood chips.
2. _Agricultural Residues_: Crop residues like corn stalks, straw, and sugarcane bagasse.
3. _Animal Manure_: Waste from livestock that can be used for biogas production.
4. _Energy Crops_: Specific crops grown for energy production, such as switchgrass and miscanthus.
5. _Organic Waste_: Food waste and other organic materials from households and industries.

Advantages and Challenges of Biomass Energy

Advantages:
1. _Renewable_: Biomass is a renewable resource that can be replenished over time.
2. _Carbon Neutral:_ It is carbon neutral because the carbon dioxide absorbed by plants during growth balances the carbon dioxide emitted during biomass combustion.
3. _Waste Reduction_: Using agricultural and organic waste for energy reduces landfill waste and associated environmental issues.
4. _Energy Security_: Biomass can be locally sourced, reducing dependence on imported fuels and enhancing energy security.

Challenges:
1. _Resource Availability_: Biomass availability can be seasonal and geographically dependent, affecting its consistent supply.
2. _Land Use_: Growing energy crops can compete with food production and lead to land use conflicts.
3. _Emission Control_: Combustion of biomass can release particulate matter and other pollutants if not managed properly.
4. _Economic Viability_: The cost of collecting, processing, and transporting biomass can be high, affecting its economic feasibility.

Basics of Biogas: Production and Usage

Anaerobic digestion of organic materials by microorganisms results in the production of biogas. Methane (CH_4) and carbon dioxide (CO_2) make up the majority of biogas, with trace amounts of other gases. Organic matter is broken down during production in an oxygen-free atmosphere, usually in a biogas digester.

Biogas Production Steps:
1. _Feedstock Collection_: Gathering organic materials such as animal manure, food waste, and agricultural residues.
2. _Anaerobic Digestion_: Placing the organic materials in a biogas digester, where microorganisms break them down to produce biogas.
3. _Biogas Capture_: Collecting the biogas produced in the digester for storage and use.
4. _Digestate Management_: The leftover material, called digestate, can be used as a nutrient-rich fertilizer.

Uses of Biogas:
1. _Cooking and Heating_: Biogas can be used directly for cooking and heating in homes.
2. _Electricity Generation_: Biogas can power generators to produce electricity.

3. *Vehicle Fuel:* With proper upgrading, biogas can be used as a renewable vehicle fuel.

Biogas in Off-Grid Living: A Sustainable Solution

For off-grid living, biogas presents a sustainable and efficient energy solution. It can be produced locally from available organic waste, providing a reliable source of energy for cooking, heating, and electricity generation. The ability to generate energy on-site enhances self-sufficiency and reduces reliance on external energy supplies.

Benefits for Off-Grid Living:

1. *Energy Independence*: Biogas systems allow off-grid communities to produce their own energy from local resources.
2. *Waste Management:* Biogas production helps manage organic waste effectively, reducing environmental pollution.
3. *Economic Savings*: By producing biogas, off-grid households can save on fuel costs and potentially generate income by selling excess energy.
4. *Environmental Impact*: Biogas systems reduce greenhouse gas emissions and reliance on fossil fuels.

Modern Technologies Enhancing Biomass and Biogas Efficiency

Technological advancements have significantly improved the efficiency and feasibility of biomass and biogas energy systems. Modern technologies aim to maximize energy output, reduce emissions, and enhance the economic viability of these renewable energy sources.

Enhanced Biomass Technologies:

1. *Advanced Combustion Systems*: When compared to conventional biomass burning, improved combustion technologies like gasification and pyrolysis offer higher efficiency and lower emissions
2. *Integrated Systems*: To construct hybrid systems that guarantee a consistent energy supply, biomass energy is combined with energy from other renewable sources, such as solar and wind.
3. *Biomass Pellets*: Compressing biomass into pellets increases energy density, making transportation and storage more efficient.

Innovative Biogas Technologies:

1. *Improved Digesters:* Modern biogas digesters are designed for higher efficiency and better methane yield. These include continuous and batch digesters, as well as advanced anaerobic reactors.
2. *Biogas Upgrading*: Technologies such as pressure swing adsorption, membrane separation, and water scrubbing can upgrade biogas to biomethane, making it suitable for use as vehicle fuel or injection into the natural gas grid.
3. *Smart Monitoring Systems*: Implementing smart sensors and monitoring systems to optimize the biogas production process, detect leaks, and ensure safe operation.

With their sustainable approaches to waste management and energy production, biomass and biogas are essential elements of the renewable energy landscape. To fully utilize these energy sources, one must grasp their foundations, benefits, and drawbacks as well as the ways in which contemporary technologies are increasing their efficiency. Biomass and biogas will become more vital as the globe moves toward more environmentally friendly practices in order to achieve energy independence and lessen our influence on the environment.

Chapter 7: Harnessing the Power of Heat: Wood Stoves and DIY Solutions

In the world of off-grid living and self-sufficiency, managing your heat source is crucial. Not only does it contribute to your overall comfort, but heating is also essential for various activities like cooking and hot water supply. One of the most popular and practical solutions to this necessity is the use of wood stoves.

What are Wood Stoves?

Wood stoves are heating devices that may burn biomass fuel produced from wood, including logs or pellets. In addition to being a useful cooking stove, a wood stove can be utilized as a home's main source of heat. Because they are available in a range of sizes and types, you may customize them to fit your specific needs and the design of your house.

Building Your Own Wood Stove

While purchasing a commercially available wood stove is a viable option, there is also the possibility of building your own. This might seem daunting, but a DIY wood stove can be a rewarding project, both in terms of the building process and the subsequent use. Creating your own wood stove allows you to design a heating solution perfectly tailored to your needs and available resources. A homemade wood stove can be created from recycled materials such as old metal barrels, which reduces costs and promotes sustainability.

DIY Wood Stove: A Step-by-Step Guide

Creating your own wood stove can be a rewarding project. Here's a simple guide to help you build one using an old metal barrel.

Materials:

- An old metal barrel – This will be the body of your stove.
- Heat-resistant paint – To give your stove a neat, finished look.
- Metal legs or stand – For your stove to stand on.
- Pipe for the stovepipe – To guide the smoke away from the stove.
- Metal sheet for the door – Allows access to the inside of the stove.
- Hinges and handle for the door – To open and close the stove door.
- Drill – To make necessary holes for screws and the stovepipe.
- Screws, bolts, and nuts – To secure the parts of your stove together.
- Heat-resistant sealant – To ensure your stove is airtight.

Steps:

1. **Prepare the Barrel**: Clean your barrel thoroughly, removing any residue or rust. This will ensure that the paint adheres properly and improves the longevity of your stove.
2. **Paint the Barrel**: Use a heat-resistant paint to cover your barrel. This not only makes your stove look better but also helps protect the metal from excessive heat.
3. **Install the Legs**: Attach the metal legs or stand to your barrel, ensuring it's stable and level.
4. **Cut the Door**: Decide where you want your door to be and trace it out on the barrel. Use a metal cutter to cut out the door.
5. **Install the Door**: Attach the metal sheet to the door's opening using hinges and add a handle. Make sure the door can open and close freely.
6. **Install the Stovepipe**: Drill a hole at the top of your barrel for the stovepipe. Attach the stovepipe using bolts, making sure it's secure and airtight.
7. **Seal the Stove**: Use a heat-resistant sealant around all joins to make sure your stove is airtight.
8. **Curing the Stove**: Before using the stove, it must be cured. This involves lighting a few small fires inside the stove and letting them burn out naturally.

Remember, safety is crucial when building and using your wood stove. Always ensure proper ventilation and use caution when the stove is in operation.

Once you have completed these steps, you'll have a functioning wood stove ready to warm your home and provide a heat source for cooking. By harnessing the power of heat through wood stoves, you can enhance your self-sufficiency and create a sustainable heating solution tailored to your needs.

Chapter 8: Exploring the Efficiency of Pellet Stoves

Pellet stoves are a modern alternative for home heating, offering a unique blend of aesthetics and functionality. Unlike traditional wood-burning stoves, pellet stoves utilize compressed pellets made from wood, sawdust, or other organic materials as fuel. These stoves offer a range of advantages that make them an attractive choice for those seeking to warm their homes in a more sustainable, efficient, and convenient manner.

Understanding Pellet Stoves

Pellet stoves work by feeding these pellets from a storage hopper into a burn pot via an automatic auger. This combustion area is highly efficient, burning the pellets entirely, producing a very small amount of ash and requiring less frequent cleaning than traditional stoves. Moreover, these stoves are typically equipped with a built-in fan that circulates the hot air throughout the room, providing uniform heating.

Efficiency and Sustainability

One of the most striking benefits of pellet stoves is their high energy efficiency. Depending on the model, pellet stoves can reach efficiency levels of up to 90%, significantly higher than traditional wood stoves. This means that a higher proportion of the energy contained in the fuel is converted into heat for your home, reducing waste and saving money on heating costs. From an environmental perspective, pellet stoves are also considered greener options. The pellets are often made from waste products, which would otherwise be discarded. They burn cleaner, emitting fewer particulates and less carbon monoxide than wood, making them a more eco-friendly choice.

Convenience and Control

Pellet stoves offer a high level of user convenience. They are equipped with controls that allow for easy adjustment of heat output, and some even come with programmable thermostats or remote controls. With automatic feeding systems, they can operate for long hours without the need for constant refueling. However, it's important to note that pellet stoves do require electricity to run the auger, controls, and fan. In areas with frequent power outages, a backup power source might be necessary.

Installation and Maintenance

Installing a pellet stove involves positioning the stove, providing an external vent, and making an electrical connection. While it can be a DIY project for those with some technical skills, it's usually best to consult with a professional to ensure safety and proper operation.

Steps for Installation:
1. **Select the Location**: Choose a location that provides easy access for refueling and has adequate ventilation. Ensure it meets local building codes and manufacturer guidelines.
2. **Install the Venting System**: Follow the stove's manual for venting. This typically involves cutting a hole through an exterior wall and installing a vent pipe.
3. **Connect the Electrical Components**: Pellet stoves need to be plugged into an electrical outlet. Ensure the connection is safe and secure.
4. **Position the Stove**: Place the stove on a non-combustible surface. Use floor protection if needed.
5. **Test the System**: Once installed, run the stove to ensure everything works correctly.

Maintenance Tips:
- **Daily**: Empty the burn pot and ensure it's free of ash and debris.
- **Weekly**: Clean the heat exchanger and check the hopper for pellet residue.
- **Monthly**: Inspect the venting system for obstructions and clean the exhaust fan.
- **Annually**: Have a professional inspection to ensure the stove is operating safely and efficiently.

With their high efficiency, eco-friendliness, and convenience, pellet stoves are a worthy contender for home heating solutions. As with any significant home improvement project, understanding your specific needs, the features of different models, and their maintenance requirements will help you make the best choice for your situation. By incorporating a pellet stove into your home, you can enjoy a warm, comfortable living space while reducing your environmental footprint.

Chapter 9: Embracing the Warmth: Propane Furnaces and Portable Heaters

When it comes to heating our homes, many different technologies and fuel sources are available. Among them, propane furnaces and portable heaters are increasingly recognized as reliable, cost-effective, and energy-efficient options. In this chapter, we will delve into the world of propane heating, explaining what these systems are, how they work, and why they might be a suitable choice for your heating needs.

Propane Furnaces: Power and Efficiency

A propane furnace is a heating system that uses propane gas as its fuel source. Compared to other types of heating systems, propane furnaces offer several advantages.

Great Energy Efficiency: Propane furnaces are mostly renowned for having a high energy efficiency. They can achieve up to 98% efficiency ratings, which means that practically all of the energy in the propane is transformed into heat for your house. Over time, you may save a lot of money on your energy expenses because to this great efficiency.

Powerful Heat Output: Additionally, propane furnaces are recognized for their powerful heat output. They can produce hotter air than electric heat pumps, making them a preferred option for those living in colder climates. This ability to produce higher temperatures quickly makes propane furnaces an excellent choice for regions that experience severe winters.

Portable Propane Heaters: Flexibility and Convenience

Compact and Mobile: Portable propane heaters are a more flexible option. These units are compact and lightweight, designed to be moved around easily to provide heat wherever it's needed. They're perfect for heating specific rooms or outdoor spaces, such as patios or garages.

Off-Grid Capabilities: Moreover, because they don't require electricity, portable propane heaters can be a valuable resource during power outages or for off-grid living situations. This makes them highly versatile and practical for emergency preparedness.

Numerous Designs: There are several different types of portable propane heaters, such as forced-air, convection, and radiant models. Based on the particular heating needs and available area, each style offers advantages of its own.

Safety and Environmental Considerations

Clean-Burning Fuel: Because propane burns cleanly, it emits fewer hazardous emissions than a lot of other fossil fuels. As a result, there are less greenhouse gas and carbon dioxide emissions, which helps to clean up the environment.

Safety Precautions: However, like all gas appliances, propane furnaces and heaters must be used responsibly to ensure safety. Regular maintenance is essential to prevent gas leaks and ensure proper ventilation. It's also important to install carbon monoxide detectors in your home as an additional safety measure.

Maintenance Requirements: The installation of a propane furnace should be carried out by a qualified professional. It involves connecting the furnace to a propane tank, which may be either above or below ground. Maintenance usually involves regular inspection of the unit, checking for leaks, and cleaning or replacing filters. When it comes to portable heaters, make sure you routinely check the item for any indications of wear or damage, and always operate it safely by following the manufacturer's instructions.

Establishment and Upkeep

Expert Installation: Propane furnace installation ought to be done by an accredited specialist. It entails attaching a propane tank—which could be underground or above ground—to the furnace. For operation to be both safe and effective, proper installation is essential.

Continual Upkeep: Regular unit inspections, leak detection checks, and filter cleaning or replacements are typically included in maintenance. To keep your propane furnace operating safely and efficiently, it's best to have a professional service it once a year. When it comes to portable heaters, make sure you routinely check the item for any indications of wear or damage, and always operate it safely by following the manufacturer's instructions.

Chapter 10: Project: Setting Up a Biogas Plant

Setting up a biogas plant is an exciting and sustainable project that can provide renewable energy and efficient waste management solutions. This chapter will guide you through the process of establishing your own biogas plant, from understanding the project's objectives to gathering materials, designing the plant, and ensuring its efficient operation.

Project Objective and Expected Outcomes

The primary objective of setting up a biogas plant is to convert organic waste into biogas and digestate. Biogas can be used as a renewable energy source for cooking, heating, and electricity generation, while digestate serves as a valuable fertilizer. The expected outcomes of this project include:

Renewable Energy Production: Generating biogas to meet household or small-scale energy needs.

Waste Management: Efficiently managing organic waste from kitchens, gardens, and farms.

Environmental Benefits: Reducing greenhouse gas emissions and reliance on fossil fuels.

Economic Savings: Lowering energy costs and potentially generating income from excess biogas or digestate.

Gathering Necessary Materials and Tools

Before starting your biogas plant project, gather the following materials and tools:

Digester Tank: A large, airtight container for anaerobic digestion, such as a plastic or metal tank.

Gas Holder: A floating drum or gas bag to collect and store biogas.

Inlet and Outlet Pipes: PVC pipes for feeding organic waste into the digester and removing digestate.

Gas Outlet Pipe: A flexible pipe to transport biogas from the digester to the storage system.

Pressure Regulator: To control the flow and pressure of biogas.

Valves and Fittings: For secure and leak-proof connections.

Sealants: High-quality waterproof sealants to ensure airtight connections.

Basic Tools: Drills, saws, wrenches, nuts, bolts, and screwdrivers.

Safety Gear: Gloves, goggles, and protective clothing.

Designing Your Biogas Plant: A Step-by-Step Guide

Step 1: Site Selection and Preparation

Choose a suitable location for your biogas plant. The site should be flat, well-drained, and easily accessible. It should also receive adequate sunlight to maintain optimal temperatures for anaerobic digestion. Ensure the site is safe from flooding and away from residential areas to avoid odor issues.

Step 2: Building the Digester and Gas Holder

Digester Construction: Clean the digester tank and drill holes for the inlet and outlet pipes. Install the pipes and seal the connections to ensure airtightness.

Gas Holder Setup: Install the gas holder above the digester. If using a floating drum, ensure it can move freely as gas accumulates. If using a gas bag, secure it to prevent leaks.

Step 3: Installing Gas Collection and Storage Systems

Gas Outlet Pipe: Connect a flexible pipe from the digester's gas outlet to the gas holder. Use a pressure regulator to control the gas flow.

Gas Storage: Ensure the gas storage system is durable and leak-proof. Install valves to manage the flow of biogas to appliances.

Step 4: Setting Up the Piping and Appliance Connections

Piping Installation: Install pipes to transport biogas from the storage system to appliances such as stoves, heaters, or generators. Ensure all connections are secure and leak-proof.

Appliance Connections: Connect biogas-compatible appliances to the piping system. Use pressure regulators to ensure safe and efficient operation.

Feeding the Biogas Digester: Dos and Don'ts

Dos:

Diverse Feedstock: Use a variety of organic waste, including kitchen scraps, garden waste, and animal manure, to ensure a balanced nutrient mix.

Chop and Mix: Chop large pieces of organic waste and mix them with water to create a slurry. This improves digestion efficiency.

Regular Feeding: Add feedstock regularly to maintain consistent biogas production.

Dont's:

Avoid Non-Biodegradables: Do not add plastics, metals, or non-biodegradable materials to the digester.

Limit Fats and Oils: Excessive fats and oils can inhibit the digestion process. Add them in moderation.

No Chemicals: Avoid adding chemicals, pesticides, or antibiotics, as they can disrupt the microbial activity in the digester.

Testing and Monitoring Your Biogas Plant

Initial Testing:

Gas Production: After setting up the plant, wait for a few weeks for the bacteria to start producing biogas. Test for gas production by lighting a small amount of the collected gas.

System Checks: Ensure there are no leaks in the piping and storage systems. Use a soap and water solution to check for bubbles indicating gas leaks.

Monitoring:

Regular Checks: Monitor the temperature, pH, and moisture levels in the digester. Optimal conditions are crucial for efficient biogas production.

Gas Quality: Check the methane content of the biogas. Higher methane content indicates better quality biogas.

Feedstock Management: Keep track of the types and quantities of feedstock added to the digester to maintain a balanced diet for the microbes.

Maintenance, Safety, and Troubleshooting

Maintenance:

Leak Checks: Regularly inspect the system for leaks, especially around connections and seals.

Cleaning: Clean the digester and gas storage systems periodically to remove any sludge or residue buildup.

Equipment Inspection: Regularly check the condition of valves, pipes, and pressure regulators.

Safety:

Proper Ventilation: Ensure the biogas plant is well-ventilated to prevent the buildup of gases.

Protective Gear: Always wear safety gear when handling feedstock, chemicals, or performing maintenance tasks.

Emergency Procedures: Know how to shut down a system in an emergency, and keep first aid and fire extinguishers nearby.

Troubleshooting:

Low Gas Production: Check for issues such as inadequate feedstock, low temperatures, or pH imbalances. Adjust feeding rates and conditions as needed.

Gas Leaks: Identify and seal any leaks promptly. Use a soap and water solution to detect leaks.

Poor Gas Quality: Ensure the digester is receiving a balanced mix of feedstock. Check for and remove any inhibitory substances.

Setting up a biogas plant is a rewarding project that contributes to renewable energy production, efficient waste management, and environmental sustainability. By following this comprehensive guide, you can successfully establish and maintain a biogas plant that meets your energy needs and promotes a self-sufficient lifestyle Embrace biogas's capacity to move toward a more environmentally friendly future.

MODULE E - WATER ENERGY

Chapter 1: Harnessing the Power of Water: Building Your Own Hydropower System

Water is not only essential for life but also a powerful energy source. Hydropower is one of the most reliable and constant renewable energy sources, making it ideal for off-grid living. This chapter explores the fundamentals of hydropower, its components, and the steps required to build a small-scale, DIY hydropower system.

Unleashing the Potential of Hydropower

Hydropower systems convert the kinetic energy of moving water into electricity using a turbine or water wheel connected to a generator. This method has been used for centuries, from ancient water wheels grinding grain to modern hydroelectric dams. Unlike solar and wind energy, a well-designed hydropower system can generate electricity 24/7, making it an incredibly reliable power source.

Essential Components of a Hydropower System

Creating a small-scale hydropower system involves several key components:

- **Water Source:** A source of running water with sufficient flow rate and head (vertical distance the water falls). These factors determine the potential energy of the water.
- **Intake:** The entry point for water, ideally equipped with a screen to prevent debris from entering and damaging the turbine.
- **Penstock:** A pipe that carries water from the intake to the turbine, controlling the flow.
- **Turbine:** transforms falling or streaming water's kinetic energy into mechanical energy. Different settings are acceptable for different types of turbines, such as impulse and response turbines.
- **Generator:** Coupled with the turbine, it converts mechanical energy into electrical energy. Small-scale systems can use modified alternators or purpose-built generators.
- **Controller:** Regulates the generator's output to match the electrical system's needs and manage battery charging to prevent overcharging.
- **Batteries and Inverter:** Necessary for storing energy and converting the generated DC power into AC power.

Building Your Own Hydropower System

Constructing your own hydropower system is a significant undertaking that requires technical knowledge, physical resources, and patience. Here are the steps in more detail:

1. **Site Assessment:** Survey your property to find a suitable water source. Consider the flow rate, available head, and local regulations related to water usage.
2. **System Design:** Once you understand your site's specifics, design your system. Calculate the potential power generation and select the appropriate turbine and generator types.
3. **Material Acquisition:** Purchase or repurpose the necessary materials based on your design. This includes the turbine, generator, controller, penstock, batteries, inverter, and construction materials like pipes, fittings, and wiring. Buy extra materials to account for potential errors and replacements.
4. **Building the System:** Assemble the turbine, connect it to the generator, set up the intake and penstock, and install the controller. Pay close attention to safety during this stage. If uncertain, consult or hire a professional.
5. **Testing and Adjustment:** Test the system by allowing water to flow through it and ensure everything functions as intended. This stage may require tweaking and adjustments, such as fixing penstock leaks, adjusting turbine positioning, or modifying the generator and controller configuration.
6. **Regular Maintenance:** After the system is operational, perform regular maintenance to ensure its efficiency. This include clearing the intake, inspecting the penstock for leaks, and making sure the controller, generator, and turbine are operating as intended.

How to Build a Small-Scale Hydropower Generator

Here is a basic guide for constructing your hydropower generator:

Materials Required:

- PVC pipes (for penstock)

- PVC T-joint (for turbine housing)
- Plastic spoons (for turbine blades)
- Metal rod (for turbine shaft)
- DC motor (acts as a generator)
- Wires (for connections)
- Multimeter (for measurements)
- Epoxy (for bonding)
- Battery and Inverter (for energy storage and conversion)

Step-by-Step Guide:

1. **Building the Turbine:**
   o Mark equally spaced points along the metal rod for attaching the plastic spoons (turbine blades).
   o Attach the plastic spoons to the rod using epoxy, forming a basic turbine.
   o Ensure the spoons are securely attached and allow time for the epoxy to fully set.
   o Insert the rod through the PVC T-joint, with the turbine sitting in the perpendicular section and the rod extending out both ends of the longer section.

2. **Connecting the DC Motor:**
   o Attach the DC motor to one end of the rod, ensuring it fits onto the motor shaft. The DC motor will serve as your generator.
   o Secure the DC motor to the PVC T-joint using additional epoxy or by creating a custom mount.
   o Ensure the DC motor is firmly attached and allow time for the epoxy to set if using epoxy.

3. **Constructing the Penstock:**
   o Use PVC pipes to create a pathway for the water, with one end connecting to the PVC T-joint above the turbine and the other end positioned in your water source.
   o Ensure proper sealing of the pipes to prevent leakage.

4. **Establishing Electrical Connections:**
   o Attach the DC motor's wires to the battery, ensuring the positive and negative terminals align.
   o Connect wires from the battery to the inverter to convert the generated DC power into AC electricity for typical home use.

5. **Installing the System:**
   o Position your hydropower system at the selected site, ensuring the penstock effectively collects water and that the water hits the turbine blades as it passes through.
   o Secure the system to prevent movement or damage from water flow.

6. **Testing Your System:**
   o Once the system is installed, allow water to flow and check if the turbine spins effectively.
   o Use a multimeter to measure the voltage output of the generator, ensuring it is functioning correctly.
   o Monitor the system over several days, making adjustments as necessary to achieve the most efficient power generation.

Building a small-scale hydropower system is a significant project but offers an excellent way to harness a renewable energy source. By understanding the principles of hydropower and the necessary components, you can create a system that provides a consistent, reliable source of electricity for your off-grid living.

Chapter 2: Exploring Water Wells: An In-depth Look at Dug, Drilled, and Driven Wells

Access to clean and reliable water is vital for any self-sufficient lifestyle. A well-planned water well can become the cornerstone of your off-grid living, providing you with a continuous supply of water. This chapter delves into the three main types of wells: dug, drilled, and driven wells.

Digging Deeper into Dug Wells

A dug well is the most ancient and simplest form of well, created by digging a hole in the ground using shovels or digging tools. Typically, dug wells are 10 to 30 feet deep and are lined with stone or brick to prevent cave-ins. However, due to their shallow depth, dug wells are susceptible to contamination from surface water.

Steps to Construct a Dug Well:

1. *Site Selection*: Choose a high elevation site to minimize contamination.
2. *Excavation*: Dig until water is struck, often a labor-intensive process.
3. *Reinforcement*: Line the well with stone or brick masonry to maintain stability.
4. *Maintenance:* Regularly check and clean the well to ensure it doesn't dry up and stays free from contaminants.

Understanding Driven Wells

A small-diameter pipe is driven into soft soil, like sand or gravel, to produce a driven well. These wells are typically up to 50 feet deep, making them less prone to contamination compared to dug wells. Driven wells involve a well point at the end of the pipe, which has openings to allow water to enter while keeping sediment out.

Steps to Construct a Driven Well:

1. *Site Selection*: Choose an area with soft earth.
2. *Driving the Pipe*: Use a heavy-duty driver to push the well point and pipe into the ground.
3. *Assembly*: Connect additional pipe lengths as needed until you reach the desired depth.
4. *Water Testing*: Test the water quality regularly to ensure it's safe for consumption.

Examining Drilled Wells

Drilled wells are created using percussion or rotary-drilling machines and can reach depths of more than 1,000 feet, though most household wells are usually between 100-500 feet deep. Given their depth, drilled wells are less likely to be contaminated, providing a more reliable water source.

Steps to Construct a Drilled Well:

1. *Professional Drilling*: Hire professional drilling services to reach the aquifer.
2. *Casing Installation*: Insert a steel or plastic casing into the drilled hole to prevent it from collapsing.
3. *Grouting:* Fill the area around the casing with grout to create a sanitary seal and prevent surface contaminants from entering the well.
4. *Pump Installation*: Install a well pump to draw water from the well to your home.
5. *Regular Maintenance*: Periodically inspect and maintain the well and pump system to ensure ongoing water quality and system integrity.

Additional Water Sourcing and Filtration Techniques

In off-grid living, relying on a single water source might not always be feasible. Weather conditions, soil composition, and geographical location can all affect the reliability of a water source. Therefore, it's beneficial to explore additional water sourcing techniques.

Surface Water Collection:

- *Uses*: Surface water from lakes, rivers, and streams can be used for irrigation, washing, and cooling.
- *Filtration*: If used for drinking, the water needs proper filtration and treatment to remove potential contaminants.

Dew and Fog Collection:

- *Method:* Use collection surfaces that condense water from the air into a reservoir.
- *Limitations*: This method doesn't produce large quantities of water but can be useful in survival scenarios.

Snow and Ice Melting:
- *Use:* Melting snow and ice for water consumption is viable in colder climates.
- *Energy Requirement*: This method is energy-intensive and should be a last resort if other sources are unavailable.

Water Filtration Techniques
Once you've sourced your water, it's critical to ensure it's safe for use. Here are some techniques for water filtration and purification:

Boiling:
- *Method*: Boiling water kills bacteria, viruses, and parasites.
- *Use:* Ideal for making water safe to drink.

Water Filtration Systems:
- *Options:* Various filters are available, from portable personal filters to larger household systems.
- *Considerations:* Choose based on the volume of water you need to filter and the types of contaminants present.

Solar Water Disinfection (SODIS):
- *Method:* Uses UV radiation from the sun to kill pathogens in water.
- *Requirements:* Only plastic PET bottles and direct sunlight are needed.

Chemical Treatment:
- *Options:* Chlorine or iodine can be used to treat water.
- *Drawbacks*: May leave a residual taste, so it should be used as a last resort.

Overview of Waterborne Pathogens and Contaminants
Understanding potential pathogens and contaminants in water is crucial for effective filtration and purification. Common waterborne pathogens include bacteria (e.g., E. coli, Salmonella), viruses (e.g., Hepatitis A, Norovirus), and parasites (e.g., Giardia, Cryptosporidium). Contaminants can also include chemicals (e.g., pesticides, heavy metals) and physical debris (e.g., sediment, organic material).

Mechanical Filtration Methods
Sediment Filters:
- *Use:* Remove larger particles such as sand, dirt, and rust.
- *Installation:* Typically the first stage in a multi-stage filtration system.

Ceramic Filters:
- *Use:* Trap bacteria and protozoa but allow water to pass through.
- *Maintenance*: Clean the outer surface regularly to maintain flow rate.

Chemical Purification Methods
Chlorination:
- *Use:* Adds chlorine to water to kill pathogens.
- *Considerations:* Effective but may leave a chlorine taste.

Iodine Treatment:
- *Use:* Uses iodine tablets or solutions to disinfect water.
- *Drawbacks:* Not suitable for long-term use due to potential health risks from prolonged iodine consumption.

Activated Carbon:
- *Use:* Adsorbs organic compounds and improves taste and odor.
- *Installation:* Often used as a secondary filter to enhance water quality.

Ultraviolet (UV) Purification
Principle:
- *Method:* Uses UV light to kill bacteria, viruses, and protozoa by damaging their DNA.
- *Requirements:* Requires electricity and clear water for maximum effectiveness.

Distillation as a Purification Technique
Principle:
- *Method*: Boils water to produce steam, which is then condensed back into liquid form, leaving most contaminants behind.

- *Effectiveness:* Removes a wide range of impurities, including heavy metals and salts.
- *Drawbacks:* Energy-intensive.

Comparing Efficiency and Cost of Modern Purification Techniques
Boiling:
- *Pros:* Highly effective.
- *Cons:* Energy-intensive.

Filtration Systems:
- *Pros:* Vary in cost and effectiveness; suitable for ongoing use.
- *Cons:* May require regular maintenance and replacement parts.

SODIS:
- *Pros:* Free and effective.
- *Cons:* Slow and dependent on sunlight.

Chemical Treatment:
- *Pros:* Inexpensive and portable.
- *Cons:* Can leave a taste.

UV Purification:
- *Pros:* Effective and fast.
- *Cons:* Requires clear water and electricity.

Distillation:
- *Pros:* Very effective.
- *Cons:* High initial and operational cost.

By mastering these additional sourcing and filtration techniques, you can make the most of the resources available to you and ensure a reliable water supply for your off-grid survival project.

Chapter 3: Harnessing the Skies: A Guide to Collecting Rainwater

In the journey towards self-sufficiency, rainwater collection is a sustainable and practical method for securing water. This chapter covers the essentials of setting up and using a rainwater harvesting system.

Understanding Rainwater Harvesting

Gathering, storing, and utilizing rainwater for a variety of uses—such as drinking, toilet flushing, and irrigation—requires rainwater harvesting. This water is typically collected from roofs, directed via gutters and downspouts into a storage system.

Benefits of Rainwater Harvesting

- **Water Conservation:** Reduces dependence on traditional water sources.
- **Cost Savings:** Can significantly reduce water bills.
- **Ideal for Irrigation:** Naturally soft and free from chemicals.
- **Emergency Backup:** Serves as a valuable resource during supply interruptions.

Setting Up Your Rainwater Collection System

Catchment Surface:
- *Material:* Metal roofs are ideal for collecting potable water.
- *Cleaning:* Ensure the roof is clean and free from contaminants.

Gutters and Downspouts:
- *Installation:* Attach gutters along the roof edge, sloping towards the downspouts.
- *Gutter Guards:* Optional, but recommended to prevent debris from entering.

First-Flush Diverter:
- *Purpose:* Diverts the initial flow of water to remove contaminants from the roof.
- *Installation:* Attach to the downspout to redirect the first few gallons of water away from the storage tank.

Storage Tanks or Barrels:
- *Size:* Depends on your water needs and available space.
- *Position:* Place on a stable, elevated platform near the downspouts.
- *Cover:* Use covers to prevent evaporation, algae growth, and mosquito breeding.

Delivery System:
- *Components:* Include pumps, pipes, and hoses.
- *Filtration and Treatment:* Necessary for drinking water, involving filtration, disinfection, and sometimes boiling.

Building a Rainwater Collector: A Step-by-Step Guide

Materials Needed:
- Rain barrel or large storage container
- Roofing material
- PVC pipe
- Pipe fittings
- Mesh screen
- Sealant
- Faucet
- Concrete blocks

Steps:
1. *Position Your Rain Barrel:*
   - Place the barrel under a downspout on a stable, elevated surface.
2. *Install the Faucet:*
   - Drill a hole near the bottom of the barrel, insert the faucet, and seal it.
3. *Connect the Downspout:*
   - Cut the downspout to sit above the barrel, attach a PVC elbow joint, and extend it over the barrel.
4. *Install the Roof-Washing Filter:*

  o Attach the filter to the PVC pipe to divert the initial, contaminated flow.
5. _Install the Mesh Screen:_
  o Secure the screen over the barrel to keep out debris and insects.
6. _Seal All Connections:_
  o Use sealant to ensure all connections are secure and leak-free.
7. _Wait for Rain:_
  o Your system is ready to collect rainwater.

By following these steps, you can set up a functional rainwater collection system that enhances your off-grid living setup. Regular maintenance is key to ensuring the system operates efficiently and provides a reliable source of water.

Chapter 4: Crafting Cleanliness: DIY Water Distillation – An Expanded Look

Water distillation is an essential skill for anyone striving for self-sufficiency, especially in situations where water quality is compromised. This chapter delves deeper into the process of water distillation and offers practical advice on maximizing the effectiveness of your homemade water distiller.

Understanding the Process
Distillation involves heating water to create steam, which leaves impurities behind. The steam is then condensed back into purified water. This method removes a wide range of contaminants, including bacteria, viruses, salts, and heavy metals.

Building Your Own Water Distiller: A Step-by-Step Guide
Materials Needed:
- Large stainless steel pot with lid
- Small glass or stainless steel bowl
- Heat-resistant silicone or rubber tubing
- Stove or other heat source
- Ice
- Drinking water storage containers

Step-by-Step Guide:
1. *Prepare Your Equipment:*
   - Ensure all components are clean. The pot should hold enough water for distillation without touching the small bowl when it floats.
2. *Set Up the Pot:*
   - Place the pot on the stove and fill it halfway with the water you want to distill. Leave enough space for the small bowl to float.
3. *Place the Bowl:*
   - Float the small bowl in the center of the pot. It should not touch the bottom.
4. *Attach the Tubing:*
   - Make a small hole in the lid of the pot and insert one end of the tubing. The other end should be directed towards your collection container.
5. *Cover the Pot:*
   - Place the lid upside down on the pot, ensuring the tubing extends out to the collection container.
6. *Heat the Water:*
   - Turn on the heat source and bring the water to a boil. Once boiling, reduce the heat to maintain a steady boil.
7. *Enhance Condensation:*
   - Place ice on the inverted lid to help condense the steam. As the steam rises, it will hit the cool lid, condense, and drip into the small bowl.
8. *Collect the Distilled Water:*
   - The condensed water will flow through the tubing into the storage container.
9. *Monitor the Process:*
   - Check the setup regularly to ensure the pot doesn't boil dry and that the distillation process is working efficiently.

Improving Your Water Distillation Setup
Ensuring a Good Seal:
- Use a silicone or rubber ring around the pot's rim to create an airtight seal, minimizing steam loss.

Temperature Control:
- Maintain a gentle boil to avoid rapid evaporation, which can carry impurities.

Cooling System:
- For better efficiency, consider a more advanced cooling system, like a cooled tube or coil, to condense the steam more effectively.

Safety Considerations

Handling Equipment:

- Always handle the pot, tubing, and other components carefully to avoid burns from hot water or steam.

Water Source:

- Start with the cleanest water possible, as distillation may not remove all contaminants, especially volatile organic compounds.

Benefits and Limitations

Advantages:

- Removes a broad range of contaminants, including heavy metals and salts.
- Produces very pure water.

Limitations:

- Energy-intensive process.
- Slow compared to other purification methods.
- May not remove all volatile organic compounds.

By understanding the distillation process and constructing your own water distiller, you can secure a reliable source of clean, drinkable water. This skill is invaluable for self-sufficiency and can be crucial in survival situations. Regular practice and improvements to your setup will ensure you are always prepared to produce safe water.

Chapter 5: Harnessing Outside Water Sources: A Novice's Guide

In a survival situation, access to a reliable water source is critical. While having a well or rainwater collection system is ideal, these may not always be available or feasible. Knowing how to safely utilize outside water sources becomes invaluable. This guide provides essential knowledge and practical steps for harnessing and treating water from natural sources.

Understanding Outside Water Sources

Outside water sources include streams, rivers, lakes, and ponds. These water bodies often provide a plentiful supply of water. However, while this water may look clean, it could be filled with harmful bacteria, parasites, and other contaminants. Therefore, it is critical to treat this water before using it for drinking or cooking.

Finding Outside Water Sources

Locating outside water sources may take some knowledge and skill. Here are some pointers:

Low-Lying Areas:
- Water naturally flows downhill, so low-lying areas often harbor water sources.

Vegetation:
- Lush vegetation is often a sign of a nearby water source.

Animal Trails:
- Animals also require water and often create trails leading to water sources. Following animal trails can lead you to water.

Treating Outside Water Sources

While outside water sources can be a lifesaver in a survival situation, it's essential to treat this water properly to remove potential contaminants. Here are some ways to treat outside water:

Boiling:
- Boiling is one of the most effective ways to purify water. It kills most bacteria, viruses, and parasites. Boil the water for at least one minute to ensure its safety.

Filtration:
- A portable water filter can be a great tool for purifying water from outside sources. They come in various types and sizes, with the most common being pump filters, gravity filters, and straw-style filters.

Chemical Treatment:
- Tablets or drops containing iodine or chlorine can be used to purify water. However, they may leave an unpleasant taste.

UV Light Treatment:
- Portable UV purifiers are another option. They use UV light to kill bacteria and viruses but don't remove any particulates in the water.

Building an Outside Water Collector

If you find a reliable outside water source, it might be worth building a simple water collector to ease the process of gathering water. This can be as simple as a large container placed under a fast-dripping source or a more complicated system using pipes to channel the water from the source to your storage tank.

Constructing a Simple Water Collector: A Step-by-Step Guide

Materials Needed:
- Large container (e.g., a 55-gallon drum)
- PVC pipes
- PVC fittings (elbows, tees, etc.)
- Mesh screen (to filter out debris)
- Waterproof sealant
- Basic tools (saw, drill, etc.)

Step-by-Step Guide:

1. *Choose a Collection Point:*

o Identify a spot where water naturally drips or flows, such as under a small waterfall, a natural runoff area, or a rock overhang.

2. *Prepare the Container:*
   o Clean the container thoroughly to ensure it is free from any contaminants. Drill a hole near the bottom of the container to attach a spigot or tap for easy water access.

3. *Install the Mesh Screen:*
   o Place the mesh screen over the opening of the container to filter out large debris and insects. Secure it in place with waterproof sealant.

4. *Set Up the Collection System:*
   o Connect the PVC pipes and fittings to channel water from the collection point into the container. Ensure the pipes are secured and angled properly to allow gravity to direct the water flow.

5. *Seal All Connections:*
   o Use waterproof sealant on all pipe connections to prevent leaks and ensure that the water flows smoothly into the container.

6. *Position the Collector:*
   o Place the container in a stable, elevated position to facilitate water collection and easy access to the spigot.

7. *Regular Maintenance:*
   o Check the collector regularly for any blockages or leaks, and clean the mesh screen to maintain optimal water flow.

Safety Tips for Using Outside Water Sources

Avoid Contaminated Areas:
* Stay away from water sources near industrial areas, agricultural runoff, or where animals defecate.

Filter Before Treating:
* Always filter the water to remove particulates before applying chemical treatments or UV light purification.

Test for Safety:
* If possible, use water testing kits to check for contaminants and ensure the water is safe to drink.

Identifying, gaining access to, and treating external water sources is an essential component of being self-sufficient. Even though it could appear overwhelming at first, you can safely utilize these priceless resources if you have the correct information and resources. To protect your health, always remember to treat any water you get from outside sources. The safety of your water is just as important as its accessibility.

Chapter 6: Understanding and Implementing Greywater Treatment Systems

As self-sufficiency and sustainability become more important, managing water efficiently is crucial. One effective method is utilizing a greywater treatment system. This chapter explains what greywater is, its benefits, and how to implement a system in your home.

What is Greywater?
Greywater refers to the relatively clean wastewater from baths, sinks, washing machines, and other kitchen appliances. It's not as contaminated as blackwater from toilets but still requires treatment before reuse.

Benefits of a Greywater System
- *Water Conservation*: Reusing greywater significantly reduces the demand for fresh water, which is beneficial in water-scarce areas.
- *Reduced Strain on Septic Systems*: Diverting greywater to irrigation can take a considerable load off your septic system, prolonging its life.
- *Nutrient Utilization*: Greywater often contains nutrients like nitrogen and phosphorus, which are beneficial to plants.

Implementing a Greywater Treatment System
Building a greywater treatment system can be simple or complex, depending on your needs. Here are the steps and materials for a basic system:
Materials:
- Collection bucket or drum
- PVC pipes and connectors
- A filter (e.g., cloth or sponge)
- Garden hose or drip irrigation system
- Non-toxic, biodegradable soap and detergent
Steps:
1. *Choose Your Sources:*
   o The best sources for greywater are your washing machine, bathtub, bathroom sinks, and shower.
2. *Collect the Greywater:*
   o Connect your sources to a central collection point using PVC pipes. This could be a simple bucket or a larger drum.
3. *Filter the Greywater:*
   o Before using the greywater, filter it to remove large particles that could clog your irrigation system. Use a cloth or sponge for this.
4. *Apply to Your Garden:*
   o Use a garden hose or drip irrigation system to apply the filtered greywater directly to your plants. Use the greywater within 24 hours.
5. *Choose the Right Products:*
   o Since greywater will be used to water plants, it's essential to use non-toxic, biodegradable soap and detergent to avoid harming your plants or the surrounding soil.

Types of Greywater Treatment Systems
- *Direct Use Systems: These systems use greywater directly from the source to irrigate plants after simple* filtration.
- *Treatment and Reuse Systems: These systems involve treating greywater to a level where it can be* stored and reused, involving filtration, disinfection, and sometimes nutrient removal.

Potential Problems and Solutions
- *Odor: Greywater can start to smell if not used quickly. Use it within 24 hours to prevent this.*

- *Clogging: Particles in greywater can clog irrigation systems. Regular maintenance and good filtration can* help prevent this.
- *Plant Damage: Harmful substances like bleach or salt in greywater can damage plants. Use plant-friendly* products to avoid this.

Safety and Hygiene Considerations

- *Avoid Contact: While greywater is relatively clean, it can still contain bacteria and other microorganisms.* Avoid direct contact whenever possible.
- *Don't Use on Edibles: Greywater shouldn't be used to irrigate plants that produce food that can be eaten* raw, such as salad greens, to avoid potential contamination.
- *Regular System Maintenance: Maintaining the system regularly ensures that it runs smoothly and* hygienically.

Implementing a greywater treatment system requires some effort but offers undeniable benefits. By reusing water, you conserve resources, reduce strain on your septic system, and utilize nutrients beneficial for plants. Always ensure safety and regular maintenance to avoid any health risks.

Chapter 7: The Art and Science of Water Filtration: An Essential Guide

Clean, drinkable water is fundamental to life and survival, particularly in a self-sufficient lifestyle. Not all water is safe for consumption directly, which is where water filtration comes into play. This chapter explores various water filtration methods, emphasizing the importance and types of systems you can implement.

The Need for Water Filtration

Even water that appears clean can harbor microscopic contaminants that cause illness. These contaminants can come from soil, agricultural runoff, industrial waste, or the atmosphere. Filtration is essential to remove these impurities and ensure safe drinking water.

Types of Water Filtration Systems

There are various types of water filtration systems, each designed to remove specific types of contaminants:

- *Mechanical Filters:* Remove larger particles such as sediment, dirt, and particulate matter. Often the first stage in a multi-stage filtration system.
- *Activated Carbon Filters:* Remove organic compounds, chlorine, and other chemicals affecting the taste and odor of water.
- *Reverse Osmosis Filters:* Use a semi-permeable membrane to remove a wide variety of contaminants, including salts, nitrates, and some metals.
- *UV Filters:* Use ultraviolet light to kill bacteria, viruses, and other microorganisms.
- *Ceramic Filters:* Have microscopic pores that filter out bacterial contaminants.

Selecting the right filtration system depends on the specific contaminants in your water. Often, a combination of methods provides the best results.

Building a Basic Water Filtration System

Creating a simple water filtration system at home can significantly improve water quality. Here's a step-by-step guide to building a basic filter:

Materials Needed:

- Large plastic or glass container
- Gravel
- Sand
- Activated charcoal
- Cotton or coffee filter
- Rubber band

Instructions:

1. *Prepare the Container:*
   - Clean the container thoroughly. This will serve as the body of your filter.
2. *Layer the Materials:*
   - Start with a layer of cotton or a coffee filter at the bottom to prevent other materials from falling through.
   - Add a layer of activated charcoal. This removes organic contaminants and improves taste and odor.
   - Add a layer of sand. This removes finer particles.
   - Add a layer of gravel. This removes larger debris and supports the sand layer.
3. *Assemble the Filter:*
   - Secure the filter materials in place using a rubber band.
4. *Filter the Water:*
   - Pour the water slowly into the top of the filter. Collect the filtered water in a clean container as it drips through the layers.
5. *Test the Water:*
   - Use a water testing kit to ensure the filtered water is safe for drinking.

Purifying Your Water Using UV Light: A Step-by-Step DIY Guide

UV purification is an effective way to eliminate harmful microorganisms without adding chemicals to the water. Here's how to set up a UV purification system:

Materials Needed:
- UV water purifier
- Plumbing tools
- Protective gloves and eyewear
- Water source

Instructions:
1. _Understand the Principle:_
   - UV light kills harmful bacteria and other microorganisms by disrupting their DNA.
2. _Purchase a UV Water Purifier:_
   - Choose a model suitable for the volume of water you wish to purify.
3. _Install the Purifier:_
   - Follow the manufacturer's instructions. Mount the purifier in the main water supply pipe.
4. _Connect the Water Source:_
   - Attach the purifier to your water source.
5. _Turn on the UV Lamp:_
   - Let it warm up before starting the water flow.
6. _Run the Water:_
   - The water will pass through the UV light chamber, killing microorganisms.
7. _Test the Water:_
   - Ensure the water is free from harmful bacteria using a water testing kit.
8. _Regular Maintenance:_
   - Clean the quartz sleeve and replace the UV lamp annually. Check and replace the pre-filter regularly.

Exploring More Water Filtration Methods

Beyond the methods already discussed, there are several other effective water purification techniques for survival situations:

- _Ceramic Filters:_ Simple, portable, and effective for removing bacteria and sediment. Can be made using clay and combustible materials.
- _Charcoal Filters:_ Excellent for removing certain chemicals and improving taste and odor. Can be made using a plastic bottle filled with gravel, sand, and activated charcoal.
- _Solar Disinfection (SODIS):_ Uses sunlight to kill pathogens. Fill a clear bottle with water and leave it in the sun for at least six hours.
- _Chemical Disinfection:_ Uses chlorine or iodine to kill pathogens. Effective but may leave an unpleasant taste.

Each method has pros and cons, and the best choice often depends on the specific situation and the quality of the water source.

Understanding and implementing water filtration is crucial for ensuring a safe water supply in a self-sufficient lifestyle. By mastering various filtration and purification techniques, you can protect yourself and your family from waterborne illnesses, ensuring a steady supply of clean, safe drinking water.

Chapter 8: PROJECT: Constructing a DIY Water Pump

A water pump is an essential component for any self-sufficient homestead, as it allows for the movement of water from one location to another. Whether you need to extract water from a well, irrigate your garden, or establish a plumbing system, a water pump is a valuable tool for managing your water supply. In this chapter, we will explore the construction of a DIY water pump using recycled materials, providing an affordable and hands-on solution for your homestead.

Materials Needed:
- Plastic water bottle
- Old garden hose
- Epoxy resin or waterproof adhesive
- Two one-way valves (available online or at hardware stores)
- PVC pipe and fittings (to match your hose size)
- Bicycle inner tube

Step-by-Step Guide:

1. Prepare Your Bottle Start with a clean and dry plastic water bottle. Remove the bottom of the bottle to create a cylinder shape. This will serve as the main body of your pump.

2. Connect the Hose Cut two sections of the garden hose. One section should be long enough to reach from your water source to the desired delivery location. The other section should be approximately one foot long. Attach one end of the shorter hose to the top of the bottle (where the cap goes) and secure it using epoxy resin or waterproof adhesive. This will ensure a tight seal and prevent leaks.

3. Install One-Way Valves Attach a one-way valve to the free end of each hose, ensuring that the valves are set to allow water to be sucked into the long hose and pushed out through the short hose. The valves will ensure water flows in the correct direction and prevent backflow.

4. Assemble the Pump Connect the other end of the long hose to a PVC pipe fitting that matches your hose size. Repeat the same process for the short hose, connecting it to another PVC pipe fitting. Ensure all connections are secure and watertight using epoxy resin or waterproof adhesive.

5. Create a Handle Cut the bicycle inner tube to match the length of your bottle. Connect the ends of the inner tube to form a loop. Fix this loop to the middle of the plastic bottle, creating a pump handle. This handle will be used to manually operate the pump.

6. Use Your Pump To operate the pump, submerge the free end of the long hose into the water source. Hold the bottle upright and push down on the handle (inner tube) to create a vacuum that draws water up into the bottle and hose. Release the handle to allow water to be pushed through the short hose and delivered to your desired location.

Additional Considerations:

Performance and Limitations: Please note that this DIY pump is a basic design and may not have a high flow rate or the ability to pump water uphill over long distances. It is intended for small-scale water transfer and educational purposes. For more robust off-grid water solutions, consider commercially-made manual pumps or solar-powered pump systems.

Maintenance: Regularly check all connections for leaks and ensure that the one-way valves are functioning correctly. Clean the hoses and fittings periodically to prevent blockages and maintain efficiency.

Safety: When constructing and operating your DIY water pump, ensure that all tools and materials are handled safely. Use protective gear, such as gloves and safety glasses, when cutting materials and applying adhesives.

Enhancements and Upgrades:

Increase Flow Rate: To increase the flow rate, consider using larger diameter hoses and more powerful one-way valves. This will allow more water to be pumped with each stroke.

Add a Pressure Tank: Incorporating a pressure tank into your system can help maintain a consistent water pressure and flow rate. This can be particularly useful for irrigation or household water supply systems.

Solar-Powered Pump: For a more advanced project, explore the possibility of integrating a solar-powered pump. This would provide a continuous and automated water supply, further enhancing your homestead's self-sufficiency.

Automated Pump System: Consider upgrading to an automated pump system with a timer or float switch to regulate water levels and flow. This can be particularly useful for maintaining water levels in ponds or reservoirs.

Chapter 9: PROJECT: Building an Automated Rainwater Collection and Purification System

Introduction and Objective of the Project

Water is a precious resource, and managing it efficiently is crucial for sustainability, especially in an off-grid or self-sufficient living scenario. This chapter guides you through the process of building an automated rainwater collection and purification system. The objective is to create a reliable source of clean water by capturing rainwater, filtering it, purifying it, and automating the process to ensure minimal manual intervention. This project will enhance your self-sufficiency and contribute to water conservation efforts.

List of Materials and Tools Required
Materials:
- Roofing material (for catchment area)
- Gutters and downspouts
- Gutter guards (optional)
- First flush diverter
- Storage tanks or barrels (food-grade)
- Gravel and sand (for basic filtration)
- Activated carbon filter
- UV purification system or chlorine tablets
- PVC pipes and fittings
- Water pump
- Sensors (rain sensor, water level sensor)
- Control unit (microcontroller like Arduino or Raspberry Pi)
- Electrical wiring
- Waterproof housing for electronics

Tools:
- Ladder
- Measuring tape
- Hacksaw or pipe cutter
- Drill with bits
- Screwdriver set
- Silicone sealant
- Pipe wrenches
- Safety gloves and goggles

Preparing the Catchment Area

The catchment area is typically the roof of your house or another structure. Ensure the roofing material is clean and suitable for collecting potable water. Metal roofs are ideal, while asphalt shingles can impart unwanted chemicals into the water.

1. *Clean the Roof*: Remove debris, leaves, and dirt from the roof surface.
2. *Inspect for Damage*: Ensure there are no leaks or damage to the roofing material.
3. *Install Gutter Guards*: If necessary, install guards to prevent debris from entering the gutters.

Installing Gutter and Downspouts

Gutters and downspouts are essential for directing rainwater from the roof to the storage system.

1. *Measure and Cut:* Measure the perimeter of your roof to determine the length of gutters required. Cut the gutters to size.
2. *Install Gutters*: Attach the gutters along the roof edge using brackets and screws, ensuring a slight downward slope towards the downspouts.
3. *Attach Downspouts*: Secure the downspouts to the gutters and direct them towards the storage tanks.

Setting up the First Flush System

A first flush system diverts the initial flow of rainwater, which often contains contaminants from the roof, away from the storage tank.

1. *Install Diverter*: Attach the first flush diverter to the downspout.
2. *Configure Diverter*: Set the diverter to redirect the first few gallons of rainwater away from the storage tank.

Installing Storage Tanks

Storage tanks should be positioned close to the downspouts and on a stable, elevated platform to facilitate water flow.

1. *Prepare the Base*: Level the ground and place a stable base (concrete or gravel) where the tanks will sit.
2. *Install Tanks*: Position the tanks on the prepared base. Connect the downspouts to the tanks using PVC pipes.

Setting up Filtration Units

Filtration is crucial for removing sediment, debris, and some contaminants from the collected water.

1. *Basic Filtration*: Set up a basic filtration unit using gravel and sand. Place this filter at the tank inlet.
2. *Activated Carbon Filter*: Install an activated carbon filter to remove organic contaminants and improve water taste and odor.

Integrating a Purification System

Purification ensures the collected water is safe for drinking.

1. *UV Purification*: Install a UV purification system after the filtration units. Follow the manufacturer's instructions for installation and operation.
2. *Chemical Purification (Optional):* Alternatively, use chlorine tablets for chemical purification. Follow dosage instructions carefully.

Automation and Monitoring: Implementing Sensors and Controls

Automating the system reduces manual intervention and ensures efficient operation.

1. *Rain Sensor:* Install a rain sensor on the roof to monitor rainfall and control the water collection process.
2. *Water Level Sensor*: Place a water level sensor in the storage tank to monitor water levels and prevent overflows.
3. *Control Unit*: Set up a microcontroller (e.g., Arduino or Raspberry Pi) to automate the system based on sensor inputs. Program the controller to manage the pump, open/close valves, and operate the purification system.

Maintenance and Troubleshooting

Regular maintenance is essential to keep the system running smoothly.

1. *Inspect Gutters and Downspouts*: Regularly check for and remove any blockages or debris.
2. *Clean Filters*: Clean or replace filtration units periodically to maintain efficiency.
3. *Check Sensors and Electronics*: Ensure all sensors and electronic components are functioning correctly. Replace any faulty components.
4. *Monitor Water Quality*: Regularly test the water quality to ensure the purification system is effective.

By following this guide, you can build an efficient, automated rainwater collection and purification system that provides a reliable source of clean water. This project not only enhances your self-sufficiency but also promotes sustainable living by conserving water resources. With proper maintenance and monitoring, your system will serve you well for years to come.

MODULE F: SHELTER AND SECURITY

Chapter 1: Self-Reliant Sanctuary: Fortified Shelter Design

Designing a self-reliant sanctuary involves creating a fortified shelter that offers protection and sustainability. Such a design ensures the ability to withstand natural disasters and human intrusions. A fortified shelter must incorporate robust materials and structural reinforcements for long-term durability and security.

Key Elements of Fortified Shelter Design

1. Structural Reinforcement:
- *Foundations*: Deep, reinforced concrete foundations provide stability and resistance to seismic activity.
- *Walls*: Reinforced concrete or steel-reinforced walls offer superior strength. Bulletproof materials or blast-resistant coatings can be added for enhanced protection.
- *Roof:* A solid, reinforced roof structure with layers of ballistic material ensures protection from aerial threats.

2. Strategic Location:
- *Natural Barriers*: Choose locations with natural barriers like hills or forests for additional protection. Avoid flood-prone areas and ensure accessibility to water and arable land.

3. Secure Entry Points:
- *Reinforced Doors and Windows*: High-security locks and shatterproof glass are essential. Incorporate hidden or reinforced escape routes for emergencies.

4. Technological Integration:
- *Security Systems*: Install surveillance cameras, motion detectors, and alarm systems powered by renewable energy sources like solar panels for continuous operation.

Principles of Resilient Home Design

Resilient home design prioritizes the home's ability to withstand and adapt to various challenges over time, ensuring functionality, safety, and sustainability.

Core Principles:

1. Durability:
- Use materials and construction techniques that offer long-lasting performance. Weather-resistant materials like treated wood and corrosion-resistant metals maintain structural integrity.

2. Adaptability:
- Design spaces that can be easily modified to meet changing needs. Flexible layouts, modular furniture, and multi-functional rooms enhance adaptability.

3. Sustainability:
- Incorporate eco-friendly practices and materials to minimize environmental impact. Use renewable energy sources, implement water conservation systems, and select sustainable building materials.

4. Redundancy:
- Build redundant systems for critical functions like power, water, and communication to ensure continuous operation during emergencies. Backup generators, water storage tanks, and alternative communication methods are vital.

Building in Harmony with Nature: Natural and Sustainable Materials

Utilizing natural and sustainable materials reduces the environmental footprint and enhances the health and comfort of the home's occupants. These materials provide superior insulation, breathability, and aesthetic value.

Types of Natural and Sustainable Materials:

1. Wood:
- Responsibly sourced wood, like cross-laminated timber (CLT), offers adaptability and warmth.

2. Stone:
- Stone provides excellent thermal mass and natural beauty. Local sourcing reduces transportation emissions.

3. Rammed Earth:

- This ancient technique involves compacting natural earth materials to create solid, energy-efficient walls with high thermal mass.

4. Bamboo:
- A fast-growing, renewable resource, bamboo is strong and flexible, ideal for various structural and decorative applications.

5. Recycled Materials:
- Using recycled metal, glass, and plastic reduces waste and demand for new raw materials. These materials can be incorporated into structural elements and finishes.

Enhancing Home Security
Ensuring home security involves a comprehensive approach combining physical barriers, technological solutions, and strategic planning.

Strategies for Enhancing Home Security:

1. Physical Barriers:
- *Fencing:* Sturdy fencing acts as the first line of defense. Options include metal, composite materials, or natural barriers like thorny bushes.
- *Reinforced Doors and Windows*: High-security locks, shatterproof glass, and reinforced frames provide critical protection.
- *Lighting:* Adequate lighting around entry points and pathways deters intruders. Motion-activated lights are particularly effective.

2. Technological Solutions:
- *Surveillance Systems*: Security cameras strategically placed around the property help monitor and record activity. Advanced systems offer remote access and alerts.
- *Alarm Systems:* Integrating alarms that trigger upon unauthorized entry can alert residents and authorities promptly.
- *Smart Home Integration*: Utilizing smart home technology allows for remote monitoring and control of security systems via smartphones and other devices.

3. Safe Rooms:
- Designing a safe room within the home provides a secure place during emergencies. Safe rooms should be reinforced, well-stocked, and equipped with communication devices.

4. Emergency Planning:
- Develop and regularly update an emergency plan, including evacuation routes, meeting points, and communication protocols. Regular drills ensure everyone knows their role.

Underground and Earth-Sheltered Homes: A Hidden Fortress
Earth-sheltered or subterranean homes offer unique benefits in terms of security, energy efficiency, and environmental integration. These dwellings provide natural insulation and blend seamlessly with their surroundings.

Advantages:

1. Security:
- The natural barrier provided by the earth enhances protection against intruders and severe weather. The low profile makes these homes less visible and more difficult to target.

2. Energy Efficiency:
- Earth-sheltered homes benefit from the insulating properties of the surrounding soil, maintaining stable interior temperatures and reducing the need for artificial heating and cooling.

3. Environmental Integration:
- These homes have minimal impact on the landscape, preserving natural aesthetics and promoting biodiversity. Green roofs and walls can further enhance ecological benefits.

4. Disaster Resilience:
- Underground homes are inherently resistant to many natural disasters, including tornadoes, hurricanes, and wildfires, due to their robust construction and protective earthen cover.

5. Sustainable Living:
- Incorporating practices like rainwater harvesting, solar panels, and natural ventilation systems enhances the eco-friendly nature of earth-sheltered homes.

Chapter 2: Innovations in Building Materials

An Overview of Sustainability in the Construction Industry
Sustainability in construction refers to designing and building structures that are resource- and environmentally-conscious throughout their lifecycle. This approach enhances occupant health and well-being while reducing negative environmental impacts.

Key Aspects of Sustainable Construction:

1. Energy Efficiency:
- *Renewable Energy*: Installing solar panels, wind turbines, or geothermal systems. These systems harness natural energy sources, significantly reducing electricity bills and lowering the carbon footprint.
- *Energy-Efficient Systems*: Utilizing LED lighting, energy-efficient HVAC systems, and Energy Star-rated appliances. Smart thermostats optimize heating and cooling, saving energy and money.

2. Water Efficiency:
- *Low-Flow Fixtures:* Installing low-flow toilets, showerheads, and faucets to reduce water consumption. Dual-flush toilets offer different flush options to save water.
- *Rainwater Harvesting*: Collecting and storing rainwater for landscape irrigation or non-potable uses. Systems can range from simple barrels to complex underground cisterns.

3. Material Selection:
- *Sustainable Materials*: Choosing materials like bamboo, recycled metal, or cork, which have a low environmental impact and require less energy to produce and transport.
- *Life Cycle Assessment*: Evaluating the environmental impact of materials from production to disposal to select those with minimal negative impact.

4. Indoor Environmental Quality:
- *Natural Lighting*: Maximizing natural light reduces the need for artificial lighting and improves occupant well-being. Skylights and large windows enhance daylighting.
- *Non-Toxic Materials*: Using low-VOC paints, adhesives, and finishes to improve indoor air quality, reducing the risk of respiratory issues.

5. Waste Reduction:
- *Construction Waste Management*: Implementing practices to reduce, reuse, and recycle construction debris, minimizing landfill waste.
- *Modular Construction*: Prefabricated modules reduce material waste and construction time, and they can be disassembled and reused.

Using Contemporary Insulation Materials to Save Energy
Proper insulation is crucial for energy efficiency and maintaining comfortable indoor temperatures. Modern insulation materials offer enhanced performance and sustainability.

Types of Modern Insulation Materials:

1. Spray Foam Insulation:
- *Closed-Cell Foam*: High R-value per inch and moisture barrier, ideal for spaces requiring maximum insulation.
- *Open-Cell Foam*: Good insulation and soundproofing, suitable for interior walls and ceilings.

2. Fiberglass Insulation:
- *Batts and Rolls*: Easy to install, widely used in walls, attics, and floors.
- *Blown-In Fiberglass*: Ideal for insulating irregular spaces, providing uniform coverage.

3. Cellulose Insulation:
- *Recycled Content*: Made from recycled paper, offers good thermal and acoustic insulation.
- *Dense-Pack Application*: Blown into cavities at high density to prevent settling and provide consistent insulation.

4. Rigid Foam Boards:
- *Extruded Polystyrene (XPS):* High moisture resistance, used below grade and in exterior walls.
- *Polyisocyanurate (PIR):* Highest R-value per inch, suitable for roof and wall insulation.

5. Natural Fiber Insulation:
- *Cotton:* Made from recycled denim, offering good thermal performance and sound absorption.

- *Sheep's Wool*: Naturally fire-resistant and helps regulate indoor humidity.

6. Aerogel Insulation:
- *High Performance*: Extremely low thermal conductivity, ideal for thin insulation applications.
- *Flexible Sheets*: Used in walls, roofs, and around pipes to prevent heat loss.

Durable and Eco-Friendly Construction Materials
Selecting durable and eco-friendly materials ensures buildings are long-lasting and have a minimal environmental footprint.

Examples of Durable and Eco-Friendly Materials:

1. Recycled Steel:
- *Strength and Durability*: Ideal for structural elements, reducing the need for mining new materials.
- *Recyclability:* Can be recycled indefinitely without losing properties.

2. Bamboo:
- *Rapid Growth*: Renewable resource used for flooring, cabinetry, and structural elements.
- *Strength and Flexibility*: Comparable to steel in tensile strength.

3. Rammed Earth:
- *Natural Materials*: Provides excellent thermal mass and reduces the need for artificial heating and cooling.
- *Aesthetics:* Offers a unique, natural look.

4. Reclaimed Wood:
- *Sustainable Sourcing*: Salvaged from old structures, reducing demand for new timber.
- *Character and History*: Adds unique character with its aged appearance.

5. Recycled Concrete Aggregate (RCA):
- *Waste Reduction*: Utilizes crushed concrete from demolished structures.
- *Versatility:* Used in road construction, foundations, and as base material for new concrete.

6. Green Roof Systems:
- *Insulation and Energy Savings*: Vegetation on rooftops provides insulation and reduces energy costs.
- *Stormwater Management*: Absorbs rainwater, reducing runoff.

7. Low-VOC Paints and Finishes:
- *Healthier Indoor Air:* Reduces the release of harmful chemicals.
- *Wide Range of Options*: Available in various colors and finishes.

8. Cross-Laminated Timber (CLT):
- *Engineered Wood:* Strong and stable material suitable for multi-story buildings.
- *Sustainable Construction*: Reduces construction time and waste.

Emerging Technologies in Construction for Off-Grid Living
Innovative technologies enhance sustainability, efficiency, and self-sufficiency in construction, especially for off-grid living.

Emerging Technologies:

1. 3D Printing:
- *Rapid Construction*: Prints entire structures quickly with minimal waste.
- *Customization*: Allows for complex and custom designs.

2. Modular and Prefabricated Construction:
- *Efficiency and Precision:* High quality and reduced construction time.
- *Scalability:* Easily scalable and reconfigurable.

3. Solar Roof Tiles:
- *Integrated Energy Generation*: Solar panels embedded in roofing materials.
- *Durability:* Designed to withstand harsh weather.

4. Smart Home Systems:
- *Automation and Control*: Remote control of lighting, heating, and security.
- *Energy Management*: Optimizes energy usage.

5. Water Purification and Recycling Systems:
- *Self-Sufficiency*: Advanced systems enable the use of greywater and rainwater.
- *Conservation:* Reduces dependence on external water sources.

Chapter 3: Securing Off-Grid Living

Living off-grid offers numerous benefits, including independence and sustainability, but it also comes with unique security challenges. This chapter aims to equip you with the knowledge and tools needed to secure your off-grid home, ensuring the safety of your property and loved ones.

1. Evaluating Off-Grid Security Requirements Transitioning to an off-grid lifestyle necessitates a thorough evaluation of security needs. Begin by conducting a comprehensive risk assessment, taking into account local crime rates, potential wildlife threats, and environmental hazards such as floods or fires. Identify valuable assets that require protection, including solar panels, water systems, and livestock. Create a detailed security plan that outlines the measures needed to address identified risks, considering both physical and digital threats. In this section, we'll also explore various risk assessment tools and techniques to ensure you have a solid understanding of your security needs.

2. Physical Defense Strategies: Barriers, Illumination, and Monitoring Physical security measures are crucial for protecting off-grid properties. This includes installing robust fencing options such as electric fences or using natural barriers like dense hedges. Effective lighting solutions, powered by renewable energy, can significantly enhance security by deterring intruders and improving visibility. Surveillance systems, including high-resolution cameras and drone monitoring, provide real-time oversight of your property. This section will delve into the installation, maintenance, and integration of these physical security measures, ensuring they work seamlessly together to provide comprehensive protection.

3. Innovative Tech: Solar-Powered Security Systems Harnessing solar power for security systems offers a sustainable and reliable solution for off-grid living. Explore various solar-powered security devices, including motion detectors, automated gates, and alarm systems. Learn about the installation process, the necessary maintenance, and how to ensure these systems remain effective even during prolonged periods of low sunlight. We will also discuss the integration of these systems with smart home technology, allowing for remote access and monitoring through smartphones and other devices, enhancing overall security and convenience.

4. Emergency Communication Networks Reliable communication systems are vital for off-grid living, especially during emergencies. This section will cover the range of communication options available, from satellite phones and ham radios to emergency beacons and two-way radios. Understand the operational capabilities of each device, their advantages, and limitations. We will also discuss the creation of an emergency communication plan, including regular testing of devices, establishing communication protocols, and designating contact points. This ensures that you and your family can maintain contact with the outside world and receive assistance when needed.

5. Digital Defense: Safeguarding Your Off-Grid Tech Protecting your off-grid technology from cyber threats is as important as physical security. Learn about implementing robust cybersecurity measures, such as firewalls, encryption, and anti-malware software. This section will also cover the importance of securing your network, using secure passwords, and keeping software updated to protect against vulnerabilities. Educate all household members on best practices for online safety and the importance of being vigilant against phishing and other cyber-attacks. By taking these steps, you can ensure that your off-grid systems remain secure and operational.

6. Community Strength: Collaborative Security Efforts Building a strong, cooperative community is key to enhancing security in an off-grid environment. Establishing a neighborhood watch program can create a sense of shared responsibility and vigilance among residents. This section will explore how to set up and maintain such programs, including organizing regular meetings, developing communication strategies, and coordinating patrols. Additionally, we will discuss the benefits of community training sessions on emergency response, first aid, and security protocols. By fostering a collaborative spirit, off-grid communities can enhance their overall security and resilience.

Tips and Tricks for Everyday Security
- Regularly check and maintain all security systems to ensure they are functioning correctly.
- Keep a detailed inventory of valuable items and update it regularly.
- Use camouflage techniques to make your property less visible from a distance.

Chapter 4: Constructing an Eco-Friendly Insulated Cabin

Project Goals and Design Blueprint

Building an eco-friendly insulated cabin begins with defining clear objectives and creating a comprehensive design blueprint. Your goals should focus on minimizing environmental impact, maximizing energy efficiency, and using locally sourced materials. This section will guide you through setting these sustainability goals and selecting appropriate cabin designs. Key elements include passive solar heating, natural ventilation, and efficient space utilization. Detailed planning ensures the project remains on track and within budget while aligning with your eco-friendly aspirations. Draft floor plans, select sustainable materials, and integrate eco-friendly features from the outset.

Steps to Get Started:
- *Define Sustainability Goals*: Outline what you aim to achieve regarding environmental impact, energy efficiency, and material use.
- *Create a Blueprint*: Draft detailed floor plans that incorporate eco-friendly features.
- *Research and Select Designs*: Explore various designs that focus on passive solar heating, natural ventilation, and space efficiency.

Sourcing Materials and Tools

Gathering necessary materials and tools is critical. Choose sustainable, high-quality materials such as reclaimed wood, recycled insulation, and non-toxic finishes. This section provides a comprehensive list of tools required, from basic hand tools to specialized equipment, and offers tips on sourcing materials locally to reduce costs and environmental impact. Additionally, the benefits of using energy-efficient tools and machinery will be covered.

Materials and Tools:
- *Sustainable Materials*: Reclaimed wood, recycled insulation, non-toxic finishes.
- *Basic Tools*: Hammer, saw, measuring tape, level.
- *Specialized Equipment*: Energy-efficient tools, solar-powered machinery.
- *Sourcing Tips:* Buy locally, look for second-hand options, and choose high-quality, durable materials.

Selecting and Preparing the Site

Choosing the right location for your cabin is crucial for sustainability and comfort. Factors to consider include sunlight exposure, wind patterns, and proximity to natural resources. Proper site preparation is essential, involving responsible land clearing, grading for drainage, and minimal disruption to the local ecosystem. This section also discusses obtaining necessary permits and adhering to zoning regulations.

Site Preparation Steps:
- *Criteria for Selection*: Sunlight exposure, wind patterns, proximity to resources.
- *Land Preparation*: Clear responsibly, grade for drainage, preserve local ecosystems.
- *Permits and Regulations*: Obtain necessary permits, follow zoning laws.

Constructing the Foundation

A strong foundation is crucial for your cabin's longevity. Explore eco-friendly foundation options such as pier and beam, slab-on-grade, and earthbag foundations. Detailed instructions for laying out and constructing the foundation, including setting footings, pouring concrete, and ensuring proper insulation and moisture barriers, will be provided.

Foundation Construction:
- *Foundation Types*: Pier and beam, slab-on-grade, earthbag.
- *Construction Steps*: Set footings, pour concrete, ensure insulation and moisture barriers.
- *Eco-Friendly Tips*: Use fly ash in concrete mix, recycled materials for insulation.

Framing and Insulation Installation

Building the frame and installing insulation are key steps in creating an energy-efficient cabin. This section guides you through framing techniques using sustainable lumber and advanced framing methods to reduce material usage and increase efficiency. Eco-friendly insulation options like cellulose, wool, and hemp will be detailed, along with installation techniques to ensure optimal thermal performance.

Framing and Insulation:
- *Framing Techniques*: Use sustainable lumber, advanced framing methods.
- *Insulation Options*: Cellulose, wool, hemp.
- *Installation Techniques:* Ensure thermal performance, use thermal mass strategies, airtight construction.

Roofing, Siding, and Installing Windows and Doors

The exterior must be durable and energy-efficient. This section covers roofing materials and techniques, including green roofs, metal roofing, and solar shingles. Siding options like reclaimed wood, fiber cement, and natural stone are explored for their aesthetic and environmental benefits. Guidance on selecting and installing energy-efficient windows and doors is also provided.

Exterior Construction:
- *Roofing Options*: Green roofs, metal roofing, solar shingles.
- *Siding Materials*: Reclaimed wood, fiber cement, natural stone.
- *Windows and Doors*: Energy-efficient options, double or triple glazing, proper sealing techniques.

Interior Finishing and Furnishing

Eco-friendly options for flooring, wall finishes, and cabinetry are discussed, along with sustainable furnishing choices. Natural and low-VOC paints and finishes ensure a healthy indoor environment. Tips on creating a cozy, functional, and eco-friendly living space are provided, including optimizing natural light and ventilation and using multi-functional furniture.

Interior Finishing:
- *Finishing Materials*: Eco-friendly flooring, low-VOC paints, sustainable cabinetry.
- *Furnishing Tips*: Second-hand furniture, reclaimed materials, multifunctional pieces.
- *Living Space Optimization:* Maximize natural light and ventilation.

Integrating Eco-friendly Utilities and Final Review

The final step is integrating sustainable utilities and conducting a thorough inspection. This section covers installing solar panels, rainwater harvesting systems, composting toilets, and energy-efficient heating and cooling systems. Tips for maintaining your eco-friendly cabin and making future improvements are included, along with exploring smart home technology to monitor energy use and manage utilities efficiently.

Utility Integration and Final Review:
- *Eco-Friendly Utilities*: Solar panels, rainwater systems, composting toilets, energy-efficient HVAC.
- *Inspection and Maintenance*: Ensure all systems function correctly, create a maintenance schedule.
- *Smart Home Technology*: Monitor energy use, manage utilities efficiently.

By following these detailed steps, you can construct a sustainable, eco-friendly insulated cabin that aligns with your environmental and self-sufficiency goals. Each phase, from planning and sourcing materials to construction and integration of utilities, contributes to creating a comfortable and sustainable living space.

MODULE G: MODERN SOLUTIONS FOR INDEPENDENT LIVING

Chapter 1: Innovations in Off-Grid Technology and Communication

Exploring New Horizons in Off-Grid Radio Technology

The landscape of off-grid living is continually evolving, with advancements in radio technology playing a pivotal role. This section delves into the latest developments in off-grid radio technology, which have significantly improved communication capabilities for those living away from traditional infrastructure.

We will explore high-frequency (HF) and very high-frequency (VHF) radios, detailing their applications in long-range and short-range communication respectively. Digital modes such as Digital Mobile Radio (DMR) and Digital Amateur Radio also play a crucial role, offering enhanced clarity and reliability. The integration of these technologies facilitates communication across vast distances without reliance on cellular networks or internet connections.

Further, we will discuss the practicality of setting up these radio systems, including licensing requirements, selecting the appropriate equipment, and tips for optimizing signal strength. The importance of maintaining and upgrading equipment to keep pace with technological advancements will also be emphasized.

In addition, case studies and real-world examples of successful off-grid radio setups will be included to provide practical insights and inspiration for implementing these technologies.

Connecting the Dots: Off-Grid Internet and Satellite Communication

Access to the internet is no longer a luxury but a necessity, even for those living off the grid. This section covers various methods of obtaining internet access in remote locations, emphasizing the importance of connectivity for both personal and professional needs.

Satellite internet is a primary solution, with providers like Starlink offering high-speed internet access to remote areas. We will discuss the setup process, costs, and the benefits of satellite internet, such as consistent connectivity and broad coverage. Mobile broadband, using cellular networks, offers another option, though it depends on proximity to cell towers. We will explore the use of signal boosters and antennas to enhance connectivity in weak signal areas.

Additionally, we will cover the integration of these systems with existing infrastructure, ensuring a seamless connection for various devices. The potential for combining multiple internet sources to create a more robust and reliable network will also be discussed.

Detailed comparisons of different service providers, their coverage maps, and data plans will be provided to help users make informed decisions. We will also include testimonials from off-grid users who have successfully implemented these technologies.

Harnessing the Sun: Solar-Powered Communication Devices

Solar energy is a game-changer for off-grid living, particularly for powering communication devices. This section examines a range of solar-powered communication devices and their role in maintaining connectivity without reliance on traditional power sources.

We will explore portable solar chargers, ideal for small devices like phones and radios, and portable solar panels that can power larger systems. Comprehensive solar-powered communication systems, including solar-powered Wi-Fi routers and base stations, will also be discussed. These systems can provide consistent and reliable power, crucial for maintaining communication in remote areas.

Detailed insights into the selection, installation, and maintenance of these devices will be provided, including tips for optimizing efficiency and ensuring longevity. The use of battery storage systems to store excess solar energy for use during nighttime or cloudy days will also be covered.

Real-life examples of successful solar-powered communication setups will be included to illustrate best practices and innovative solutions. Additionally, we will discuss the environmental benefits of using solar power and how it contributes to sustainable living.

Staying Prepared: Emergency Radios and Signaling Techniques

In off-grid living, being prepared for emergencies is crucial. This section explores the importance of emergency radios and signaling techniques, which are vital for maintaining communication during crises.

We will discuss different types of emergency radios, including hand-crank and solar-powered models. These radios often feature NOAA weather alerts, AM/FM bands, and two-way communication capabilities, making them indispensable tools for off-grid living. Detailed guidance on selecting the right emergency radio, based on features and reliability, will be provided. In addition to radios, we will cover various signaling techniques, both traditional and modern. This includes the use of signal mirrors, flares, and whistles, as well as more advanced methods like satellite beacons and Personal Locator Beacons (PLBs). Understanding these techniques ensures that you have multiple ways to send and receive critical information during emergencies, enhancing safety and preparedness.

Case studies of emergency scenarios where these tools and techniques were effectively used will be included to provide practical insights. We will also discuss the importance of regular drills and training to ensure preparedness.

Building Connections: Networking for Off-Grid Communication

Creating a robust communication network is essential for off-grid living. This section provides a comprehensive guide to setting up and maintaining networks for off-grid communication.

We will explore various networking solutions, such as mesh networks, which allow devices to communicate with each other directly, extending coverage without relying on a central hub. Point-to-point wireless links can provide high-speed connections between distant locations, useful for larger properties or community setups.

Community-based intranets offer another layer of connectivity, enabling local communication and resource sharing even without internet access. We will discuss the necessary hardware, such as routers, repeaters, and antennas, and software options for managing these networks.

We'll go over best practices for maintaining safe and dependable communication in off-grid communities, including how to solve typical problems and enhance network efficiency. There will also be emphasis on how crucial it is to do routine maintenance and updates to maintain the network safe and operational.

We will include examples of successful off-grid networks, showcasing different configurations and the benefits they provide. Additionally, we will discuss the potential for expanding these networks to create larger, interconnected off-grid communities.

Chapter 2: Ensuring Connectivity in Off-Grid Living

The Critical Role of Communication in Off-Grid Living

Effective communication is essential for off-grid living, providing safety, social connection, and access to vital information. Without reliable communication channels, individuals living off the grid can face significant challenges, particularly during emergencies.

Safety and Emergency Response: Communication is critical for ensuring timely medical assistance, coordinating with emergency services, and receiving weather alerts. In remote areas, the ability to communicate can be lifesaving. We will discuss various scenarios where effective communication has prevented disasters and ensured safety.

Social Connection: Maintaining contact with family and friends is crucial for mental well-being. Isolation can lead to feelings of loneliness and depression, making regular communication essential. We will explore different methods of staying connected, such as using social media, email, and video calls, even in remote locations.

Access to Information: Staying informed about current events, weather forecasts, and local news is important for making informed decisions. We will discuss how off-grid residents can access news and information through various communication channels, ensuring they remain connected to the broader world.

Educational and Professional Needs: For those who work or study remotely, reliable communication is indispensable. We will explore options for maintaining a stable internet connection for professional and educational purposes, ensuring that living off the grid does not hinder personal or professional growth.

Case Studies: Real-life stories and case studies will be included to highlight the importance of communication in off-grid living, providing practical examples and insights.

Satellite vs Cellular: Comparing Off-Grid Communication Options

Choosing the right communication method is crucial for off-grid living. This section provides a detailed comparison between satellite and cellular communication options, analyzing their strengths, weaknesses, and suitability for different off-grid scenarios.

Satellite Communication: Satellite communication is ideal for remote locations where cellular signals are weak or nonexistent. We will explore the benefits of satellite communication, such as global coverage and reliability, and discuss the latest advancements in satellite technology.

Setup and Costs: Detailed guidance on setting up satellite communication systems, including selecting the right equipment, installation processes, and ongoing maintenance, will be provided. We will also discuss the costs associated with satellite communication, including initial setup fees, monthly service plans, and equipment maintenance.

Challenges: Potential challenges, such as latency issues and weather-related disruptions, will be discussed. We will provide tips on mitigating these challenges and ensuring a stable connection.

Cellular Communication: Cellular communication can be a viable option for those within range of cell towers. We will examine the benefits of cellular networks, including lower latency and generally lower costs compared to satellite services.

Enhancing Cellular Reception: The use of signal boosters, antennas, and other technologies to enhance cellular reception in remote areas will be explored. Detailed instructions on selecting and installing these devices will be provided.

Service Providers: A comparison of different cellular service providers, their coverage maps, and data plans will help off-grid dwellers make informed decisions. We will discuss how to choose the best provider based on location, usage needs, and budget.

Case Studies: Real-life examples and testimonials from off-grid users who have successfully implemented satellite and cellular communication solutions will be included to illustrate practical applications and outcomes.

Mesh Networks: Community-Driven Connectivity Solutions

Mesh networks offer a decentralized and resilient communication solution for off-grid communities. This section will explain the concept of mesh networks, how they work, and their benefits for off-grid living.

How Mesh Networks Work: We will explore the technical aspects of mesh networks, including how devices connect directly with each other to create a robust and flexible network. Detailed explanations of mesh network topology and protocols will be provided.

Setting Up a Mesh Network: Step-by-step guidance on setting up a mesh network, including selecting the right hardware (routers, nodes) and software, will be offered. We will discuss different mesh network configurations and how to optimize them for specific needs.

Benefits: The advantages of mesh networks, such as their resilience to single points of failure and ability to extend coverage over large areas, will be highlighted. We will also discuss how mesh networks can improve community cohesion and resource sharing within off-grid communities.

Maintenance and Optimization: Best practices for maintaining and optimizing mesh networks to ensure reliable performance will be provided. This includes regular software updates, troubleshooting common issues, and strategies for expanding the network as needed.

Real-World Examples: Case studies of successful mesh network implementations in various off-grid environments will be included, showcasing their effectiveness and providing practical insights.

Essential Tools for Emergency Communication

Emergency communication devices are crucial for ensuring safety and preparedness in off-grid living. This section will cover a range of emergency communication tools and techniques to ensure you can always stay connected during crises.

Emergency Radios: We will delve into the features and benefits of various emergency radios, including hand-crank, solar-powered, and battery-operated models. The importance of features like NOAA weather alerts, two-way communication, and durability will be discussed.

Selecting the Right Radio: Guidance on selecting the right emergency radio based on specific needs and environments will be provided. We will explore different brands and models, comparing their features, reliability, and cost.

Satellite Phones: Satellite phones provide a reliable communication option in emergencies, especially in areas without cellular coverage. We will explore the pros and cons of satellite phones, including their cost, reliability, and usage scenarios.

Personal Locator Beacons (PLBs) and Emergency Position-Indicating Radio Beacons (EPIRBs): These devices are essential for sending distress signals to search and rescue authorities. We will explain how they work, their range, and the different models available on the market.

Signaling Techniques: In addition to electronic devices, traditional signaling techniques like signal mirrors, whistles, and flares will be discussed. Understanding how to use these methods effectively can be life-saving in emergency situations.

Case Studies and Real-Life Scenarios: We will include real-life stories and case studies where emergency communication devices played a crucial role in rescue operations, providing practical insights into their importance and effectiveness.

Regular Drills and Training: The importance of regular drills and training to ensure preparedness will be emphasized. We will provide tips on conducting effective drills and maintaining readiness.

Chapter 3: Cutting-Edge Gadgets for Off-Grid Living

Solar-Powered Innovations: Harnessing Sunlight for Connectivity

Off-grid living is being revolutionized by solar power, which offers a dependable and sustainable energy source for a variety of devices. This section examines the newest solar-powered gadgets that improve off-grid living conditions and communications.

Power banks with solar chargers: For maintaining the charging of gadgets like phones, tablets, and GPS units, portable solar chargers and power banks are indispensable. There will be in-depth information on how to choose the best solar charger based on portability, capacity, and efficiency. We will also discuss the technology underlying solar panels, including the differences between polycrystalline and monocrystalline panels and how they impact efficiency and performance.

Solar-Powered Lights and Lanterns: Lighting is crucial for safety and convenience in off-grid living. We will explore solar-powered lights and lanterns, highlighting features such as brightness, battery life, and durability. Tips on the best placement and maintenance of these lights to maximize their effectiveness will also be included. Additionally, we will discuss innovative lighting solutions like solar string lights for outdoor areas and solar floodlights for security purposes.

Solar-Powered Communication Devices: Maintaining connectivity is vital, and solar-powered communication devices like satellite phones, Wi-Fi routers, and radios are key. This section will cover the latest advancements in these devices, focusing on their reliability, ease of use, and integration with existing off-grid setups. We will also look into the future of solar-powered communication technologies, such as advancements in battery storage and the integration of smart technology.

Case Studies: Real-life examples of off-grid residents successfully using solar-powered gadgets will be included, providing practical insights and tips for effective implementation. These case studies will illustrate how different environments and climates impact the performance of solar-powered devices.

Weather Monitoring: Essential Meteorological Gadgets

Staying informed about weather conditions is critical for off-grid living, affecting everything from safety to resource management. This section explores modern weather monitoring gadgets that provide accurate and timely meteorological data.

Portable Weather Stations: We will discuss portable weather stations that measure temperature, humidity, wind speed, and barometric pressure. Insights into selecting the right weather station based on accuracy, range, and additional features like data logging will be provided. We will also explore how to set up and calibrate these stations for optimal performance.

Weather Radios: Weather radios that receive NOAA alerts and updates are essential for staying informed about severe weather conditions. This section will cover different models, highlighting features such as alert types, battery life, and additional functionalities like two-way communication. We will discuss the integration of weather radios with other emergency preparedness tools.

Smart Weather Sensors: Advancements in smart technology have led to the development of weather sensors that can be integrated with home automation systems. We will explore these sensors, focusing on their benefits for off-grid living, such as remote monitoring and integration with other smart devices. Additionally, we will discuss how these sensors can be used to automate responses to weather changes, such as closing windows during rainstorms or adjusting solar panel angles based on sunlight.

Practical Applications: Examples of how off-grid residents use weather monitoring gadgets to make informed decisions and enhance their safety and efficiency will be included. These examples will highlight how accurate weather data can improve daily planning and long-term resource management.

Hand-Crank and Dynamo Powered Devices: Reliable Off-Grid Power Solutions

In off-grid living, having reliable, manually powered devices can be a game-changer, especially during emergencies. This section explores hand-crank and dynamo-powered gadgets that provide dependable power solutions without relying on batteries or external electricity sources.

Hand-Crank Radios: We will delve into the features and benefits of hand-crank radios, which are indispensable for receiving news and weather updates during power outages. Detailed guidance on selecting the best models based on durability, reception quality, and additional features will be provided. We will also discuss the advantages of radios with multiple power options, including solar and battery backups.

Dynamo Flashlights and Lanterns: Lighting is essential, and dynamo-powered flashlights and lanterns offer a reliable source of illumination. We will explore different models, discussing their brightness, ease of use, and battery life. Tips on maintaining these devices to ensure long-term functionality will also be included. We will also cover innovative products like hybrid flashlights that combine hand-crank, solar, and battery power.

Hand-Crank Chargers: Hand-crank chargers can power small electronic devices like phones and GPS units. This section will cover the latest models, focusing on their charging efficiency, durability, and ease of use. We will also discuss scenarios where hand-crank chargers are particularly useful, such as extended camping trips or during natural disasters.

Case Studies: Real-life stories of off-grid individuals successfully using hand-crank and dynamo-powered devices during emergencies and daily life will provide practical insights. These stories will illustrate the reliability and versatility of manually powered devices in various off-grid scenarios.

Water Purification Gadgets: Ensuring Safe Drinking Water

Access to clean drinking water is a top priority for off-grid living. This section explores modern water purification gadgets that ensure safe and reliable water sources.

Portable Water Filters: We will discuss various portable water filters, including straw filters, pump filters, and gravity filters. Detailed insights into selecting the best filter based on filtration capacity, ease of use, and maintenance will be provided. We will also explore the differences between filters that remove bacteria, protozoa, and viruses, and those that also eliminate chemicals and heavy metals.

UV Purifiers: UV purifiers use ultraviolet light to kill bacteria and viruses in water. This section will explore different models, focusing on their effectiveness, portability, and battery life. Tips on using and maintaining UV purifiers to ensure optimal performance will also be included. We will also discuss how to combine UV purifiers with other filtration methods for comprehensive water treatment.

Water Purification Tablets: In emergency situations, water purification tablets offer a quick and reliable solution. We will discuss their advantages, usage instructions, and storage tips to ensure you always have a safe water supply. We will also cover the shelf life of these tablets and how to properly store them for long-term use.

Practical Applications: Examples of off-grid residents using water purification gadgets to ensure safe drinking water in various environments will be included, providing practical insights and tips. These examples will highlight the importance of having multiple water purification options for different situations.

Outdoor and Survival Gear: Modern Innovations

Modern outdoor and survival gear enhances safety, comfort, and efficiency for off-grid living. This section explores the latest innovations in outdoor and survival equipment.

Multitools and Knives: We will discuss various multitools and knives, essential for a wide range of tasks from cooking to repairs. Detailed guidance on selecting the best tools based on functionality, durability, and ease of use will be provided. We will also explore specialized tools designed for specific tasks, such as hunting or fishing.

Fire Starters: Reliable fire starters are crucial for cooking, warmth, and signaling. We will explore different types of fire starters, including ferro rods, magnesium blocks, and waterproof matches. Tips on using and maintaining these tools to ensure they work when needed will be included. We will also discuss innovative products like electric plasma lighters that work in wet conditions.

Emergency Shelters: Portable emergency shelters provide protection in extreme weather conditions. This section will cover various options, such as bivvy sacks, tarp shelters, and portable tents, focusing on their durability, ease of setup, and portability. We will also explore the use of space blankets and thermal shelters for emergency warmth and protection.

Navigation Tools: Effective navigation is vital for off-grid living. We will discuss modern navigation tools, including GPS devices, compasses, and maps, highlighting their importance for safety and efficiency. Tips on using and maintaining these tools will also be included. We will also cover advanced GPS devices with features like topographic maps, route planning, and emergency SOS functions.

Real-Life Applications: Stories and case studies of off-grid residents successfully using modern outdoor and survival gear will provide practical insights and demonstrate the importance of having reliable equipment. These stories will highlight the versatility and necessity of having the right gear for various off-grid activities and emergencies.

Chapter 4: Building Your Off-Grid Internet System

Defining Project Goals: Assessing Your Internet Requirements
Identifying Usage Needs:
- *Basic Usage*: Tasks like emailing and browsing need lower bandwidth. Calculate data usage for these activities to determine the required speed.
- *Moderate Usage*: Streaming videos, video calls, and social media require more bandwidth. Understand typical bandwidth requirements for these activities.
- *High Usage:* Remote work, online gaming, or multiple users need higher bandwidth. Guidelines for required internet speeds will be provided.

Location Considerations:
- *Remote Locations*: Explore challenges like signal obstructions from terrain or vegetation and available solutions.
- *Environmental Factors*: Understand how weather conditions like rain, snow, or wind affect your internet connection and how to mitigate these issues.

Budget Planning:
- *Initial Costs*: Breakdown of initial costs, including equipment purchase, installation fees, and setup costs.
- *Ongoing Costs:* Monthly service fees, maintenance costs, and potential upgrade expenses to help plan your budget.

Choosing the Right Internet Service: Satellite, Cellular, or Alternatives
Satellite Internet:
- *Benefits:* Wide coverage, reliable, and suitable for most online activities.
- *Challenges:* Latency, weather sensitivity, and higher costs. Comparison of providers like Starlink, HughesNet, and Viasat.
- *Setup Process*: Steps for setting up satellite internet, including dish positioning, ensuring a clear line of sight, and configuring the modem.

Cellular Internet:
- *Benefits:* Lower latency and cost compared to satellite, easier setup, and mobility.
- *Challenges:* Limited by cellular coverage, which might be sparse in remote locations. Signal boosters can enhance reception.
- *Providers Comparison*: Compare major cellular providers, their coverage, data plans, and costs.

Alternative Options:
- *Long-Range Wi-Fi*: Suitable for community networks or sharing internet from a distant source. Setup and range extension techniques.
- *LEO Satellites*: Explore the benefits of Low Earth Orbit satellites like lower latency and higher speeds.

Case Studies:
- *Real-life Examples*: Testimonials from off-grid users highlighting pros and cons of different services.

Gathering Essential Equipment: Comprehensive Hardware Checklist
Satellite Dish and Modem:
- *Selection Tips*: Choosing the right satellite dish and modem based on location and internet needs.
- *Installation Guidance*: Steps for setting up the dish, positioning, and connecting the modem.

Cellular Modem and Booster:
- *Selection Tips*: Choosing the right cellular modem and booster based on provider and signal strength.
- *Installation Guidance*: Steps for installing cellular modems and boosters, including optimal placement.

Routers and Networking Devices:
- *Router Types:* Discussion on different types of routers (standard, dual-band, tri-band) and their features.
- *Extenders and Mesh Systems*: Benefits of using extenders or mesh networks to enhance Wi-Fi coverage.
- **Configuration Tips**: Setting up SSIDs, securing your network, and managing bandwidth.

Power Backup Systems:

- *Solar Batteries*: Choosing the right capacity and type of solar batteries.
- *UPS and Generators*: Additional power backup options for critical situations.

Installing a Solar Power System: Powering Your Connectivity
Solar Panels:
- *Selection Tips*: Choosing the right solar panels based on power requirements and available space. Compare monocrystalline vs. polycrystalline panels.
- *Installation Guidance*: Steps for mounting, wiring, and positioning solar panels for optimal sunlight exposure.

Battery Storage:
- *Selection Tips:* Choosing the right batteries, focusing on capacity, lifespan, and maintenance.
- *Installation Guidance*: Connecting batteries to the solar system and managing charge/discharge cycles.

Inverters and Charge Controllers:
- *Role Explanation*: Understanding the roles of inverters and charge controllers in a solar power system.
- *Selection and Setup*: Choosing the right models and installation guidance.

System Monitoring:
- *Tools and Techniques*: Using monitoring tools to track solar power system performance and identify issues early.

Setting Up the Antenna or Cellular Booster: Enhancing Signal Strength
Antenna Selection:
- *Types of Antennas*: Different types of antennas (directional, omnidirectional, Yagi) and their suitability.
- *Selection Tips*: Choosing the best antenna based on location and signal strength.

Installation Tips:
- *Optimal Positioning*: Positioning and mounting the antenna to maximize signal reception.
- *Avoiding Obstructions*: Tips on avoiding obstacles that can block or interfere with the signal.

Using Signal Boosters:
- *Types of Boosters*: Overview of different signal boosters and how they work.
- *Selection and Setup*: Guidance on choosing and installing the right signal booster.

Testing and Optimization:
- *Signal Testing Tools*: Using apps and tools to test and optimize signal strength.
- *Fine-Tuning Tips*: Techniques for fine-tuning antenna and booster placement for best performance.

Creating a Local Area Network (LAN): Connecting Your Devices
Network Planning:
- *Layout Planning*: Importance of planning network layout, considering device locations and interference.
- *Cabling Considerations*: Choosing the right cabling (Ethernet vs. Wi-Fi).

Wired vs. Wireless:
- *Pros and Cons:* Comparing wired and wireless LAN setups.
- *Best Practices*: Tips for optimizing wired and wireless networks.

Router and Switch Setup:
- *Configuration Basics*: Setting up and configuring routers and switches.
- *Advanced Features*: Utilizing advanced router features like QoS, guest networks, and parental controls.

Connecting Devices:
- *Compatibility Tips*: Ensuring compatibility between devices and network components.
- *Optimization Tips:* Tips for optimizing device connections for a stable network.

Implementing Security Measures: Protecting Your Off-Grid Internet
Firewall Setup:
- *Importance of Firewalls:* Understanding the role of firewalls in network security.
- *Setup Guide*: Instructions for setting up hardware and software firewalls.

Encryption:
- *Types of Encryption*: Discussion on different encryption methods like WPA3 and VPNs.
- *Setup Guide:* Setting up and managing encryption to protect your data.

Regular Updates and Maintenance:
- *Importance of Updates*: Keeping devices and software up to date to protect against vulnerabilities.
- *Automation Tips*: Automating updates and maintenance tasks.

Monitoring and Response:
- *Monitoring Tools*: Using tools to detect suspicious activity on the network.
- *Response Strategies*: Tips on responding to security incidents effectively.

Planning for the Future: Expanding and Upgrading Your Off-Grid Internet System
Scalability:
- *Designing for Expansion*: How to design your system with scalability in mind.
- *Modular Components*: Selecting components that can be upgraded over time.

Technology Trends:
- *Keeping Up with Advancements*: Discussion on emerging technologies like 5G and LEO satellites.
- *Integration Tips:* Practical tips on integrating new technologies.

Regular Assessments:
- *Performance Tracking*: Conducting regular assessments to identify areas for improvement.
- *Performance Metrics*: How to perform assessments and track performance metrics.

Budgeting for Upgrades:
- *Financial Planning:* Strategies for budgeting future upgrades.
- *Cost-Effective Options*: Leveraging cost-effective upgrade options.

MODULE H: PROFITABLE OFF-GRID LIVING
Chapter 1: Starting an Off-Grid Business

Entrepreneurial Opportunities in Off-Grid Living
In recent years, the allure of off-grid living has inspired many to pursue entrepreneurial ventures that align with their sustainable lifestyles. This section explores various business opportunities that can be undertaken while living off the grid, highlighting the benefits and challenges unique to this lifestyle.

Identifying Business Opportunities:
- *Sustainable Products*: Discuss the potential of creating and selling eco-friendly products, such as biodegradable soaps, organic farming tools, and sustainable home goods. These products cater to the growing market of environmentally conscious consumers.
- *Services for the Off-Grid Community*: Explore service-based businesses like consulting for new off-grid converts, offering maintenance services for renewable energy systems, or even building tiny homes. These services are in high demand as more people transition to off-grid living.

Case Studies and Examples:
- *Provide real-life examples of successful off-grid entrepreneurs and the types of businesses they run, offering inspiration and practical insights.* For instance, highlight a business that produces solar-powered devices or another that offers eco-friendly construction services.

Overcoming Challenges:
- *Address common challenges such as limited internet access, logistical issues, and the need for self-sufficiency in various aspects of the business.* Discuss solutions like using satellite internet for better connectivity, planning logistics for product distribution, and skills training for self-sufficiency.

Remote Work and Digital Nomadism
The rise of remote work has opened up new possibilities for those living off the grid. This section will explore how to leverage digital tools and platforms to earn a living while enjoying the benefits of an off-grid lifestyle.

Setting Up a Remote Work Environment:
- *Essential Tools and Technology*: Discuss the necessary tools for remote work, such as reliable internet connections, power backup solutions, and ergonomic workspaces. Emphasize the importance of having a dedicated workspace and reliable power sources to maintain productivity.
- *Choosing the Right Job*: Explore various remote job opportunities that are well-suited for off-grid living, including freelance writing, graphic design, virtual assistance, and IT services. Provide resources for finding remote work, such as job boards and freelance platforms.

Balancing Work and Off-Grid Life:
- *Offer strategies for maintaining a work-life balance, emphasizing the importance of setting boundaries and scheduling time for both work and off-grid activities.* Discuss techniques like time blocking, taking regular breaks, and setting clear start and end times for the workday.

Success Stories:
- *Highlight individuals who have successfully transitioned to remote work while living off the grid, sharing their tips and experiences.* Include examples of how they manage their time, overcome connectivity challenges, and stay productive in an off-grid environment.

Selling Produce and Homemade Goods
For those with a green thumb or a knack for crafting, selling produce and homemade goods can be a rewarding way to generate income. This section covers the essentials of turning your garden and workshop into profitable ventures.

Growing and Selling Produce:
- *High-Value Crops:* Identify crops that are easy to grow and have high market value, such as herbs, specialty vegetables, and fruits. Discuss market trends and demand for organic produce.
- *Organic Farming Techniques***:** Discuss the benefits of organic farming and how to achieve certification, enhancing the marketability of your produce. Provide tips on sustainable farming practices, pest management, and soil health.

Creating and Selling Homemade Goods:
- *Crafts and Artisan Products***:** Explore the types of homemade goods that are popular in local markets, such as candles, soaps, pottery, and textiles. Highlight the importance of quality craftsmanship and unique designs.
- *Online and Offline Sales Channels***:** Provide guidance on selling products through farmers' markets, local stores, and online platforms like Etsy. Discuss marketing strategies, pricing, and building a brand.

Financial Planning for Off-Grid Living
Effective financial planning is crucial for sustaining an off-grid lifestyle. This section provides a comprehensive guide to managing finances, ensuring long-term stability and growth.

Budgeting and Cost Management:
- *Initial Investment***:** Outline the initial costs of setting up an off-grid home, including land, renewable energy systems, and essential infrastructure. Provide a sample budget and tips for cost-effective planning.
- *Ongoing Expenses***:** Discuss ongoing costs such as maintenance, food, and utilities, offering tips for reducing expenses through self-sufficiency practices. Highlight the importance of tracking expenses and adjusting the budget as needed.

Income Diversification:
- *Multiple Income Streams***:** Emphasize the importance of diversifying income sources to mitigate risks and ensure financial stability. This includes combining remote work, selling goods, and offering services. Discuss strategies for creating multiple income streams and managing them effectively.

Savings and Investments:
- *Building a Safety Net:* Provide strategies for saving money and creating an emergency fund to cover unexpected expenses. Discuss the importance of financial security and planning for emergencies.
- *Sustainable Investments***:** Explore investment opportunities that align with off-grid values, such as renewable energy projects and sustainable agriculture. Provide guidance on making informed investment decisions and growing wealth sustainably.

Chapter 2: Making Money from Off-Grid Living

Embracing Self-Sufficiency for Income
Food Production:
- *Financial Benefits*: Growing your own fruits, vegetables, and herbs can significantly reduce grocery bills. Selling excess produce at local farmers' markets or to neighbors can provide a steady income. Highlight success stories of off-grid communities thriving through sustainable agriculture.
- *Preservation Methods*: Techniques like canning, drying, and fermenting extend the shelf life of produce, reducing waste and creating value-added products for sale year-round. Provide step-by-step guides and safety tips for food preservation.

Livestock and Poultry:
- *Potential Earnings*: Raising chickens, goats, sheep, or bees can be profitable through selling eggs, milk, meat, wool, or honey. Include financial projections based on different scales of operations.
- *Sustainable and Ethical Practices*: Emphasize ethical treatment and sustainable practices in animal husbandry, such as organic feed, rotational grazing, and humane slaughter methods. Highlight the market for ethically produced animal products.

Handmade and Artisan Goods:
- *Creating and Selling Handmade Items*: Items like candles, soaps, knitwear, and home decor have a dedicated market. Discuss creating high-quality handmade goods and turning a hobby into a business.
- *Local Markets and Online Platforms*: Insights into participating in local craft fairs and farmers' markets. Discuss online platforms like Etsy, eBay, and Shopify for reaching a global audience. Include tips on photography, product descriptions, and customer service for online sales.

Leveraging Natural Resources for Financial Gain
Timber and Firewood:
- *Income from Harvesting*: Potential earnings from selling timber and firewood. Information on local regulations, permits, and sustainable harvesting practices to maintain forest health.
- *Responsible Forestry Practices:* Highlight replanting trees, managing forest health, and using eco-friendly logging techniques. Discuss certifications like FSC (Forest Stewardship Council) that add value to timber products.

Herbs and Medicinal Plants:
- *Market for Medicinal Plants*: Growing demand for herbs like lavender, chamomile, and echinacea. Discuss cultivation techniques, harvest times, and processing methods for optimal potency and quality.
- *Potential Products*: Identify products such as teas, essential oils, tinctures, and dried herbs. Discuss packaging, labeling, and marketing strategies to attract health-conscious consumers.

Renewable Energy:
- *Producing and Trading Extra Energy*: Install solar or wind turbines to produce energy. Discuss selling excess energy back to the grid to generate additional income and lower energy costs.
- *Regulatory and Logistical Aspects*: Explain connecting to the grid, necessary permits, and regulations. Insights into government incentives, tax credits, and grants for renewable energy installations.

Crafting and Selling Handmade Products
Identifying Market Trends:
- *Current Trends*: Analyze trends in the handmade market, such as eco-friendly products, minimalist designs, and personalized items. Identify market gaps and capitalize on emerging trends.
- *Popular Handmade Items*: Examples include handmade jewelry, knitted garments, pottery, and woodwork. Emphasize the importance of uniqueness and quality.

Production Techniques:
- *Efficient Production*: Tips on maintaining high quality while increasing output. Discuss consistency, time management, and using sustainable materials.
- *Sustainable Materials:* Use eco-friendly materials like organic cotton, recycled metals, and natural dyes. Provide sources for obtaining these materials and discuss their benefits.

Marketing and Sales Strategies:
- *Marketing Handmade Products*: Strategies for marketing and selling products, including creating an attractive brand, developing a strong online presence, and engaging with customers through social media.
- *Building a Brand*: Importance of branding, including creating a memorable logo, consistent packaging, and a compelling brand story. Tips on standing out in a competitive market.

Teaching and Hosting Workshops: Education as a Revenue Stream
Identifying Skills and Knowledge:
- *Valuable Skills for Teaching*: Identify valuable skills and knowledge to teach, such as sustainable living practices, renewable energy, organic gardening, and traditional crafts.
- *Popular Workshop Topics*: Examples include beekeeping, soap making, herbal medicine, and permaculture design. Highlight the growing interest in self-sufficiency and sustainability.

Setting Up Workshops:
- *Organizing Workshops*: Practical advice on selecting a venue, pricing, and marketing strategies. Benefits of partnering with local community centers, educational institutions, and other organizations.
- *Promotion and Marketing*: Strategies for promoting workshops, such as using social media, creating flyers, and leveraging word-of-mouth. Importance of testimonials and reviews in attracting participants.

Online Education:
- *Opportunities for Online Courses*: Potential of offering online courses and webinars to reach a broader audience. Tools and platforms for creating and hosting online educational content.
- *Creating Online Content*: Tips on producing high-quality videos, developing engaging course materials, and interacting with students online. Benefits of passive income from recorded courses.

By diversifying income sources and leveraging the unique opportunities presented by off-grid living, individuals can create sustainable and rewarding businesses that align with their values and lifestyle.

Chapter 3: Profiting from Surplus and Eco-Tourism

Market Research and Identifying Profitable Opportunities
Market Research:
- *Conducting Market Research:* Use surveys, interviews, and online research to understand local demand. Look for gaps in the market that you can fill with your produce or handmade goods.
- *Examples of Profitable Items:* High-demand crops like heirloom tomatoes, exotic herbs, and organic berries can command premium prices. Livestock such as free-range chickens and heritage breed pigs are popular. Handmade items like natural soaps, beeswax candles, and wooden crafts also have strong market potential.

Organic Certification:
- *Obtaining Certification:* Outline the steps to become certified organic, including understanding standards, preparing your farm, and passing inspections. Mention reputable certifying bodies like USDA Organic.
- *Maintaining Standards:* Emphasize adhering to organic practices, such as using organic feed, avoiding synthetic pesticides, and maintaining detailed records. Certification enhances marketability and product pricing.

Programs for Community Supported Agriculture (CSA)
CSA Configuration:
- *Setting Up a CSA:* Outline key steps including deciding on CSA size, membership fees, and distribution schedules. Explain how to manage subscriptions and handle payments.
- *Benefits of CSA Programs:* Discuss how CSAs provide upfront capital, create a loyal customer base, and reduce the risk of unsold produce. Highlight benefits for consumers, such as access to fresh, local produce and a connection to the farming process.

Marketing and Management:
- *Attracting and Retaining Members:* Market your CSA through social media, local events, and word of mouth. Offer incentives like early-bird discounts and referral bonuses to attract new members.
- *Effective Communication:* Emphasize clear communication with CSA members, providing regular updates about produce availability, delivery schedules, and farm news. Use newsletters, emails, and social media to keep members engaged and informed.

Farmers' Markets and Local Supply Chains
Participating in Farmers' Markets:
- *Selecting Markets:* Choose markets based on location, customer demographics, and vendor mix. Participate in markets that align with your product offerings and target audience.
- *Preparing for Market Days:* Ensure your stall is attractive and organized, with clear signage and pricing. Bring enough inventory to meet demand and offer samples to entice customers. Accept multiple forms of payment, including cash, credit cards, and mobile payments.
- *Building Relationships:* Foster relationships with other vendors and regular customers. Networking with fellow vendors can lead to collaborations and shared marketing efforts. Engaging with customers builds loyalty and repeat business.

Local Supply Chains:
- *Supplying Local Businesses:* Establish connections with local restaurants, grocery stores, and co-ops. Offer competitive pricing and consistent quality to build long-term relationships.
- *Ensuring Reliability:* Ensure reliable and timely delivery of your produce and products. Maintain high standards of quality and consistency to meet the expectations of your business partners.

Eco-Tourism: Turning Your Off-Grid Lifestyle into a Destination
Introduction to Eco-Tourism:
- *Growing Trend:* Discuss the increasing popularity of eco-tourism and its benefits, such as generating income, promoting sustainability, and educating visitors about off-grid living. Highlight successful eco-tourism destinations and their unique offerings, such as farm stays, workshops, and nature tours.

Setting Up an Eco-Tourist Destination:
- _Accommodations and Activities_: Offer tips on setting up comfortable and eco-friendly accommodations, such as cabins, yurts, or tiny homes. Plan activities like hiking, organic farming workshops, and wildlife watching. Ensure amenities like composting toilets, solar showers, and communal kitchens are sustainable and functional.
- _Sustainable Infrastructure_: Emphasize eco-friendly infrastructure, such as renewable energy systems, rainwater harvesting, and waste recycling. Showcase your commitment to sustainability through educational tours and hands-on activities.

Marketing and Promotion:
- _Marketing Strategies_: Utilize online platforms like Airbnb, eco-tourism websites, and social media to market your destination. Develop a professional website with detailed information about your offerings, booking options, and visitor testimonials.
- Partnerships and Collaborations: Partner with travel agencies, eco-tourism platforms, and local tourism boards to reach a wider audience. Collaborate with other local businesses to offer package deals and cross-promotions.

Sustainable Practices:
- _Waste Management:_ Implement comprehensive waste management practices, including composting, recycling, and minimizing single-use plastics. Use energy-efficient appliances and renewable energy sources to reduce your carbon footprint.
- _Environmental Education_: Provide educational materials and workshops to inform visitors about sustainable living practices. Create a memorable experience that inspires guests to adopt eco-friendly habits in their own lives.

By leveraging surplus production and eco-tourism, off-grid residents can create profitable and sustainable income streams. These ventures not only support financial stability but also promote a deeper connection with the environment and the community.

MODULE I: SUSTAINABLE COMMUNITY LIVING
Chapter 1: Establishing Resilient Communities and Support Networks

Creating and Integrating into Off-Grid Communities
Understanding Community Dynamics:
- **Types of Off-Grid Communities:** Explore different models such as eco-villages, intentional communities, and cooperative housing. Discuss their unique features, goals, and the lifestyles they support.
- **Finding the Right Fit:** Highlight the importance of shared values and goals. Provide tips for evaluating potential communities, such as visiting multiple times, engaging in community activities, and discussing long-term plans with current members.

Steps to Form a Community:
- **Initial Planning:** Outline the vision and mission of the community. Discuss setting goals, defining values, and creating a roadmap for development.
- **Legal and Logistical Considerations:** Explore zoning laws, land acquisition processes, and choosing the right legal structure, such as forming a cooperative, a non-profit, or a trust.

Joining an Existing Community:
- **Research and Outreach:** Guide on researching existing communities through websites, social media, and community networks. Highlight the importance of communication and visiting potential communities.
- **Integration Process:** Tips for a smooth integration, including participating in community workdays, respecting established norms, and building relationships with current members.

Maximizing Shared Resources and Mutual Aid
Resource Sharing:
- **Common Facilities:** Discuss the benefits of shared facilities such as communal kitchens, workshops, and laundry rooms. Explain how these reduce costs and resource consumption.
- **Tools and Equipment:** Highlight the advantages of sharing tools and equipment, including gardening tools, construction equipment, and renewable energy systems. Provide examples of successful resource-sharing programs.

Mutual Aid Systems:
- **Skill Sharing:** Emphasize the importance of skill sharing, covering trades like carpentry, plumbing, medical care, and educational services. Discuss setting up a skill-sharing database or schedule.
- **Emergency Support:** Develop strategies for mutual aid during emergencies, such as creating emergency plans, establishing communication protocols, and organizing regular training sessions.

Creating Systems for Resource Management:
- **Organizing Resource Pools:** Tips for creating and managing communal resource pools, including fair access policies, maintenance schedules, and contribution systems.
- **Governance of Shared Resources:** Discuss different governance structures for managing shared resources, ensuring transparency, equity, and accountability.

Effective Conflict Resolution and Governance
Conflict Resolution:
- **Common Sources of Conflict:** Identify common sources of conflict, such as resource allocation, personal differences, and decision-making processes. Provide case studies illustrating these conflicts.
- **Resolution Techniques:** Discuss various conflict resolution techniques, including active listening, mediation, and restorative justice. Provide a step-by-step guide for implementing these techniques within the community.

Governance Structures:
- **Types of Governance:** Explore different governance models, such as consensus-based decision-making, sociocracy, and democratic assemblies. Discuss the pros and cons of each model.

NO GRID SURVIVAL PROJECTS BIBLE

- **Creating a Governance Charter:** Provide guidelines for creating a governance charter that outlines roles, responsibilities, decision-making processes, and conflict resolution methods.

Ensuring Participation and Inclusivity:
- **Encouraging Participation:** Strategies for encouraging active participation from all community members, such as rotating leadership roles, creating inclusive discussion spaces, and ensuring transparency in decision-making.
- **Inclusivity:** Discuss the importance of inclusivity and diversity in decision-making processes. Offer tips for ensuring all voices are heard, such as using facilitation techniques that encourage quieter members to speak up.

Building a Support Network for Sustainability

Internal Support Systems:
- **Health and Wellness:** Discuss the importance of supporting the physical and mental health of community members through shared health resources, wellness programs, and mental health support groups.
- **Educational Initiatives:** Explore opportunities for education and skill development within the community, such as organizing workshops, creating mentorship programs, and encouraging lifelong learning.

External Support Networks:
- **Connections with Nearby Communities:** Highlight the benefits of forming alliances with nearby off-grid or on-grid communities for mutual support, resource sharing, and joint initiatives.
- **Partnerships with Organizations:** Discuss potential partnerships with non-profits, government agencies, and other organizations that support sustainable living. Provide examples of successful partnerships and the benefits they bring.

Long-Term Sustainability Strategies:
- **Continuous Improvement:** Emphasize the importance of regularly evaluating and improving community practices and systems. Discuss methods for gathering feedback and implementing changes.
- **Adaptability and Resilience:** Strategies for maintaining flexibility and resilience in the face of changing circumstances and challenges, such as economic shifts, climate change, and evolving community needs.

Analysis and Improvements

Structure and Completeness: The chapter is well-structured and covers a comprehensive range of topics essential for establishing resilient off-grid communities. Each section provides actionable advice and detailed steps, making it practical and informative.

Content Enhancement:
1. **Detailed Case Studies:** Including more real-life examples and case studies would add depth and provide practical insights into how different communities handle challenges and opportunities.
2. **Visual Aids:** Adding diagrams, flowcharts, or infographics to illustrate community structures, resource management systems, and governance models would enhance understanding.
3. **Resource Links:** Providing links to additional resources, such as books, online forums, and organizations, would offer readers further avenues for research and support.
4. **Interactive Elements:** Suggesting interactive elements like community assessment checklists, governance templates, or skill-sharing databases could provide tangible tools for readers to implement the concepts discussed.

Chapter 2: Creating and Sustaining Off-Grid Communities

Historical Context:
- **Traditional Practices:** Ancient and indigenous communities lived sustainably by relying on communal resources and cooperation. They practiced methods like crop rotation, communal hunting, and shared housing, which minimized their environmental footprint and fostered social cohesion.
- **Modern Resurgence:** The revival of these practices today is driven by environmental concerns, economic instability, and a desire for self-sufficiency. Communities are increasingly adopting sustainable living to reduce their reliance on external systems and promote environmental stewardship.

Core Principles:
- **Self-Sufficiency:** Emphasizes the importance of producing one's own food, energy, and resources to reduce dependency on external supplies and increase resilience.
- **Sustainability:** draws attention to methods that reduce their negative effects on the environment, like the use of renewable energy sources, permaculture, trash reduction, and biodiversity promotion.
- **Community:** Discusses the value of strong social bonds, mutual support, and shared goals in fostering a resilient community. Community living enhances mental and emotional well-being and provides a robust support network during times of need.

Benefits of Community Living in Off-Grid Settings
Shared Resources:
- **Economies of Scale:** Combining resources for infrastructure, food, and energy can save expenses and boost productivity dramatically. Energy, water, and waste management shared systems maximize resource utilization and reduce personal costs.
- **Skill Sharing:** A diverse skill set within the community enhances self-sufficiency. Community members can exchange skills in carpentry, gardening, healthcare, education, and more, ensuring that everyone benefits from collective knowledge.

Social Support:
- **Mental and Emotional Health:** Living in a supportive community reduces stress and increases happiness. Regular social interactions, communal activities, and mutual support systems promote a sense of belonging and well-being.
- **Collective Security:** Communities can provide enhanced security through mutual vigilance and coordinated response plans during emergencies. Shared resources for security, such as surveillance systems and emergency protocols, increase overall safety.

Environmental Impact:
- **Reduced Footprint:** Community living can reduce individual environmental footprints through shared resources, efficient land use, and collaborative environmental practices. This includes shared transportation, communal energy systems, and collective waste management.
- **Biodiversity and Conservation:** Community-led conservation efforts can have a significant impact on local biodiversity. Practices like sustainable farming, habitat restoration, and native species planting support environmental health and resilience.

Infrastructure and Shared Resources: Building the Foundation
Energy Systems:
- **Renewable Energy:** Community-scale renewable energy systems, including solar, wind, and micro-hydro, can provide sustainable power. Guidelines for system design, installation, and maintenance ensure reliable energy supply.
- **Energy Storage and Distribution:** Efficient energy storage solutions, such as batteries and thermal storage, coupled with an effective distribution infrastructure, support consistent energy availability within the community.

Water Management:

- **Water Sourcing:** Methods for sourcing water, such as rainwater harvesting, wells, and natural springs, ensure a sustainable water supply. Guidelines for water quality assurance and sustainable use are crucial.
- **Wastewater Treatment:** Eco-friendly wastewater treatment systems, including constructed wetlands, composting toilets, and greywater recycling, minimize environmental impact and conserve water.

Food Production:
- **Community Gardens:** Benefits and logistics of establishing community gardens include garden design, crop selection, and maintenance. Gardens provide fresh produce and enhance food security.
- **Permaculture and Agroforestry:** Advanced sustainable farming techniques, integrating trees and perennial plants with crops and livestock, support ecosystem health and productivity.

Shelter and Construction:
- **Sustainable Building Materials:** Natural and locally sourced materials, such as straw bales, cob, and reclaimed wood, reduce environmental impact and enhance building sustainability.
- **Community Buildings:** Communal spaces, such as meeting halls, workshops, and kitchens, foster social interaction and collective activities. Design and construction tips ensure these buildings meet community needs effectively.

Challenges and Solutions: Ensuring Community Longevity

Social Dynamics:
- **Conflict Resolution:** Common sources of conflict, such as resource allocation and personal differences, require effective resolution strategies. Techniques like mediation, consensus-building, and restorative justice help maintain harmony.
- **Governance and Decision-Making:** Different governance models, such as consensus-based decision-making, sociocracy, and democratic assemblies, support fair and inclusive decision-making. Creating a governance charter outlines roles, responsibilities, and processes.

Economic Sustainability:
- **Financial Management:** Strategies for managing community finances, including budgeting, fundraising, and financial planning, ensure economic stability.
- **Income Generation:** Potential income sources, such as ecotourism, educational workshops, and selling surplus produce and crafts, diversify revenue streams and enhance financial resilience.

Environmental Challenges:
- **Resource Management:** Sustainable management of natural resources, including water, soil, and energy, ensures long-term viability.
- **Adaptation to Climate Change:** Adaptation strategies, such as diversifying crops, improving water management, and enhancing infrastructure resilience, address the impacts of climate change on off-grid communities.

Health and Safety:
- **Healthcare Access:** Ensuring access to healthcare services through partnerships with local health providers, training community members in basic healthcare, and promoting preventative health measures.
- **Safety Protocols:** Enhancing community readiness and responsiveness involves establishing safety measures for various events, such as medical emergencies, natural catastrophes, and security threats.

Continuous Improvement:
- **Regular Assessments:** Regular assessments and feedback loops identify and address issues proactively. Continuous improvement practices ensure the community remains adaptive and resilient.
- **Learning and Adaptation:** Encouraging a culture of continuous learning and adaptation promotes innovation and resilience within the community. Sharing knowledge and experiences strengthens community bonds and fosters sustainable growth.

Enhancements and Practical Additions

Comprehensive Case Studies: Using case studies and real-world examples gives readers a deeper understanding of how various communities respond to opportunities and difficulties. For example, profiling a successful eco-village or an intentional community can illustrate effective strategies and innovative solutions.

Visual Aids: Adding diagrams, flowcharts, or infographics to illustrate community structures, resource management systems, and governance models enhances understanding. Visual representations of community layouts, energy systems, and water management can make the concepts more tangible.

Chapter 3: Networking and Support Systems

Building Connections
Community Bonds:
- *Importance*: Strong relationships within your community are essential for mutual support, resource sharing, and emotional well-being.
- *Benefits:* Enhances social cohesion and resilience.

External Networks:
- *Importance:* Connecting with other off-grid communities and sustainable living experts broadens your support system.
- *Benefits:* Provides access to additional resources, knowledge, and collaborative opportunities.

Resource Accessibility:
Knowledge Sharing:
- *Methods:* Utilize networks for exchanging knowledge and expertise on topics like gardening and renewable energy.
- *Benefits:* Regular knowledge-sharing sessions or online forums help disseminate valuable information.

Resource Pooling:
- *Methods:* Pool resources such as bulk purchasing supplies or sharing specialized equipment.
- *Benefits:* Reduces costs and improves efficiency through collective resource management systems.

Support During Crises:
Emergency Response:
- *Methods:* Networks provide crucial support during emergencies by offering aid and resources.
- *Benefits*: A well-organized emergency response plan within the network ensures timely assistance.

Mental Health:
- *Methods:* Strong support networks offer companionship and assistance during challenging times.
- *Benefits:* Regular social activities and mental health resources help maintain emotional well-being.

Resource Sharing and Barter Systems: Traditional Methods with Modern Benefits
Establishing Barter Systems:
Identifying Needs and Offerings:
- *Methods*: Guide community members to identify needed goods and services and what they can offer in return.
- *Benefits:* Creating an inventory of skills and resources streamlines the barter process.

Creating a Barter Network:
- *Methods:* Steps include creating a directory, establishing trade values, and tracking exchanges.
- *Benefits:* Regular community meetings facilitate the process.

Benefits of Barter Systems:
Economic Efficiency:
- *Methods:* Barter systems reduce reliance on cash economies.
- *Benefits:* Foster cooperation and reduce waste.

Strengthening Community Bonds:
- *Methods:* Regular exchanges strengthen relationships and trust.
- *Benefits*: Promotes social cohesion and mutual support.

Examples of Successful Barter Systems:
Case Studies:
- *Methods:* Provide examples of successful communities.
- *Benefits:* Highlight how these systems enhance community resilience and self-sufficiency.

Practical Tips:
- *Methods*: Offer tips for maintaining fair and efficient barter systems, such as clear communication and record-keeping.
- *Benefits:* Ensures the system operates smoothly and fairly.

Educational Workshops and Skill-Sharing: Platforms for Growth

Organizing Workshops:
Identifying Skills and Interests:
- *Methods*: Conduct surveys or hold community meetings to gather information.
- *Benefits:* Tailors workshops to meet community needs.

Logistics and Planning:
- *Methods:* Choose locations, set schedules, secure materials, and ensure accessibility.
- *Benefits*: Organizes successful workshops.

Promoting Skill-Sharing:
Creating a Skill Database:
- *Methods:* Maintain a database of community members' skills and expertise.
- *Benefits:* Allows everyone to access and utilize the skills available.

Regular Skill-Sharing Events:
- *Methods:* Organize monthly skill swaps or seasonal workshops.
- *Benefits:* Keeps the community engaged and continuously learning.

Benefits of Educational Workshops:
Skill Development:
- *Methods:* Continuous learning and development through workshops.
- *Benefits*: Contributes to personal growth and community resilience.

Community Engagement:
- *Methods:* Increased engagement through workshops.
- *Benefits:* Strengthens social bonds and promotes cooperation.

Examples of Workshops and Skill-Sharing Initiatives:
Successful Initiatives:
- *Methods:* Provide examples of successful workshops.
- *Benefits:* Detail their structure and impact on the community.

Practical Tips:
- *Methods:* Offer tips for ensuring the success of these initiatives.
- *Benefits:* Effective promotion, participant feedback, and adapting to community needs.

Off-Grid Forums and Social Media Groups: Bridging the Distance
Benefits of Online Platforms:
Knowledge Exchange:
- *Methods:* Online platforms facilitate idea exchange among off-grid communities.
- *Benefits:* Provides space for asking questions, sharing solutions, and learning from others.

Support Networks:
- *Methods:* Offer emotional support, troubleshooting, and inspiration.
- *Benefits:* Build connections with like-minded individuals across distances.

Choosing the Right Platforms:
Popular Forums and Groups:
- *Methods*: Overview of popular online forums and social media groups.
- *Benefits:* Helps in selecting platforms dedicated to off-grid living and sustainable practices.

Evaluating Platforms:
- *Methods:* Tips for evaluating and choosing the right platforms.
- *Benefits:* Ensures platforms meet specific needs.

Participating in Online Communities:
Effective Participation:
- *Methods:* Strategies for active engagement and constructive interactions.
- *Benefits:* Fosters a positive community atmosphere.

Building Relationships:
- *Methods*: Importance of building relationships within online communities.
- *Benefits:* Leads to real-world connections and collaborations.

Creating Your Own Online Community:
Starting a Forum or Group:
- *Methods:* Step-by-step guide to creating an online forum or group.

- *Benefits*: Establishes a productive environment with clear guidelines and active moderation.

Maintaining Engagement:
- *Methods*: Tips for maintaining engagement and activity within the community.
- *Benefits*: Keeps members involved through regular updates and interactive content.

Creating a Supportive Off-Grid Network: Long-Term Strategies

Long-Term Planning:

Vision and Goals:
- *Methods*: Importance of having clear vision and goals.
- *Benefits:* Ensures alignment with community values and needs.

Sustainable Practices:
- *Methods:* Highlight the need for sustainable practices in network management.
- *Benefits:* Ensures viability and long-term benefits.

Building Strong Relationships:

Regular Communication:
- *Methods:* Emphasize the importance of regular communication.
- *Benefits:* Maintains strong relationships and addresses issues promptly.

Trust and Reciprocity:
- *Methods*: Encourages fair exchanges and mutual aid.
- *Benefits:* Strengthens trust and reciprocity within the network.

Adapting to Changes:

Flexibility:
- *Methods:* Highlight the importance of being flexible and adaptable to changes.
- *Benefits:* Fosters innovation and resilience.

Continuous Improvement:
- *Methods:* Regularly assess the network's effectiveness and make necessary adjustments.
- *Benefits:* Refines practices through feedback and learning from experiences.

Examples of Successful Networks:

Case Studies:
- *Methods:* Provide examples of successful off-grid networks.
- *Benefits:* Detail their structure, strategies, and outcomes.

Lessons Learned:
- *Methods:* Share lessons learned from successful networks.
- *Benefits:* Guides the development of your own network.

Resources and Tools:

Online Tools:
- *Methods*: Suggest tools for building and maintaining a supportive network.
- *Benefits*: Aids in collaboration and communication.

Educational Resources:
- *Methods*: Provide a list of books, articles, and online courses.
- *Benefits:* Offers further guidance on networking and community building.

By creating strong networks, off-grid communities can enhance resilience, share resources, and provide mutual support. These strategies help build a cohesive and sustainable living environment.

Chapter 4: Personal Narrative: Building a Thriving Community

Defining the Vision

Core Values and Goals:
- *Importance:* Establish the community's core values, such as sustainability, self-sufficiency, and cooperation.
- *Action:* Set long-term goals to guide the development and ensure alignment with these values.

Sustainable Practices:
- *Commitment:* Adopt practices like renewable energy use, waste reduction, and organic farming.
- *Action:* Make these practices central to the community's daily operations and overall vision.

Initial Planning and Outreach:

Gathering Information:
- *Research:* Study existing off-grid communities and sustainable living practices.
- *Action:* Learn from their successes and challenges to inform your planning.

Building Interest:
- *Strategies:* Use social media campaigns, community events, and informational meetings.
- *Action:* Generate interest and attract like-minded individuals to join the initiative.

Crafting the Community Blueprint:

Mission Statement:
- *Development:* Create a concise mission statement reflecting the community's vision, values, and objectives.
- *Action:* Use this as a guiding document for all members.

Strategic Plan:
- *Creation:* Develop a detailed plan with timelines, resource allocation, and key milestones.
- *Action:* Ensure structured development and track progress regularly.

Assembling a Like-Minded Group: The Core of the Community

Finding Members:

Outreach Strategies:
- *Methods:* Use social media, local events, and word-of-mouth to reach potential members.
- *Action:* Implement diverse outreach methods to attract a wide range of individuals.

Screening and Selection:
- *Process:* Ensure potential members align with the community's values and goals through interviews, trial periods, and background checks.
- *Action:* Establish a thorough screening process for selecting committed members.

Building Cohesion:

Team-Building Activities:
- *Activities:* Organize workshops, social gatherings, and collaborative projects.
- *Action:* Foster trust and camaraderie among members.

Communication Practices:
- *Methods:* Use regular meetings, newsletters, and digital tools for clear communication.
- *Action:* Maintain transparency and unity within the community.

Roles and Responsibilities:

Defining Roles:
- *Action:* Create job descriptions and assign tasks based on members' skills and interests.
- *Benefit:* Ensures smooth operation and accountability.

Rotation and Flexibility:
- *Action:* Encourage role rotation to prevent burnout and enhance skill diversity.
- *Benefit:* Keeps members engaged and promotes a dynamic community structure.

Overcoming Initial Challenges: The Learning Curve
Financial Hurdles:
Fundraising and Investment:
- *Methods*: Use crowdfunding, grants, and personal investment.
- *Action:* Host fundraising events and apply for relevant grants to gather necessary capital.

Budgeting:
- *Action*: Create a budget accounting for setup fees, recurring charges, and emergency savings.
- *Benefit:* Regularly review and adjust the budget based on actual expenses.

Logistical Challenges:
Land Acquisition:
- *Research*: Consider location, size, and legal requirements for land.
- *Action:* Engage with local authorities and experts to navigate zoning laws and land use regulations.

Infrastructure Development:
- *Planning:* Develop systems for water, energy, and waste management.
- *Action:* Prioritize sustainable solutions like rainwater harvesting, solar panels, and composting toilets.

Social Dynamics:
Building Trust:
- *Methods*: Use transparent decision-making, shared experiences, and consistent communication.
- *Action:* Foster trust among members.

Conflict Resolution:
- *Strategies*: Implement mediation, group discussions, and conflict resolution training.
- *Action:* Address issues openly and respectfully to maintain harmony.

Achieving Self-Sufficiency: A Collective Triumph
Food Production:
Gardening and Farming:
- *Methods:* Use permaculture, crop rotation, and organic pest control.
- *Action:* Ensure a steady food supply through sustainable practices.

Animal Husbandry:
- *Practices*: Raise livestock ethically for food, manure, and other resources.
- *Action:* Maintain sustainable practices in animal care.

Energy Independence:
Renewable Energy Systems:
- *Installation:* Use solar panels, wind turbines, and micro-hydro systems.
- *Action:* Achieve energy independence through renewable energy.

Energy Conservation:
- *Strategies:* Implement energy-efficient appliances, optimize insulation, and educate members.
- *Action:* Promote best practices for conserving energy.

Water Management:
Sourcing and Conservation:
- *Methods:* Use rainwater harvesting, wells, and natural springs.
- *Action:* Promote water conservation techniques like low-flow fixtures and drip irrigation.

Purification and Recycling:
- *Systems:* Install water purification and greywater recycling systems.
- *Action:* Ensure a sustainable and safe water supply.

Economic Sustainability:
Income Generation:
- *Activities*: Sell surplus produce, host workshops, and offer eco-tourism experiences.
- *Action:* Develop income-generating activities to support the community financially.

Financial Management:
- *Management:* Use savings plans, careful budgeting, and investment in community projects.
- *Action*: Ensure transparency and collective decision-making in financial matters.

Reflections and Future Plans: Sustaining the Momentum
Reflecting on Achievements:
Celebrating Milestones:
- *Events:* Recognize community achievements through events, awards, and public acknowledgments.
- *Action:* Celebrate contributions and successes.

Evaluating Progress:
- *Methods:* Use feedback from members, data on resource use, and financial records.
- *Action:* Regularly evaluate progress and identify areas for improvement.

Planning for the Future:
Vision Renewal:
- *Process:* Revisit and update the community's vision and goals periodically.
- *Action:* Engage all members in this process to ensure collective ownership.

Long-Term Strategies:
- *Development:* Create strategies for long-term sustainability, such as diversifying income sources and expanding infrastructure.
- *Action:* Foster continuous learning and innovation.

Adapting to Change:
Flexibility and Resilience:
- *Methods*: Develop contingency plans and promote a culture of adaptability.
- *Action*: Maintain flexibility to adapt to external changes.

Innovation and Growth:
- *Culture:* Encourage new ideas and techniques to continuously improve practices.
- *Action:* Promote a culture of innovation and growth.

Inspiring Others:
Sharing the Journey:
- *Methods:* Share experiences through storytelling, publications, and public speaking.
- *Action:* Document lessons learned to inspire others.

Mentorship and Support:
- *Support:* Provide guidance and encouragement to aspiring off-grid communities.
- *Action:* Share knowledge and resources to help others succeed.

MODULE L: HUNTING AND FISHING
Chapter 1: A Deeper Dive into Freshwater Fishing

Getting started in freshwater fishing entails more than just grabbing a rod and heading to the nearest pond. To make your fishing experience enjoyable and successful, it's essential to understand the intricacies, including legal requirements, choosing the right clothing, and understanding the gear.

The Right to Go Fishing: Navigating Legalities
Fishing laws, often regulated at a regional level, are put in place to protect aquatic ecosystems and fish populations. Before fishing in any body of water, familiarize yourself with local regulations. Here's a breakdown of the legal aspects you might encounter:

Fishing License: A fishing license is a permit that grants you legal access to fish in certain bodies of water. The fees often contribute to conservation efforts.
Seasons: Depending on fish spawning cycles, there may be specific seasons when fishing is allowed. This ensures species have ample time to reproduce and replenish their numbers.
Bag Limits: These are the maximum number of fish you can catch and keep in a day.
Size Limits: To protect juvenile fish, minimum size limits are often set.

Appropriate Clothing: Dress for Success
The correct attire will keep you comfortable and safe during your fishing trip.
Layering: Weather near water bodies can be unpredictable. Wear layers to adjust as needed.
Waterproof Footwear: Invest in quality waterproof boots or waders if you plan to wade into water.
Hat and Sunglasses: A wide-brimmed hat and polarized sunglasses offer sun protection and reduce water glare, aiding visibility beneath the surface.

Understanding Your Gear
A deeper understanding of your fishing gear will elevate your fishing experience:
Fishing Rods: Rods come in various lengths and actions. Medium-action rods, which bend in the top half, are versatile and suitable for beginners.
Reels: Spinning reels are user-friendly and ideal for beginners. As you advance, consider baitcasting reels for greater control and accuracy.
Fishing Line: Monofilament lines are affordable and suitable for a variety of fishing situations. However, fluorocarbon lines, while pricier, are virtually invisible underwater and resist abrasion better.
This overview provides a foundation for freshwater fishing. In the following chapters, we'll delve into the art of casting, choosing the right bait, and more!

NO GRID SURVIVAL PROJECTS BIBLE

Chapter 2: The Float - An Essential Component for Success

The float, also known as the bobber, is an invaluable tool for anglers. Not only does it indicate when a fish is biting, but it also controls the depth of your bait in the water. The choice of float can be influenced by many factors including the type of fish you're targeting, the conditions of the water, and your personal preferences.

Here is a simple guide on choosing the right float based on the fish species, recommended hook size, and key features:

Fish Species	Recommended Hook Size	Key Float Features
Trout	6-10	Light,thin, subtle
Bass	1-6	Larger, visible, sturdy
Catfish	1/0-8/0	Durable, big, buoyant
Crappie	6-8	Small,light,sensitive
Bluegill	8-12	Small, light, subtle
Carp	2-6	Big, sturdy, visible

Trout: Trout are often cautious feeders. Use a light, thin, and subtle float that doesn't spook them.

Bass: Bass are aggressive and powerful. Larger, visible, sturdy floats are effective for handling their bites.

Catfish: Catfish are strong fighters that pull hard. Durable, big, and buoyant floats are needed to withstand their powerful bites.

Crappie: Crappie are known for their soft bites. Small, light, and sensitive floats are ideal for detecting these light bites.

Bluegill: Similar to Crappie, Bluegill also have light bites. Small, light, and subtle floats work best.

Carp: Carp are large and powerful. Big, sturdy, visible floats are effective for carps.

Remember, these are just starting points. You may need to experiment and adjust based on your unique fishing circumstances.

Chapter 3 - Mastering the Art of Freshwater Fishing: An In-depth Look at Different Techniques

Float Fishing Revisited:

Float fishing can be an exciting and visually engaging method of freshwater fishing. It requires keen observation skills and patience. You will need to 'read' the float as it dances and dips on the water, looking for signs of a fish bite. For this method, it is best to use live baits, such as worms or insects, to attract a variety of fish species. Varying the depth of your hook beneath the float can help in reaching fish that are feeding at different water depths. Remember, practice makes perfect with float fishing.

Touch Fishing Expanded:

Touch fishing or tickling, is a hands-on approach, used for centuries. This method involves wading in the water and actually feeling for fish with your hands before trying to grab them quickly. It's typically used for species like catfish or trout that tend to hide under ledges or in burrows. It is important to approach silently, to not scare the fish away. This method requires skill and patience, but it can be incredibly rewarding once mastered.

Ledgering Fishing Elaborated:

Ledgering is a method of fishing where the bait is presented on the bottom of the water body, with a weight or 'ledger' used to hold it in place. The rod is usually propped up on a stand, with the line taut. A bite is indicated by the movement of the tip of the rod. Ledgering is ideal for bottom-feeding fish species. It's a passive fishing technique, and you can even set up multiple rods at a time. Consider using bite alarms for this method, which signal when a fish is biting.

Fixed Rod Fishing Expanded:

This method is more about skill and technique than the equipment used. The fixed rod method requires you to have a good understanding of casting and reeling techniques, as well as fish behavior. It is ideal for river fishing or when you are targeting a specific species or size of fish. This method requires a sturdy and responsive rod, and the ability to react quickly to bites. Bait can vary widely based on the species you're targeting.

Remember, each fishing method requires practice and patience. The fun is in the process as much as in the catch. Good luck and tight lines!

Chapter 4 - A Sea of Opportunities: An Introduction to Sea Fishing

Sea fishing or saltwater fishing, is a world apart from freshwater fishing, offering its unique challenges, a broad variety of fish species, and exciting experiences that make it a highly sought-after form of angling. From casting off the pier to deep-sea fishing, there's an adventure that fits every angler's preference.

1. Saltwater vs Freshwater Fishing:

The primary difference between sea and freshwater fishing lies in the species of fish available. Saltwater fish are generally larger and put up a tougher fight than their freshwater counterparts, making the catch even more rewarding. Additionally, the tackle used in saltwater fishing is typically more robust due to the powerful fish and corrosive sea environment. Saltwater reels and rods are built to withstand these conditions.

2. Types of Sea Fishing:

There are several ways to fish in the sea, and each one provides a unique experience:

Shore Fishing: This is probably the simplest way to start saltwater fishing. It can be done from any point where land meets the sea, such as beaches, rocks, or piers. It requires minimal gear - a good rod, suitable bait, and a basic understanding of the tides.

Boat Fishing: Done from a small boat near the shore, or offshore in deep waters, this type of fishing allows you to target a wider range of species. Depending on the depth of the water, different techniques like trolling, bottom fishing, or drift fishing can be employed.

Deep Sea Fishing: This is the most adventurous form of sea fishing. It is done far out at sea, usually where the water depth is at least 100 feet. Anglers can catch large and exotic species that are not found in shallow waters.

3. Essential Sea Fishing Gear:

Saltwater gear needs to be more durable to withstand the harsh marine environment and the size of the sea fish. The key components include:

Rod and Reel: Saltwater rods are generally longer, and reels have a larger line capacity. They are made from corrosion-resistant materials like stainless steel or ceramic.

Line: Monofilament lines are popular for their stretch and versatility, but braided lines are preferred for their strength, especially when targeting big fish.

Hooks and Lures: Saltwater fish species are diverse, and so are the baits and lures used to catch them. You'll need a variety of sizes and types for different species and fishing techniques.

Additional Gear: Other essential items include a tackle box, a fishing knife, a variety of sinkers, a good-quality fishing vest, and appropriate clothing for protection from sun and water.

Remember, the key to successful sea fishing is understanding the tides, currents, and, most importantly, the habits of the fish you're targeting. Good luck with your saltwater adventure!

Chapter 5 - Sea Fishing Styles: Discovering the Variety

Sea fishing, in all its forms, is a diverse and exciting discipline. Understanding the different styles can help you choose the one that suits you best and enrich your sea fishing experiences. This chapter explores some of the most popular types of sea fishing, focusing on fly fishing, surfcasting, mooring, and bottom fishing.

1. Fly Fishing:
Fly fishing is a technique that initially emerged for freshwater fishing but has found its way into the sea. It involves using a lightweight lure (or "fly") to mimic the natural food of the fish you're targeting, making it ideal for species that feed on the water's surface.
The fly is cast using a specially designed rod and a uniquely weighted line. This method requires finesse and a fair amount of practice but can be incredibly rewarding, offering a high degree of control and precision.

2. Surfcasting:
Surfcasting (or beach casting) is performed from the shoreline and involves casting your line out into the sea. It's a popular method for targeting species that roam the surf zone, such as bass or mullet.
Surfcasters typically use long rods (ranging from 12 to 16 feet) to cast their bait or lure far out into the water. These rods, combined with suitable reels and line, enable the angler to reach significant distances from the shore.

3. Mooring:
Mooring fishing is a common technique where the angler casts their line from a stationary boat. Depending on the target species and location, this can involve either dropping your bait directly beneath the boat or casting it out and allowing it to drift naturally with the tide and current.
This approach is particularly effective for species that inhabit or feed near the sea floor, and it can be combined with different methods such as bottom fishing or lure fishing.

4. Bottom Fishing:
As the name suggests, bottom fishing targets species that dwell near the seafloor. This method involves casting your bait and letting it sink to the bottom, waiting for a fish to bite.
Bottom fishing can be performed from a boat (at varying depths) or the shore. It is effective for many species, including snapper, grouper, cod, and flatfish. Rigs for bottom fishing are typically designed to keep your bait near the sea floor and can range from simple setups to more complex rigs for specific species or conditions.
Remember, each style of sea fishing has its unique challenges and rewards, and the best choice depends on your location, target species, and personal preference. Additionally, the right equipment, bait or lures, and knowledge of local regulations are crucial for a successful and enjoyable sea fishing experience.

Chapter 6 - Introduction to Hunting: A Timeless Pursuit

Hunting, one of the oldest practices of humankind, is far more than the pursuit of wildlife. It's a richly woven tapestry of skills, ethics, conservation, and a unique relationship with nature. As we delve into the world of hunting, we begin with an overview to appreciate its multifaceted nature.

1. The Practice of Hunting:
Hunting has evolved from a survival necessity to a recreational activity and wildlife management tool. Its practice involves tracking and pursuing animals, culminating in their capture or kill. This might sound straightforward, but hunting involves a complex combination of skills, including stalking, tracking, marksmanship, field dressing, and much more.

2. Types of Hunting:
Hunting's diversity is represented in the variety of methods used. These range from traditional methods such as still hunting, where the hunter carefully stalks their prey, to modern forms such as hunting with rifles, shotguns, or bows. Some hunters prefer using hunting dogs to help track and retrieve game.

3. Game Species:
"Game" refers to the animals hunted. They're usually categorized as big game (such as deer, elk, and bear), small game (like rabbits and squirrels), furbearers (such as foxes and raccoons), migratory birds (like ducks and geese), and upland game birds (like pheasants and quails). Each of these species presents unique challenges and requires specific hunting techniques.

4. Ethics and Conservation:
Ethics are central to responsible hunting. Respecting wildlife, following hunting laws, and practicing fair chase principles are essential ethical considerations. Additionally, hunters play a crucial role in conservation. The sale of hunting licenses, tags, and stamps is a primary source of funding for many wildlife conservation efforts.

5. The Hunting Community:
Hunting often fosters a sense of community, connecting people through shared experiences and traditions. Many hunters learn the ropes from experienced family members or friends, and hunting clubs and online communities provide spaces for hunters to share stories, tips, and advice.

As we delve deeper into the world of hunting in the following chapters, remember that hunting is a privilege, not a right. It requires a deep understanding of and respect for the animals pursued, their habitats, and the ecosystems in which they live. Hunting is an immersive way to connect with nature, offering opportunities for personal growth, challenge, and fulfillment. Whether you're a novice or experienced hunter, the chapters that follow aim to deepen your understanding and appreciation of this complex, rewarding activity.

Chapter 7 - Hunting Gear: Understanding Weapons, Ammunition, and More

To set out on a hunting journey, it's essential to understand the gear involved. One of the most critical elements is choosing the right weapon, ammunition, and practicing safety. In this chapter, we will begin to delve into these topics in more detail.

1. Hunting Weapons:
Different hunting scenarios call for various types of weapons. Let's take a deeper look:

<u>Rifles:</u> These long-barreled firearms are designed for long-range shooting and are perfect for targeting big game like deer, elk, or moose. The bullets fired by rifles are driven down a spirally grooved bore, imparting a rapid spin that stabilizes the bullet, providing the hunter with a high level of accuracy over long distances. The power and caliber of a rifle must be chosen according to the size of the game to ensure a clean, ethical kill.

<u>Shotguns:</u> Shotguns are primarily used for hunting birds and small mammals. Unlike rifles, shotguns fire shells containing multiple small pellets (or a single slug for larger game). When discharged, the pellets scatter, increasing the chances of hitting the target, especially when it's moving quickly, like a flying bird or a running rabbit. The gauge of a shotgun (a measure of its bore size) is an essential factor to consider based on the game and hunting style.

<u>Bows:</u> Bow hunting is a challenging and rewarding form of hunting that requires a lot of practice and skill. Traditional recurve bows and modern compound bows are common choices. The key to successful bow hunting is draw weight (the force needed to pull back the bowstring) and shot placement. Archers need to be much closer to their target than gun hunters, as the effective range for a bow is considerably less.

<u>Handguns:</u> Handgun hunting is not as common as the other methods due to the short range and lower power of handguns, but it presents an exciting challenge for experienced hunters. Handguns can range from revolvers to semi-automatic pistols, and they're usually used for smaller game or as a backup weapon in case of emergency.

As we've started our exploration of hunting weapons, it's crucial to remember that the best weapon for you depends on your skill level, the game you're pursuing, and local laws and regulations.

2. Ammunition:
Each type of weapon requires a specific kind of ammunition:

<u>Rifle ammunition:</u> The choice of rifle ammunition is vast, with a variety of calibers and bullet designs to choose from. The type of game you're hunting will dictate your ammunition choice. Larger game requires a heavier bullet, which will penetrate deeper to reach vital organs.

<u>Shotgun ammunition:</u> Shotgun shells are filled with either birdshot (small pellets for small game and birds), buckshot (larger pellets for larger game), or slugs (a single, large projectile used for big game). The type of shell needed depends on the game being hunted and the hunting environment.

<u>Bow ammunition:</u> Arrows, used by bowhunters, come in various materials like carbon, aluminum, and wood. They're tipped with broadheads - sharp blades designed to take down game efficiently.

<u>Handgun ammunition:</u> As with rifles, handgun ammunition comes in various calibers, with larger calibers being more suitable for larger game.

3. Safety Mechanisms:
Every firearm is equipped with a safety mechanism that prevents the gun from firing accidentally. It's essential to familiarize yourself with the safety mechanisms on your weapon and to always engage the safety when not intending to fire.

4. The Viewfinder or Scope:
A scope, or viewfinder, is an essential piece of equipment for accurate shooting, especially over long distances. Scopes come in a variety of magnifications, with larger magnifications allowing for more precise shots over greater distances. However, larger scopes can also be heavier and more challenging to handle, so choose a scope that fits your specific hunting needs.

5. Cleaning your weapons:
Keeping your hunting weapons clean and well-maintained is crucial for their performance and longevity. A well-maintained

weapon will function correctly, shoot accurately, and last for many years. Cleaning involves removing dirt, dust, and residue from firing, oiling moving parts, and preventing rust.

6. Shooting Position:

The position you take when shooting can greatly affect your accuracy. There are several shooting positions you can adopt, including standing, kneeling, sitting, or prone (lying down), with each position offering different stability levels. Practice shooting from various positions to find what works best for you.

Understanding your hunting gear, from the type of weapon and ammunition to its safety mechanisms and maintenance, is critical for a successful hunting experience. It ensures your safety and improves your chances of securing your target. In the next part of this chapter, we will continue to delve into other essential hunting topics.

Chapter 8 - Mastering the Hunt: Proven Hunting Strategies

Hunting is an ancient practice that calls for patience, discipline, and an understanding of animal behavior. To maximize your hunting experience, adopting various proven strategies can significantly increase your success rate. In this chapter, we'll examine some of the best hunting strategies used by experienced hunters.

1. Spot and Stalk:
This method involves identifying the game from a distance, then carefully approaching it for a clear shot. It requires patience and stealth, as well as an understanding of wind direction to prevent your scent from alerting the animal. It's essential to move slowly and stop frequently to blend into the environment.

2. Still Hunting:
Contrary to what the name suggests, still hunting isn't about sitting still but involves moving through the hunting area at a slow pace, looking for signs of game. It requires a high level of patience and the ability to walk quietly, listen for sounds, and spot subtle signs of wildlife.

3. Ambush Hunting (Stand Hunting):
This is where a hunter waits in one spot, often in a tree stand or ground blind, near known animal trails, feeding areas, or watering holes. The key here is to blend in with the surroundings and remain quiet and motionless to avoid detection.

4. Drive Hunting:
In drive hunting, a group of hunters works together to 'drive' animals toward a line of hunters waiting for a shot. It requires significant coordination and safety measures to ensure no hunter is in the line of fire.

5. Calling and Decoying:
Many hunters use calls to mimic animal sounds and lure them into range. Decoys can also be used to attract animals. It requires a knowledge of the species you're hunting and its behavior.

6. Tracking:
This technique requires following an animal's tracks and signs to get within shooting range. It requires a good knowledge of the animal's habits and the ability to read signs like footprints, droppings, feeding signs, etc.

7. Hunting with Dogs:
Some hunters use dogs to find, flush out, or retrieve game. The breed of dog used depends on the type of game being hunted. Each of these strategies can be effective depending on the circumstances and type of game being hunted. Knowledge, patience, practice, and a respect for the animals and the environment are the true keys to success in hunting. These strategies form a toolbox from which you can choose, depending on your hunting situation and the specific behavior of the game you are pursuing. Expanding upon our initial hunting strategies, let's delve into a few more tactics that seasoned hunters commonly use to secure their game.

8. Stalking:
Stalking, similar to spot and stalk, involves closely and stealthily following your prey once you've spotted it. This method calls for acute patience, impeccable timing, and sound knowledge of the landscape. Stalking can be both physically and mentally challenging as it involves moving quietly and patiently for hours while keeping your focus sharp.

9. Posting:
Posting is a strategy where hunters position themselves along escape routes, waiting for the game to pass through. This method requires knowledge about the animal's preferred paths and can be very effective when hunting in groups.

10. Ground Blinds:
Ground blinds are structures designed to conceal hunters on the ground level. They can range from simple natural blinds made of vegetation to complex commercially made blinds. They provide excellent concealment and can be particularly effective in areas where trees suitable for stands are scarce.

11. Elevated Stands:
An elevated stand is a platform built on trees where hunters perch to get a better viewpoint and stay out of the direct line of sight of the game. These can be particularly useful when hunting deer or other game that rely heavily on their sense of smell, as being elevated can help keep the hunter's scent from reaching the animals.

12. Game Calling:

Different from the basic calling, game calling involves using specialized tools to mimic the specific sounds that animals make, whether it's the call of a potential mate or the distress call of a young animal. This strategy can be incredibly effective, but it requires a sound understanding of the animal's behavior and communication.

13. Driving:

Driving, a group hunting strategy, involves some members acting as drivers who walk in a line and push the game towards hunters waiting at the end of a predetermined route. This method requires careful planning and coordination among the group members.

14. Flushing:

Flushing is a strategy used to drive animals out of their hiding places. Hunters often use dogs or birds of prey to aid in this method. The goal is to make the game run or fly out into the open, providing a clear shot.

While some of these tactics may be challenging to master, they can significantly increase your success and efficiency in hunting. Remember, the key is to choose a strategy that best suits your target species, your hunting terrain, and your personal hunting style. Patience, understanding of animal behavior, and practice are your best allies in mastering these hunting strategies.

MODULE M: SUSTAINABLE ORCHARD AND GARDEN

Chapter 1: How to Design Your Orchard

Designing an orchard is an essential first step toward cultivating a thriving space for fruit trees and plants. A well-planned orchard can increase yields, reduce maintenance, and provide a serene and beautiful environment. In this chapter, we'll explore the key steps and considerations for designing your orchard.

Evaluate Your Land

The first thing you need to do is evaluate your land. This includes assessing the soil quality, topography, and climate of the area.

- *Soil Quality*: The soil is the foundation for your trees. Get a soil test to understand the pH, nutrient levels, and texture. Fruit trees generally prefer well-draining soil with a pH of 6.0 to 6.5. However, some trees have specific soil requirements. Consider incorporating organic matter or compost to improve soil structure and fertility.
- *Topography*: Consider the lay of the land. The ideal site for an orchard is a gently sloping hill, which allows for good air and water drainage. Avoid areas prone to frost pockets or water accumulation.
- *Climate:* The climate determines what type of fruit trees you can grow. Make sure the trees you want to plant are suitable for your region's temperature ranges, and consider factors like chilling hours for temperate fruit trees. Research the average rainfall, humidity, and seasonal temperature variations in your area.

Choose the Right Trees

Selecting the right fruit trees is crucial. Consider the following when making your choices:

- *Compatibility with your climate and soil:* Ensure that the trees you choose are well-suited to your specific soil type and climate conditions.
- *Pollination requirements*: Some trees need cross-pollination, so you may need to plant more than one variety. Check if the trees are self-pollinating or require a pollinator partner.
- *Harvest seasons:* Planting trees with different harvest seasons can extend your harvest period, providing fresh fruit over a longer duration.
- *Tree size*: Dwarf and semi-dwarf trees are easier to manage and harvest. Consider the mature size of the trees and choose varieties that fit your space and maintenance capabilities.

Plan the Layout

Now it's time to decide on the layout of your orchard. Consider the space each tree needs to grow, both vertically and horizontally. A good rule of thumb is to plant trees at least 12 to 20 feet apart, depending on the mature size of the tree.

- *Sunlight:* Ensure that all trees will receive ample sunlight, which is crucial for fruit production. Plant the taller trees to the north of shorter ones to avoid shading.
- *Access Paths:* Plan access paths wide enough for equipment and foot traffic, ensuring that you can easily move through the orchard for maintenance and harvesting. Consider the future growth of the trees and allow enough space for movement and equipment access.
- *Wind Protection*: If your area is prone to strong winds, consider planting windbreaks like hedges or rows of tall trees around the perimeter of your orchard to protect the fruit trees. Windbreaks can also help reduce soil erosion and create a microclimate that is beneficial for the orchard.

Irrigation and Drainage

Efficient irrigation is essential for a fruitful orchard. There are various irrigation methods, such as drip irrigation, sprinklers, or furrow irrigation. Choose the one that best suits your orchard's needs and conditions.

- *Irrigation Systems*: Drip irrigation is highly efficient, delivering water directly to the root zones with minimal evaporation. Sprinklers are useful for larger areas, while furrow irrigation can be effective in certain terrains.
- *Drainage:* Ensure that your orchard has good drainage. This is especially important in areas with heavy rainfall to prevent waterlogging, which can harm the roots of the trees. Consider installing drainage tiles or creating raised beds to improve drainage.

Plan for Pest and Disease Control

Having a plan for pest and disease control is vital. This can include natural methods, such as introducing beneficial insects or using organic pesticides. Being proactive and monitoring your orchard for signs of pests or disease can save you a lot of trouble down the line.

- *Integrated Pest Management (IPM):* Implement IPM strategies that combine cultural, biological, and mechanical methods to manage pests and diseases. This approach minimizes the use of chemical pesticides and promotes a healthier orchard ecosystem.
- *Beneficial Insects:* Encourage beneficial insects like ladybugs, predatory beetles, and parasitic wasps that prey on common orchard pests. Planting companion plants that attract these beneficial insects can help maintain a balanced ecosystem.
- *Regular Monitoring*: Inspect your trees regularly for early signs of pests and diseases. Early detection allows for prompt intervention and can prevent minor issues from becoming major problems.

Once you have a plan in place, it's time to start planting. Remember that patience is key, as it may take a few years for your trees to start bearing fruit. However, with careful planning and diligent care, you can create a fruitful and sustainable orchard. Designing an orchard is an ongoing process. As your trees grow, you might need to make adjustments to your plans. Always be observant and willing to learn and adapt. Regularly update your knowledge on orchard management practices and stay connected with local agricultural extension services or orchardist communities for the latest information and support.

Chapter 2: The Best Fruit Trees for Your Orchard and How to Care for Them

Choosing the right fruit trees for your orchard is a mix of personal preference, climate adaptability, and ease of care. Here we will explore a selection of popular fruit trees that can bring variety and a bountiful harvest to your orchard.

Apple Trees
Apples are perhaps the most traditional choice for an orchard. Hardy and adaptable, apple trees can grow in a wide range of climates, though they prefer cooler winters. There are thousands of apple varieties to choose from, each with its own unique flavors, colors, and harvest times.
Care Tips:
- *Pruning:* Prune apple trees in late winter to encourage a strong structure and increase air circulation, which can prevent disease. Remove any dead, damaged, or diseased branches.
- *Watering:* Regular watering is essential, especially during dry periods. However, avoid overwatering as it can lead to root rot.
- *Fertilizing***:** Use a balanced fertilizer in early spring to support growth.

Pear Trees
Pear trees are another excellent choice for an orchard. Like apples, they can withstand cold climates and come in a variety of types.
Care Tips:
- *Soil Requirements***:** Pear trees require well-drained soil and plenty of sunlight.
- *Pruning***:** They are pruned similarly to apple trees, typically during the winter or early spring. Focus on maintaining an open canopy to improve air circulation.
- *Pest Management:* Watch for common pests such as pear psylla and codling moths, and use appropriate pest control measures.

Peach Trees
Peach trees bring a burst of pink blossoms in the spring and juicy fruit in the summer. They prefer warmer climates and well-draining, slightly acidic soil.
Care Tips:
- *Pruning:* Peach trees require more maintenance than some other fruit trees, including regular pruning to prevent diseases and pests. Prune in late winter or early spring before new growth starts.
- *Thinning:* Thin fruits to about 6-8 inches apart to ensure larger, healthier peaches.
- *Fertilizing:* Fertilize in early spring with a balanced fertilizer.

Plum Trees
There are many varieties of plum trees, including Japanese, European, and American types, each with different flavors, colors, and care needs.
Care Tips:
- *Soil Requirements***:** Plums generally prefer well-drained soil and full sun.
- *Pruning:* Proper pruning is essential for healthy plum trees, as it can help prevent disease and encourage a good harvest. Prune in late winter to remove dead or diseased wood.
- *Pollination:* Some plum varieties require cross-pollination, so plant compatible varieties close together.

Cherry Trees
Cherry trees can be divided into two main types: sweet cherries, perfect for fresh eating, and sour cherries, excellent for baking.
Care Tips:
- *Soil and Sunlight***:** Cherry trees need a well-drained, sunny location, and the soil pH should be between 6.0 and 7.0.
- *Pruning:* Careful pruning in the early years will ensure a good shape and promote higher fruit yields. Prune in late winter to early spring.

- *Bird Protection*: Use netting or other protective measures to prevent birds from eating the fruit.

Fig Trees
Fig trees are highly resilient and can adapt to a variety of climates and soils. They produce sweet fruits that are delicious fresh or dried.

Care Tips:
- *Pruning*: Fig trees are low-maintenance and usually don't require much pruning. Lightly prune in late winter to remove dead or weak branches.
- *Watering:* Regular watering is important, especially during dry spells.
- *Winter Protection*: In colder climates, protect fig trees during the winter by wrapping them in burlap or other insulating materials.

Citrus Trees
If you live in a warmer climate, citrus trees like oranges, lemons, and grapefruits can be an excellent addition to your orchard.

Care Tips:
- *Soil and Sunlight*: Citrus trees need well-drained soil and plenty of sunlight to thrive.
- *Pruning:* Prune citrus trees to maintain their shape and size and to remove any dead or diseased wood. Prune in late winter or early spring.
- *Fertilizing:* Use a citrus-specific fertilizer to provide essential nutrients.

Choosing the right trees for your orchard and taking proper care of them can result in years of plentiful harvests. Be sure to understand the unique needs of each type of tree, from sunlight and soil conditions to pruning and pest control. Additionally, consider diversifying your orchard with a mix of fruit trees to spread out the harvest season and reduce the risk of total crop failure due to pests or diseases.

Chapter 3: Mastering Soil Management in Your Orchard

Maintaining healthy soil is one of the most critical tasks in managing an orchard, as the success of your fruit trees is heavily dependent on the soil in which they grow. In this chapter, we will dive deep into the various aspects of soil management that contribute to a thriving orchard.

Understanding Soil Types
The first step to effective soil management is understanding your soil type. The three primary types of soil are sand, silt, and clay, each having unique properties that affect water drainage, nutrient availability, and root growth. Most fruit trees prefer well-draining soil, often found in loamy soil, a balanced mixture of sand, silt, and clay.

Soil Characteristics:
- *Sandy Soil*: Drains quickly and may not retain nutrients well.
- *Clay Soil:* Holds water and nutrients but may drain poorly.
- *Silty Soil:* Has moderate drainage and nutrient-holding capacity.

Soil Testing
Testing your soil can give you vital information about its current state, including pH level and nutrient content. A soil pH between 6.0 and 7.0 is generally ideal for most fruit trees, although some may prefer slightly more acidic or alkaline conditions. Essential nutrients to look for include nitrogen, phosphorous, and potassium, the primary macronutrients needed by plants.

Steps for Soil Testing:
1. *Collect Samples*: Take soil samples from various locations within the orchard.
2. *Send to a Lab*: Use a local agricultural extension office or a commercial lab.
3. *Analyze Results*: Review the report to understand nutrient levels and pH.

Improving Soil Health
If your soil lacks nutrients or has a pH that is too high or low, don't worry—soil health can be improved. Compost, manure, or soil amendments can be added to increase nutrient content. Lime can raise the pH of overly acidic soil, while sulfur can lower the pH of overly alkaline soil.

Methods for Improving Soil:
- *Organic Matter*: Add compost, well-rotted manure, or green manure crops.
- *Adjusting pH*: Use lime to increase pH or sulfur to decrease it.
- *Nutrient Amendments*: Apply fertilizers based on soil test recommendations.

Cover Crops and Mulching
Cover crops, such as clover or rye, can be grown to improve soil health between tree rows. These plants can add organic matter to the soil, reduce erosion, and even fix nitrogen in the soil if you choose legume cover crops. Mulching around your trees with wood chips or straw can help maintain soil moisture, keep roots cool, and suppress weeds.

Benefits of Cover Crops and Mulching:
- *Soil Enrichment:* Adds organic matter and nutrients.
- *Erosion Control:* Reduces soil erosion on sloped areas.
- *Weed Suppression:* Mulch helps control weed growth.

Preventing Soil Erosion
On sloped land, soil erosion can be a problem. Planting ground cover plants or creating contour lines with rows of trees can help prevent soil from being washed away by rain.

Erosion Control Techniques:
- *Ground Covers*: Use plants like clover or vetch.
- *Terracing:* Create terraces on steep slopes.

- *Contour Planting*: Align rows of trees along the contour lines of the slope.

Irrigation and Drainage
Proper water management is crucial to maintain good soil health. Overwatering can lead to waterlogged soil and root problems, while underwatering can lead to dry, unproductive soil. Ensure your land has good drainage, and consider installing an irrigation system if necessary.

Irrigation Methods:
- *Drip Irrigation*: Efficiently delivers water to the root zone.
- *Sprinklers:* Useful for larger areas but may increase humidity and disease risk.
- *Furrow Irrigation:* Channels water along trenches but may lead to uneven distribution.

Drainage Solutions:
- *Tile Drains*: Installed below the surface to remove excess water.
- *French Drains*: Gravel-filled trenches with perforated pipes.
- *Raised Beds:* Improve drainage in heavy clay soils.

Maintaining Soil Health
Maintaining healthy soil is a continuous process that involves monitoring, amending, and careful management. Regular soil tests, observation of plant health, and timely interventions are key to ensuring that your soil provides a robust and nurturing environment for your fruit trees to thrive.

Ongoing Practices:
- *Regular Monitoring*: Keep an eye on soil moisture, structure, and plant health.
- *Seasonal Amendments*: Apply compost or organic matter regularly.
- *Weed Management:* Use mulch and cover crops to keep weeds at bay.

By paying close attention to your soil, you can ensure that it provides a robust and nurturing environment for your fruit trees to thrive. Regular maintenance and proactive management will yield a healthy, productive orchard capable of delivering bountiful harvests for years to come.

Chapter 4: Shielding Your Sanctuary: Comprehensive Guide to Orchard Protection

Protecting an orchard from the varied and often unpredictable threats can seem a daunting task. The health and productivity of your fruit trees can be challenged by diseases, pests, and wildlife intruders. As an orchard owner, understanding these threats and implementing proper safeguarding measures is vital. This chapter provides a detailed guide to identifying and tackling these issues, ensuring the longevity and productivity of your orchard.

Identifying Common Pests and Diseases

The first crucial step in managing threats is the correct identification of pests and diseases. Each fruit tree species comes with its unique set of potential issues, hence a keen awareness of the signs of each problem can lead to prompt and effective management. Key signs to look out for are changes in leaf color, texture, and shape, unusual deformations or spots on fruits, and an unexplained increase in certain types of insects.

Common Pests:

- *Aphids:* Small, soft-bodied insects that suck sap from leaves, causing them to curl and distort.
- *Codling Moth*: Larvae burrow into fruit, particularly apples and pears, leading to internal damage.
- *Spider Mites*: Tiny arachnids that cause stippling on leaves and can lead to leaf drop.
- *Fruit Flies*: Attack ripening fruit, leading to rot and spoilage.

Common Diseases:

- *Apple Scab:* Fungal disease causing dark, scabby lesions on leaves and fruit.
- *Fire Blight*: Bacterial disease that blackens blossoms and branches, common in pears and apples.
- *Brown Rot*: Fungal infection causing fruit rot and cankers on branches.
- *Powdery Mildew*: Fungal disease that covers leaves and fruit in a white, powdery substance.

Implementing Pest Control

Pest control in your orchard can range from entirely organic methods to the more extreme usage of chemical interventions. Natural predators are an orchard's best friend in this battle. Encouraging the presence of birds and beneficial insects can help keep destructive pests at bay.

Organic Pest Control Methods:

- *Natural Predators*: Ladybugs, lacewings, and parasitic wasps can control aphids and other pests.
- *Insect Traps*: Pheromone traps for codling moths and sticky traps for flies.
- *Horticultural Oils:* Neem oil or insecticidal soap to suffocate insects on contact.
- *Companion Planting:* Planting garlic, marigold, or nasturtium to repel pests.

Chemical Pest Control:

- *Selective Pesticides*: Use as a last resort and choose pesticides that target specific pests to minimize harm to beneficial insects.
- *Application Timing*: Apply during times when non-target organisms are least active, such as early morning or late evening.

Disease Mitigation Strategies

Proactive measures are the most effective approach to handle diseases in your orchard. This includes implementing regular pruning to allow good air circulation, a watering routine that avoids wetting foliage, and regularly examining your trees for early signs of disease.

Organic Disease Control:

- *Pruning:* Remove and destroy infected plant parts to prevent the spread of disease.
- *Copper Sprays:* Effective against a variety of fungal and bacterial infections.
- *Bordeaux Mixture*: A combination of copper sulfate and lime for fungal diseases.
- *Sulfur*: Useful for controlling powdery mildew and other fungal diseases.

Chemical Disease Control:
- *Targeted Fungicides:* Use specific fungicides for resistant diseases, following label instructions to avoid overuse.
- *Systemic Treatments:* For severe infections, systemic fungicides can provide longer-lasting protection.

Wildlife Management: Friends and Foes
Wildlife interactions can be both a boon and a bane for an orchard. While some creatures like bees and certain birds can be beneficial, others like deer, rodents, or fruit-eating birds can inflict serious damage.

Beneficial Wildlife:
- *Pollinators:* Bees and butterflies are crucial for fruit set and should be encouraged.
- *Birds:* Certain birds can help control insect populations.

Problematic Wildlife:
- *Deer:* Can cause significant damage by browsing on young trees and fruit.
- *Rodents:* Voles and mice can girdle tree trunks and roots.
- *Birds:* Starlings and other fruit-eating birds can decimate crops.

Wildlife Deterrence Methods:
- *Fencing:* A high fence (8 feet) can deter deer. Mesh guards around tree bases can protect against rodents.
- *Netting:* Bird netting can protect fruit from birds.
- *Repellents:* Use taste or smell-based repellents for deer and rodents.
- *Scare Tactics:* Reflective tapes, noise makers, and predator decoys can help deter wildlife.

Developing a Comprehensive Protection Plan
By understanding the diverse threats to your orchard and the tools at your disposal, you can develop an effective protection plan. With vigilance, consistent care, and swift response to problems, your orchard can flourish, offering bountiful harvests for years to come.

Steps to Create a Protection Plan:
1. *Regular Monitoring:* Schedule regular inspections to identify problems early.
2. *Integrated Pest Management (IPM):* Combine biological, cultural, mechanical, and chemical control methods.
3. *Record Keeping:* Maintain detailed records of pest and disease occurrences and control measures applied.
4. *Community Resources:* Join local agricultural groups or forums to stay informed about regional pest and disease trends.

Protecting your orchard requires a multifaceted approach that balances proactive measures with responsive actions. By staying informed and prepared, you can ensure the health and productivity of your orchard, reaping the rewards of your efforts through plentiful and high-quality harvests.

Chapter 5: The Art and Science of Pruning: Shaping Your Orchard's Success

Understanding the Importance of Pruning

Pruning is not an optional chore but a necessity for maintaining the health and productivity of your fruit trees. It helps control the tree's size, ensuring that sunlight and air circulation reach all parts of the tree, reducing the likelihood of disease. Furthermore, pruning affects the balance between vegetative growth and fruit production, guiding the tree to yield more fruits over excessive foliage.

Key Benefits of Pruning:

- *Disease Prevention*: Removing diseased or dead wood reduces the risk of infection spreading.
- *Improved Light Penetration*: Ensures that sunlight reaches all parts of the tree, enhancing photosynthesis and fruit ripening.
- *Enhanced Air Circulation*: Reduces humidity within the canopy, which helps prevent fungal diseases.
- *Increased Fruit Production*: Pruning encourages the growth of fruiting wood, leading to better yields.

When to Prune

Timing is crucial when it comes to pruning. For most fruit trees, late winter or early spring is the best time to prune. Pruning in late winter encourages healthy new growth during the spring. However, for certain species like apricots, cherries, or peaches, which are prone to disease, a late spring or summer pruning can be more beneficial.

General Pruning Guidelines:

- *Late Winter/Early Spring*: Ideal for most fruit trees, as it promotes vigorous growth and healing.
- *Late Spring/Summer:* Better for trees prone to disease, as it reduces the risk of infection.
- *Avoid Fall Pruning*: Can stimulate new growth that is vulnerable to winter damage.

Mastering Pruning Cuts

Understanding different types of cuts and their effects can make the difference between a thriving tree and a struggling one. The two main types of cuts are "thinning cuts" and "heading cuts."

- *Thinning Cuts*: Remove entire branches or limbs at their point of origin. This technique opens up the interior of the tree to light and air movement, preserving the tree's natural shape.
- *Heading Cuts*: Involve cutting a branch at a point along its length, encouraging the growth of lateral branches. This type of cut stimulates growth near the cut and is useful in shaping the tree and encouraging bushier growth.

Tools of the Trade

Having the right tools is as important as knowing the techniques. The three essential tools you'll need for pruning are hand pruners, lopping shears, and a pruning saw. Keeping your tools clean and sharp ensures precise cuts and reduces the risk of transmitting diseases between trees.

Essential Pruning Tools:

- *Hand Pruners*: Ideal for small branches and precise cuts.
- *Lopping Shears*: Suitable for thicker branches, providing more leverage.
- *Pruning Saw*: Necessary for cutting larger limbs.

Tool Maintenance Tips:

- *Cleaning:* Regularly clean tools with a disinfectant to prevent disease spread.
- *Sharpening*: Keep blades sharp to ensure clean cuts and reduce damage to the tree.
- *Lubrication*: Apply oil to moving parts to keep tools functioning smoothly.

Pruning by Age

Pruning should be carried out differently according to the age of the tree.

Young Trees:

- *Establishing Structure*: Pruning helps establish a strong structural foundation. This is when you select the tree's "scaffold" branches that define its basic framework.

NO GRID SURVIVAL PROJECTS BIBLE

- *Shaping:* Guide the tree's growth to develop a balanced form that supports future fruit production.

Mature Trees:
- *Maintenance:* The goal shifts to maintaining the tree's structure, health, and productivity. Remove dead or diseased wood, thin out crowded limbs, and possibly lower the tree's height to make harvesting easier.
- *Renewal:* Encourage the growth of new fruiting wood and manage the balance between vegetative growth and fruit production.

Advanced Pruning Techniques
For orchard enthusiasts looking to refine their pruning skills, several advanced techniques can be employed to optimize tree health and productivity.

Espalier Training:
- *Design*: Train trees to grow flat against a wall or fence in decorative patterns.
- *Benefits:* Saves space, improves light exposure, and makes maintenance and harvesting easier.

Crown Thinning:
- *Technique:* Selectively remove branches from the crown of the tree to reduce its density.
- *Benefits:* Enhances light penetration and air circulation throughout the tree.

Rejuvenation Pruning:
- *Purpose*: Revitalize old or neglected trees by cutting back major limbs to stimulate new growth.
- *Method:* Typically involves more severe pruning and should be done gradually over several seasons to avoid shocking the tree.

Remembering the Pruning Process
Pruning is a process, not a one-time event. Each cut is a call to the tree to grow in a particular way, a silent conversation between you and the tree. Over time, regular and mindful pruning will lead to healthier trees and bountiful harvests, the rewards of your patience and diligence.

Key Reminders:
- *Regular Inspections*: Monitor trees regularly to identify and address issues promptly.
- *Seasonal Adjustments*: Adapt pruning techniques based on seasonal growth patterns and environmental conditions.
- *Ongoing Education:* Stay informed about best practices and new techniques in orchard management.

By mastering the art and science of pruning, you can ensure the long-term health and productivity of your orchard, shaping it into a thriving sanctuary of fruit-bearing trees.

Chapter 6: Why A Prepper's Guide

When a young person joins the Boy Scouts of America, they are exposed to essential skills that educate them to defend themselves and be ready for anything. Preparedness devotees, also known as "preppers," make an effort to be ready for a variety of catastrophes and crises, including natural disasters and civil unrest. They frequently stockpile emergency medical supplies, food, water, and other necessities. Even though not everyone engages in "prepping," anyone can assemble a survival kit that can be useful in emergency situations.

The Necessity of a Prepper's Guide
A prepper's guide serves as an essential resource for those looking to prepare for potential disasters and crises. The creation of a survival garden is a fundamental aspect of this preparation, necessitating careful consideration of several factors:

1. **Crop Failure Possibility**
   o Understand the risks and have backup plans, such as alternative crops or methods like hydroponics.
2. **Limited Time**
   o Develop efficient gardening practices that maximize yield with minimal time investment.
3. **Limited Water**
   o Implement water-saving techniques like drip irrigation or rainwater harvesting.
4. **Limited Resources**
   o Focus on cost-effective solutions and the use of available materials.
5. **Brief Growing Season**
   o Select crops with short growing cycles and use season extenders like greenhouses.
6. **Need for Adequate Protection**
   o Protect your garden from pests and environmental threats through fencing, netting, and natural repellents.

The Growing Dome Solution
A Growing Dome greenhouse can address many challenges associated with setting up a survival garden. This structure is a comprehensive preparation instrument offering several benefits:

1. **Year-Round Growth**
   o The Growing Dome utilizes active and passive solar technologies to provide a consistent and energy-efficient environment for growing plants throughout the year, regardless of your location.
2. **Durability**
   o The robust structure withstands environmental adversities like wind, snow, and hail, ensuring the safety of your food supply from various threats, including predators and other animals.
3. **Ease of Installation**
   o Greenhouse packages are designed for cost-effective and high-quality solutions, with DIY installations facilitated by detailed manuals and videos. These kits have been refined over the years for simplicity and efficiency.
4. **Long-Term Investment**
   o Growing Domes can last over 30 years and withstand hurricane winds, making them a reliable long-term investment for sustainable gardening.

Setting Up Your Growing Dome
If you prefer not to construct the Growing Dome yourself, assistance is available from private contractors, the Growing Spaces supervisor, or an installation team. For a successful survival garden, consider the following:

1. **Nutrient-Dense Crops**
   o Grow nutrient-dense fruits and vegetables that are easy to cultivate and maximize food production, such as carrots, beets, radishes, and turnips. These crops are rich in starch and can be easily preserved.
2. **Optimizing Plant Placement**
   o Plant root vegetables in the middle bed for optimal root development. Consider a fruiting tree like a fig tree to provide shade and extend the growing season for root vegetables.
3. **Fruits for Preservation**
   o Focus on fruits that can be dried or preserved, such as tomatoes, peppers, and berries, which are excellent sources of antioxidants during the winter months. Place fruiting plants like squash, green beans, and cucumbers on the south side of the garden to optimize heat and sunlight.

4. **Pollinator Attraction**
   o   Plant flowers outside the Growing Dome to attract pollinators such as bees and butterflies. Depending on the soil variety, construct raised beds or sow seeds directly into the ground.

Embracing Self-Reliance

In an effort to better prepare for an uncertain future, individuals and communities are increasingly focusing on self-reliance. Growing your own food is a crucial stage in achieving self-sufficiency, whether you are establishing a homestead or simply seeking a more self-sufficient lifestyle. By following the guidance in this chapter, you can develop a resilient and productive survival garden, ensuring a steady food supply in times of crisis.

Chapter 7: Establishing a Self-Sustaining Vegetable Garden

Creating a self-sustaining vegetable garden promotes food security, environmental sustainability, and personal well-being. This chapter guides you through essential steps to set up a productive garden that provides fresh produce year-round.

Objectives:
- *Food Security*: Ensure a reliable supply of fresh vegetables.
- *Sustainability*: Implement eco-friendly practices for a self-sustaining system.
- *Health Benefits:* Enhance physical and mental well-being through gardening.

Selecting the Right Location for Your Garden

Choosing the optimal location for your vegetable garden is crucial. Consider the following factors:

Sunlight:
- *Full Sun Exposure*: Most vegetables need 6-8 hours of direct sunlight daily.
- *Avoiding Shade:* Ensure the garden isn't shaded by trees or structures.

Soil Quality:
- *Well-Draining Soil*: Prevents waterlogging and root diseases.
- *Soil Testing:* Check pH levels and nutrient content; aim for a slightly acidic to neutral pH (6.0-7.0).

Proximity to Water Source:
- *Easy Access*: Choose a site close to a water source for easy irrigation.
- *Water Conservation*: Consider rainwater harvesting systems for a sustainable water supply.

Protection from Wind:
- *Windbreaks*: Plant hedges or install windbreaks to protect from strong winds.

Preparing the Soil

Healthy soil is the foundation of a thriving vegetable garden. Proper soil preparation ensures plants have the nutrients they need.

Clearing the Area:
- *Remove Debris*: Clear rocks, weeds, and debris to prevent competition for nutrients.
- *Weed Control*: Use mulch or cover crops to suppress weeds.

Soil Amendments:
- *Organic Matter:* Incorporate compost, aged manure, or leaf mold to improve soil structure.
- *pH Adjustment*: Amend soil with lime or sulfur based on soil test results.

Tilling and Aeration:
- *Loosening Soil*: Till to a depth of 8-12 inches for better aeration.
- *Avoid Over-Tilling*: Preserve soil structure and beneficial organisms.

Soil Fertility:
- *Cover Crops*: Grow cover crops to enhance soil fertility.
- *Soil Microorganisms*: Promote beneficial microorganisms by adding compost and avoiding synthetic chemicals.

Selecting Suitable Vegetable Varieties

Choose the right vegetable varieties based on climate, soil type, and personal preferences.

Climate Considerations:
- *Hardiness Zones*: Select vegetables suited to your region's climate.
- *Growing Season*: Choose varieties that match your growing season length.

Soil Compatibility:
- *Soil Preferences*: Match vegetables to their preferred soil conditions.

Personal Preferences:
- *Dietary Needs*: Grow vegetables you and your family enjoy.
- *Storage and Preservation*: Select varieties known for their storage qualities.

Heirloom vs. Hybrid Varieties:

- *Heirloom Varieties*: Offer better flavor and seed-saving benefits.
- *Hybrid Varieties*: Provide disease resistance and higher yields.

Planting and Sowing
Proper planting techniques are crucial for a successful garden.
Planting Seeds:
- *Seed Selection*: Use high-quality, non-GMO seeds.
- *Seed Starting*: Start seeds indoors before the last frost date.
- *Direct Sowing:* Sow root vegetables, beans, and peas directly in the garden.

Transplanting Seedlings:
- *Hardening Off:* Acclimate seedlings to outdoor conditions gradually.
- *Planting Depth*: Follow recommended depth and spacing for each variety.

Succession Planting:
- *Staggered Planting*: Ensure a continuous harvest by planting at intervals.

Companion Planting:
- *Benefits:* Improve growth, pest control, and flavor.
- *Examples:* Plant tomatoes with basil or carrots with onions.

Irrigation and Fertilization
Consistent watering and proper fertilization are critical for healthy growth and high yields.
Irrigation Techniques:
- *Drip Irrigation*: Efficiently delivers water to plant roots.
- *Mulching:* Retains soil moisture and suppresses weeds.
- *Watering Schedule*: Water early morning or late evening to reduce evaporation.

Fertilization:
- *Organic Fertilizers*: Use compost, worm castings, or fish emulsion.
- *Soil Testing*: Adjust fertilization based on soil nutrient levels.
- *Fertilization Schedule*: Follow a schedule tailored to vegetable needs.

Rainwater Harvesting:
- *Benefits:* Reduces water costs and promotes sustainability.
- *Setup*: Install gutters, downspouts, and storage tanks.

Pest and Disease Management
Managing pests and diseases is essential for a healthy garden.
Preventative Measures:
- *Crop Rotation*: Prevents pest and disease buildup.
- *Companion Planting*: Attracts beneficial insects and repels pests.

Natural Pest Control:
- *Beneficial Insects*: Introduce ladybugs, lacewings, and nematodes.
- *Homemade Remedies*: Use neem oil, insecticidal soap, or garlic spray.

Disease Management:
- *Disease-Resistant Varieties*: Reduce infection risks.
- *Sanitation:* Remove infected plants promptly.
- *Proper Spacing:* Improve air circulation to reduce fungal diseases.

Monitoring and Early Detection:
- *Regular Inspections*: Detect problems early.
- *Action Thresholds*: Intervene when pest populations reach critical levels.

Harvesting and Storage
Proper harvesting and storage maximize the shelf life and quality of your vegetables.
Harvesting Techniques:
- *Optimal Timing:* Harvest at peak ripeness for best flavor and nutrition.
- *Gentle Handling*: Avoid bruising or damaging vegetables.

Storage Methods:
- *Short-Term Storage*: Use a cool, dark place or refrigerator.

- *Long-Term Preservation*: Use canning, freezing, dehydrating, or fermenting.

Maintaining Quality:
- *Regular Inspections*: Check stored vegetables for spoilage.
- *Proper Ventilation*: Prevent mold growth with good air circulation.

Seed Saving:
- *Collecting Seeds*: Save seeds from healthy plants for future planting.
- *Seed Harvesting*: Allow seeds to mature fully before harvesting.
- *Cleaning and Drying:* Clean seeds and dry them completely before storage.
- *Storing Seeds*: Store in a cool, dark, dry place in airtight containers.

Establishing a self-sustaining vegetable garden is a dynamic process that requires continuous learning and adaptation.

Continual Learning:
- *Educational Resources*: Utilize books, online courses, and local gardening clubs.
- *Experimentation*: Try different methods and varieties.

Community Involvement:
- *Sharing Knowledge*: Engage with local gardening communities.
- *Garden Tours*: Participate in or host garden tours for inspiration.

Adaptation to Change:
- *Climate Variability*: Adjust practices in response to weather patterns.
- *Pest and Disease Management*: Stay proactive in addressing new challenges.

Sustainable Practices:
- *Reduce Waste*: Practice composting and use garden waste as compost.
- *Resource Conservation*: Conserve water, reduce energy use, and minimize chemical inputs.

Monitoring and Record-Keeping:
- *Garden Journal*: Record planting dates, weather conditions, and pest occurrences.
- *Soil Health*: Regularly monitor and test soil to maintain fertility.

By following these guidelines and embracing continuous improvement, you can establish and maintain a thriving, self-sustaining vegetable garden, providing fresh, nutritious food and promoting a sustainable lifestyle.

MODULE N: RAISING ANIMALS
Chapter 1: Selecting the right animals

Factors to consider while choosing animals to raise

Choosing the correct livestock to grow is crucial and is determined by several criteria, such as the farm's objectives, resources, and the local climate and environment. When deciding what kinds of animals to keep, it's essential to think about the following:

- First and first, it's essential to consider why you're raising animals. What exactly are you planning to use them for? What kind of animal you grow will depend on its intended use.
- Animals have varying needs regarding climate and environmental factors, including average annual temperature, humidity, and daylight hours. Select species that will do well in the typical conditions of the area.
- Land, water, and food supplies are just some resources you can access. Some species need more space and water than others, and foods that aren't suitable for all animals.
- The need for your planned output in the market is an element that must be noticed. The profitability of various livestock species varies with the demand for their respective end products.
- Care: some pets need more time and effort than others. If you have limited human resources, only get creatures you know how to care for.

Needs and requirements of different animals

Successful animal husbandry also requires familiarity with animal preferences and requirements. General recommendations for meeting the needs of several animal species are provided below.

- Chickens and ducks, for example, need a dry, well-ventilated coop outfitted with roosting bars and nesting boxes. They also need an age- and purpose-appropriate diet and access to clean water.
- Cattle need a pasture with plenty of grass, good water, and protection from the elements. They need protein, minerals, and roughage like hay or silage to be healthy.
- Goats need a warm, dry place to sleep with plenty of ventilation, fresh water, and a portion of food rich in protein, minerals, and roughage like hay or grass.
- Sheep need a pasture that provides fresh water, shade, and protection from the elements. They need protein, minerals, and roughage like hay or grass to be healthy.
- Pigs Piggybacking on the previous point, pigs need a dry, well-ventilated shelter, a steady supply of fresh water, and feed rich in minerals and protein.

There are several considerations to weigh when deciding which animals to raise, including the farm's goals, the local climate and environment, the farm's resources, the market's needs, and the available workforce. The health and happiness of animals depend on our understanding of their specific requirements and wants.

Deciding on the best fit for your homestead

There are several things to think about when deciding what would work best for your homestead, including the size of your land, your priorities, your budget, and your degree of skill. Here are some guidelines to follow when you make this critical decision for your farm:

Define your goals and priorities: Establish your objectives and top priorities. Get started on your farm by writing out your objectives and top priorities. Just what are your homesteading goals? Do you seek to ensure your food supply? Do you want to make a living wage from your property someday? Is having a wide variety of flora and animals on your farm necessary?

Assess your property: Inspect your land to understand its dimensions and potential building sites. Think about how much land you have access to, the land's geography, the soil quality, the water supply, and the local temperature and weather patterns.

Think about the tools available: Time, money, human resources, and tools. Some homesteading tasks are more labor- and resource-intensive than others, while others need just essential tools.

Research homesteading activities: Investigate various homesteading endeavors to find the best mesh with your aspirations, land, and resources. The cultivation of plants and the rearing of animals for food, fiber, and other products are everyday homesteading pursuits.

Start small and build gradually: Doing things slowly and methodically is crucial as you create your farm. You may learn from your mistakes and keep yourself from overwhelming yourself. Expand your homestead as your expertise and resources allow, but get started with a few easy tasks that fit your objectives and resources.

It is essential to consider your objectives and priorities, property, available resources, and degree of skill when determining the ideal match for your homestead. Learn as much as possible about homesteading before you go in, take baby steps, and eventually grow into a full-fledged operation.

Chapter 2: Raising poultry

Popular poultry breeds for homestead

Chickens, ducks, turkeys, and geese are some of the most common types of poultry kept on farms. Here are some well-liked varieties of each chicken species:

- Rhode Island Reds, Plymouth Rocks, Leghorns, and Orpingtons are some of the most common chicken breeds. These breeds' egg production, resilience, and calm demeanor are well-known.
- The Pekin, Muscovy, Khaki Campbell, and Indian Runner are just a few of the most common duck breeds. These breeds' meat quality, resilience, and foraging prowess are well-known.
- There are many different turkeys, but the Broad Breasted White, Narragansett, Bourbon Red, and Bronze are some of the most common. These breeds' meat quality, resilience, and foraging prowess are well-known.
- The Toulouse, Embden, and Chinese geese are the most common and well-liked goose breeds. These breeds' meat quality, resilience, and foraging prowess are well-known.

Building a suitable coop and run for poultry

The health of your chickens depends in part on your ability to construct a safe and secure coop and run for them. Some suggestions for making a chicken house and yard:

Coop: The coop should have enough room for the chickens to spread out and be secure. There should be perches for roosting and nesting boxes for depositing eggs.

Run: The birds need a large, securely gated area to roam and graze. Predators like foxes and raccoons should also be kept out of the run.

Flooring: Easy-to-maintain and clean flooring are necessary for the coop and the run. For the same reason, good drainage is essential.

Feeding and watering: Easy accessibility and cleanability of the coop and run's feeding and watering system are essential. Hanging or wall-mounted feeders and waterers fall into this category.

Light: The coop has to have enough light to keep the chickens comfortable and stimulate egg production. You may use a heat lamp or the sun to do this.

A poultry's health and happiness depend on your ability to construct a safe and secure coop and run. Think about the space, ventilation, feeding, watering, lighting, and predator protection needs of the birds you want to raise. Following these rules, you'll have a prosperous and long-lasting chicken farm.

Feeding and watering

Chickens and ducks need regular feeding and hydration to thrive. Some rules for feeding and watering your chickens:

- Protein, carbs, vitamins, and minerals are all essential parts of a healthy diet for poultry. They may be given a commercial meal designed for their age and function or a combination of commercial feed and fresh fruits, vegetables, and grains.
- Water: Always have a supply of clean water available for your chickens. A water basin may be provided, or you can utilize a wall- or ceiling-mounted waterer.
- Creating and sticking to a routine for when and how often your chickens are fed and watered is essential. This will aid in digestion regulation and lower health risks.

Egg collection and management

The welfare of your chickens depends in part on how well you gather and manage the eggs they lay. Here are some rules to follow while handling and collecting eggs:

Nesting boxes: provide your chickens with a safe place to nest and deposit their eggs. The packing containers must be sterile, airtight, and free of moisture.

Collection: Eggs should be collected regularly to reduce the risk of them getting soiled or cracked. Either a manual or automated egg-collecting method may be used.

Storage: Eggs should be kept in a clean, cold area, ideally in the fridge. Remember to start with the oldest eggs and toss any broken or dirty ones.

Dealing with common health issues

To keep your poultry healthy and happy, dealing with frequent health problems is vital. Some recurring medical issues and how to treat them are listed below.

- Infectious diseases of the respiratory system: viruses, bacteria, and fungi may all cause respiratory infections. Maintain a clean, well-ventilated environment, and don't crowd the coop to avoid respiratory diseases. Isolating the bird and giving it antibiotics or other respiratory treatments is standard for treating respiratory infections.
- Mites and lice are two examples of parasites that may irritate the skin and lead to anemia and other health problems. Parasites may be avoided by maintaining a clean, dry coop and run and by giving the chickens frequent dust baths. Use effective drugs or natural treatments to control parasite populations.
- When an egg becomes trapped in a bird's reproductive system, it is said to be "bound." Egg binding may be avoided by giving your birds a healthy diet rich in calcium. Isolating the bird and providing supportive treatment, such as a warm bath or lubricant, are effective ways to deal with egg-binding.

Common health problems, egg collecting and management, and food and water provision play significant roles in chicken production. The health and well-being of your poultry may be maintained, and high-quality eggs and meat can be produced by following these rules and getting veterinary treatment when necessary.

Chapter 3: Raising Ducks and Geese

Understanding the needs and characteristics of ducks and geese

The well-being of ducks and geese on a farm must have a firm grasp of what they need and how they behave. Following these pointers can help you better comprehend their requirements and distinguishing features:

Ducks:

- Ducks need a source of water for bathing and preening. Due to a lack of teeth, individuals must drink water to aid in digesting.
- Ducks need to eat a varied diet with the nutrients they need to thrive. Additionally, they take pleasure in going on bug and rodent hunts.
- Ducks need a safe place to live that is dry, airy and secure from predators. In addition to places to sleep and deposit eggs, they need nesting boxes.
- Ducks are gregarious creatures that like hanging out with their kind. They also form a social order with the most potent ducks at the top.
- Illnesses Respiratory infections, parasite diseases, and fungal infections are all potential problems for ducks. Consistent observation and veterinarian treatment are crucial for preventing and treating these conditions.

Geese:

- Geese are herbivores that need constant access to grass and other plants. Additionally, they take pleasure in going on bug and rodent hunts.
- Geese need to be near water so they may bathe and clean themselves. Due to a lack of teeth, individuals must drink water to aid in digesting.
- Geese need a safe place to live that is dry, has enough airflow, and is secure from predators. In addition to places to sleep and deposit eggs, they need nesting boxes.
- Geese are gregarious birds that want to be with their kind. They also form a social order with the most potent geese at the top.
- Dangerous conditions Respiratory infections, parasite diseases, and fungal infections are all potential threats to the health of geese. Consistent observation and veterinarian treatment are crucial for preventing and treating these conditions.

It's necessary for the well-being of ducks and geese on a farm to understand their demands and peculiarities. Their health, happiness, and productivity may be ensured by proper housing, nutrition, socialization, and frequent health monitoring.

Providing proper housing and nutrition

The well-being of poultry on a farm is directly related to the care and attention given to it. Some suggestions for ensuring enough shelter and sustenance are included below.

- Housing: Poultry needs a safe, secure, and comfortable living place, free from the elements and predators. Nesting boxes for eggs and perches for roosting should be provided. The housing should be large enough to hold all of the birds you want to house.
- Feeding: a poultry diet should contain a variety of protein sources, carbohydrate sources, and vitamin and mineral sources. They may be given a commercial meal designed for their age and function or a combination of commercial feed and fresh fruits, vegetables, and grains.
- Watering: Always have fresh water available for your chickens. A water basin may be provided, or you can utilize a wall- or ceiling-mounted waterer.

Breeding and hatching

The breeding and hatching process is one of the most important parts of raising chickens on a small farm. The following are some suggestions for chicken breeding and hatching:

Breeding: When breeding birds, choose those that are both healthy and genetically varied. Please give them a place to live, food, and friends to hang out with. To guarantee practical breeding, observe their habits and count eggs regularly.

Incubation: Using either an incubator or a broody hen to incubate eggs is possible. During incubation, it's essential to keep the eggs at the right temperature and humidity, give them enough air circulation and turn them often.

Hatching: After the eggs have hatched, the chicks need a safe place to live and nutritious food to grow. Always keep an eye on how they act and feel, and get them to a vet if they need it.

Dealing with Common health issues

Keeping chickens healthy and happy on a farmentails more than just preventing disease. Some frequent medical problems and how to treat them are listed below.

- Infectious diseases of the respiratory system: viruses, bacteria, and fungi may all cause respiratory infections. Maintain a clean, well-ventilated environment, and don't crowd the coop to avoid respiratory diseases. Isolating the bird and giving it antibiotics or other respiratory treatments is standard for treating respiratory infections.
- Mites and lice are two examples of parasites that may irritate the skin and lead to anemia and other health problems. Parasites may be avoided by maintaining a clean, dry coop and run and by giving the chickens frequent dust baths. Use effective drugs or natural treatments to control parasite populations.
- When an egg becomes trapped in a bird's reproductive system, it is said to be "bound." Egg binding may be avoided by giving your birds a healthy diet rich in calcium. Isolating the bird and providing supportive treatment, such as a warm bath or lubricant, are effective ways to deal with egg-binding.

Raising chickens at home requires attention to the environment, feed, breeding, hatching, and frequent health problems. The health and well-being of your poultry may be maintained, and high-quality eggs and meat can be produced by following these rules and getting veterinary treatment when necessary.

Chapter 4: Raising Rabbits

Understanding Rabbit behavior and biology

If you keep rabbits as pets or livestock on your homestead, you need to know something about their biology and behavior. To better comprehend their biology and behavior, please follow these guidelines:

- Rabbits are sociable creatures that like to hang out with their kind. There is a social order among rabbits, with the most potent individuals serving as leaders.
- Rabbits and herbivores need a high-fiber diet of hay and fresh vegetables. In addition, they always need to have access to potable water.
- Rabbits need a safe, secure, and well-ventilated home away from the reach of predators. They need a safe place to roost and lay eggs and a place to recuperate afterward.
- Throughout the year, rabbits may keep reproducing because of their high fertility. The gestation cycle of a female rabbit (a doe) is 28-32 days, and she may have anywhere from one to fourteen young (kits) at once.

Selecting the right breed for meat and fiber

- It's crucial to your homestead's success to choose the correct rabbit breed for meat or fiber production. To help you choose the best breed, consider the following:
- New Zealand, California, and Flemish Giant are three common breeds used for meat production. The meat from these animals is of high quality and overgrows.
- Angora and Jersey Wooly are two well-known fiber-producing breeds. These animals' long, luxurious fur is prized because it can be used in textile production.

Breeding and caring for young

Raising rabbit kits (babies) through their first few weeks of life is a crucial part of any rabbit farm. Here are some pointers on how to raise rabbits from birth:

Breeding: When reproducing, choose rabbits with good health and a wide range of genetic traits. Please give them a place to live, food, and friends to hang out with. Keep an eye on them and ensure they have babies to ensure your breeding efforts are fruitful.

Care of newborn kits: Kitten care includes giving the newborns a safe place to sleep and nutritious food. Always keep an eye on how they act and feel, and get them to a vet if they need it. Kits must be kept clean and warm, and the mother should be fed well to produce enough milk.

Weaning: Kits may be weaned when they are 6-8 weeks old. Ensure the weaned kits have a safe place to live and food to eat, and keep an eye on their health and behavior as they develop.

Rabbit farming on the homestead requires knowledge of rabbit biology and behavior and the correct breed selection for either meat or fiber production. You can keep your rabbits healthy and produce high-quality meat and fiber by following these rules and getting veterinarian treatment when necessary.

Dealing with common health issues

Maintaining the health and happiness of rabbits on a farm necessitates addressing frequent health problems. Some recurring medical issues and how to treat them are listed below.

- When the rabbit's digestive system slows down or stops, it is said to be in a state of gastrointestinal stasis. Causes include a bad diet, not enough exercise, and stress. Give your rabbits a high-fiber diet and plenty of activity to keep their intestines moving freely. Fluid treatment, pain medicine, and prokinetic drugs are all examples of supportive care that may be used to help alleviate gastrointestinal stasis.
- Viruses, germs, and even dust and a lack of ventilation may all play a role in triggering respiratory illnesses. Ensure the rabbit can access clean, dry, and well-ventilated housing to avoid respiratory infections. Isolating a rabbit with respiratory disease is the first step in treating it, followed by providing any necessary supportive care, including antibiotics or respiratory medicines.
- Problems with teeth may have several origins, including poor nutrition, accidents, and heredity. Pain, swelling, and abscesses are some of the symptoms. Give your rabbits a high-fiber diet and safe chew toys to keep their teeth healthy— veterinary services, like teeth trimming and abscess removal, may help with dental care.

- Mites and fleas are two examples of parasites that may irritate the skin and lead to anemia, among other problems. Maintain the rabbit in a clean environment and have it regularly dewormed and treated for parasites to keep it parasite-free.
- Problems reproducing might include miscarriage, uterine cancer, and infections of the reproductive organs. Spaying and neutering your rabbits may avoid infections in the reproductive system and other health problems. If reproductive issues are suspected, veterinarian attention should be sought.

Keeping rabbits healthy and happy on a farm requires attending to common health problems. You can keep your rabbits healthy and produce high-quality meat and fiber by following these rules and getting veterinarian treatment when necessary.

Chapter 5: Raising Goats

Different breeds of goats and their uses

Goats come in a wide variety of breeds, each with its own set of traits and applications. Some common breeds and the tasks they perform follow:

Alpine: Alpine goats are prized for their abundant milk supply and are often used in the dairy industry.

Boer: Boer goats are popular for meat because of their high meat yield.

Nubian: Nubian Goats are often used for dairy because of their excellent milk production and delicious flavor.

LaMancha: LaMancha goats are often used for dairy because of their excellent milk output and calm demeanor.

Pygmy: Pygmy goats are smaller than regular goats and are popular as pets and food sources.

Proper housing and nutrition

The well-being of goats on a farm depends on their being given enough shelter and food. Some suggestions for ensuring enough shelter and sustenance are included below.

- Goats need a safe, dry, and well-ventilated place to live away from predators. Nesting boxes for giving birth and resting perches should also be provided.
- Goats need a varied diet that includes grains or pellets in addition to roughage like hay or grass. They must also have constant access to potable water.
- Goats may need extra supplements such as minerals, vitamins, and probiotics depending on the breed and the intended use.

Breeding and caring for young goats

Goat farming on a homestead also involves the breeding and upbringing of young goats. Here are some pointers on how to raise goat kids:

- Goats should be selected for breeding based on their overall health and genetic diversity. Give them a place to live, food to eat, and friends to hang out with. Keep an eye on them to make sure they're acting normally and having babies.
- Taking care of infants entails giving them a safe place to sleep and nutritious food to eat. Always keep an eye on how they're acting and how they feel, and get them to a vet if they need it. Doe should be given high-quality food to encourage milk production and the mother should keep the young warm and clean.
- The optimal time to begin weaning a child is between 6 and 8 weeks. Make sure the weaned youngsters have a safe place to live and enough to eat and keep an eye on their health and behavior as they develop.

Successful goat farming on a homestead requires knowledge of goat breeds and their purposes, the provision of suitable shelter and nutrition, and the breeding and care of young goats. You may keep your goats healthy and provide high-quality milk, meat, or fiber by following these rules and getting veterinarian treatment when necessary.

Milking and processing goat milk

One of the most important parts of keeping goats as livestock on a small farm is milking and preparing the goats' milk. Instructions for milking goats and handling the resulting milk are provided below.

Milking: It's important to avoid infection by milking in a clean, hygienic setting. The recommended milking schedule for goats is twice daily, with intervals of roughly 12 hours. It's important to use clean, sterile containers while collecting milk.

Processing: Milk should be filtered and refrigerated to below 40 degrees Fahrenheit immediately after milking to stop the formation of harmful germs. After pasteurization, the milk may be used to produce cheese, yogurt, and other dairy goods.

Storage: Goat milk should be refrigerated or frozen immediately after purchase and kept in clean, sterile containers. It keeps well in the fridge for up to a week, or six months in the freezer.

Dealing with common health issues

It's crucial to address typical challenges encountered during goat milk production to guarantee the product's integrity and safety. Here are some often encountered problems and how to fix them:

Mastitis: Mastitis is an udder illness that may be brought on by bacteria or by trauma to the udder. To avoid mastitis, it is important to keep the milking area clean and hygienic and to look out for any indicators of udder inflammation, such as increased temperature or redness. To treat mastitis, you should quarantine the affected goat and give it antibiotics and anti-inflammatory drugs from a veterinarian.

Milk quality: Diet, environment, and cleanliness may all have an impact on milk quality. Healthy food, clean and dry quarters, and routine hygiene practices like cleaning the udder before milking will all contribute to the quality of your goats' milk.

The flavor of milk: Diet and heredity both have a role in determining how tasty milk is. Select goat breeds recognized for producing milk with a subtle flavor, and feed them a diet rich in fiber and low in odorous vegetables.

Goat husbandry on the homestead is not complete without the milking and processing of goat milk. Maintaining the purity and safety of your goat milk and your dairy products is possible by following these instructions and getting veterinarian assistance when necessary.

MODULE O: NATURAL MEDICINE
Chapter 1: Natural Health-Care

Several years of living in poverty have forced me to be prepared for whatever life sends at me. Learning the value of vegetation has saved my life on multiple occasions. Herbalism is a skill that I believe all preppers should be familiar with. Nature has always been a tried-and-true treatment for any ailment. Like any good mother, Mother Earth has provided for her offspring. It was practiced by Native Americans and the Chinese, and every holistic doctor is aware of it. There are always plants to cultivate, regardless of location. The plants in your garden that you presumably discarded as weeds (I despise that word!) have incredible medicinal properties. Even in densely populated areas, you can still find plants such as purslane, dandelion, plantain, and scallions. However, the first tenet of gardening and herb collection is to know your herbs. Mother Nature can be difficult to identify when it comes to identifying her bounty. Rose-bay Willow, for instance, is an imitator of Purple Loosestrife, which can be used to treat diarrhea caused by typhoid fever or dysentery. To novice Rose rustlers (my term for plant hunters), the two plants appear identical. Due to the unique properties of each plant, this could be hazardous. Bring a field guide if you're uncertain of what you're looking at so that you can swiftly identify it. Pick a mile away from highways - lead levels are one of the obvious explanations. Additionally, you may wish to maintain a low profile and avoid outdoor areas. There are numerous reasons to begin identifying medicinal and edible plants, but the most essential reason is to begin RIGHT NOW. You will realize that once you begin, there is no way to stop. I became obsessed with foraging when I first began. I needed to know if each plant I encountered was edible, medicinal, or both, and how to utilize it. I was constantly gaining new knowledge. Not only will you always have sustenance and medicine during difficult times, but you will also have healing knowledge to trade. Consider the matter carefully. Without the ability to obtain a prescription from a pharmacy, people will be willing to give you anything in exchange for your knowledge.

Consider asthmatics as an example. What will they do if inhalers are not used? They will approach you because you know about the New England Aster, a plant that can help them eliminate the hippopotamus on their chest. People will be willing to trade with you for medical assistance when they hear about your extraordinary healing skills through the grapevine. Similar to the days when furs and even a nice meal could be exchanged for medical care. However, you must start immediately if you wish to acquire this knowledge. Let's examine the benefits of gathering wild vegetation. In addition to the "now" factor, it is essential to know where to search and what to look for. Nobody wants to poison themselves or others. Remember that nearly every plant has imposter duplicates.

There are hundreds of plants and botanicals available for self-healing in Mother Nature's pharmacy. In this section, I will discuss six that every survivalist should be aware of and able to identify. I believe that everyone should possess Aloe Vera due to its remarkable healing properties. Simply remove one of the plant's fleshy leaves and apply the substance within for pain relief and a soothing sensation. Adding the gel extracted from a large leaf to a glass of water yields a mild laxative.

Not only are dandelion leaves tasty, but they are also rich in beta-carotene and vitamin C. This wonderful plant has bile-stimulating properties, which enhance the body's ability to eliminate impurities. This is useful if you cannot locate clean, running water and your body is constantly assaulted by bacteria. I highly recommend cultivating this aromatic plant, lemon balm. This year, this plant has produced a profusion of fragrant, lemony leaves, to my delight. As a tea, it can alleviate and calm agitation and irritability. Due to its calming influence, it can be used just before bedtime. Lemon balm is also beneficial for gastrointestinal distress. However, expectant women should avoid it because it stimulates the uterus.

This lovely aromatic flower, the New England Aster, can be found almost anywhere, but it flourishes in abandoned lots and fields. It has a broad variety of incredible applications, especially for those with asthma or COPD (Chronic obstructive pulmonary disease). New England Aster is predominantly employed as an expectorant, relieving coughs caused by the common cold and expelling phlegm. Eating its fresh blossoms induces a state of relaxation and drowsiness. Blood Flower is a beneficial plant for those who consume poisonous berries or other unidentified plants. It is related to milkweed, and its milky fluid is used as an emetic (it induces vomiting). In addition, nettle and insect stings can be soothed with the sap. In addition to driving your cat insane, I believe catnip will also drive you insane. Similar to NyQuil, it alleviates cold symptoms, can halt bleeding and swelling, and functions as an icebreaker due to its ability to induce sweating. This plant, a member of the mint family, can alleviate digestive issues, menstrual cramping, and migraines. Sage is the last plant on my list of "must-know" vegetation. Sage is most commonly associated with Thanksgiving filling. However, this is my top choice when it comes to super-healing plants. Sage is antimicrobial, anti-inflammatory, and antioxidant. Sage was used to preserve meat prior to the invention of the refrigerator, which is advantageous if you are on a meat quest.

Chapter 2: Medical Resources from Nature

Your list of home remedies is about to become much more intriguing. Although these botanicals have been used for hundreds of years, physicians and scientists now recommend using them for medicinal purposes. These natural medical resources can readily substitute for conventional treatments. The plants can heal and reduce cholesterol, high blood pressure, and arthritis discomfort, among other ailments. Some of the most effective medicinal herbs can also be used to cure cancer cells and help alcoholics quit drinking.

Herbal remedies, other natural remedies, and natural medical resources are as effective as conventional treatments. Occasionally, they are even more efficient and have no side effects. Here are some of the finest available natural medical resources. These superhealers can be added to your natural medicine or herbal products cabinet, along with your beloved recipes. Some of them, if incorporated into your daily regimen, can be beneficial to your health.

Curcuma longa possesses antioxidant, anti-inflammatory, and anti-cancer properties. This popular curry ingredient contains curcumin, which aids in the treatment of arthritis. Curcumin is a potent anti-inflammatory that functions similarly to Cox-2 inhibitor medications in reducing the Cox-2 enzyme that causes the inflammation of arthritis. In addition, turmeric is known to reduce precancerous lesions and eradicate disease-related brain plaques.

The daily consumption of cinnamon extract has been shown to reduce blood sugar and cholesterol levels. It is advantageous for type-2 diabetics and reduces cardiovascular hazards. It is essential to stay with water-soluble extracts and avoid consuming excessive amounts of the spice.

Rosemary: Rosemary extract reduces the amount of cancer-causing heterocyclic amines (HCAs) in grilled, fried, or roasting meat. It prevents carcinogens from binding to DNA and infiltrating the body, thereby preventing the development of cancer. Rosemary extract enhances the flavor of dishes when added to spice mixtures.

Ginger is renowned for its ability to alleviate motion sickness, nausea associated with pregnancy, and nausea caused by chemotherapy. It inhibits the effects of serotonin in the body, which contributes to gastric pain and nausea, and functions as a potent antioxidant.

High garlic consumption has been linked to the treatment and prevention of colorectal and ovarian cancer. It also aids in reducing blood pressure and preventing arterial blockages. Fresh, pulverized garlic provides the greatest cancer and cardiovascular health benefits.

Holy Basil: Holy basil, a pesto-specific variety, is effective for reducing tension, alleviating headaches, and promoting digestion. It increases norepinephrine and adrenaline in the organism, while decreasing serotonin. Holy basil tea leaves are an excellent source of natural pain relief.

Aloe Vera: Aloe vera has been used in traditional medicine to treat a variety of ailments, including skin disorders, constipation, infections, and fungal diseases. It has antiviral, anti-inflammatory, and antifungal properties, boosts the immune system, and is widely used in skin care cosmetics.

Feverfew has been utilized for centuries to treat headaches, toothaches, stomachaches, menstrual issues, and labor symptoms. It contains the biochemical parthenolide, which prevents the dilation of blood vessels associated with migraines and relieves allergies and arthritis discomfort.

St. John's Wort is used to heal physical symptoms in addition to alleviating mild to moderate anxiety and depression. It has the same efficacy as other medications, but none of their adverse effects.

Saw Palmetto: Men commonly use saw palmetto to treat prostate cancer and other men's health issues, including hair loss, reduced libido, and prostate enlargement. In addition, it is believed to promote relaxation, treat respiratory conditions, and boost the immune system.

Chapter 3: Medicinal Herbs For Your Bug Out Bag

Herbal remedies are extremely useful for survivalists, as first aid and healthcare are crucial in emergency situations. When you can't rely on a quick trip to the store for supplies, it's essential to investigate Mother Nature's medicine cabinet. Learn which medicinal plants should be included in your emergency supplies because they are the most beneficial and effective.

Willow Oak

As injuries and discomfort are prevalent in challenging situations, pain management is a crucial aspect of survival. The history of the willow tree's pain-relieving properties dates back to ancient Greece. Salicin glucoside, found in willow bark, is a potent pain reliever. In contrast to synthetic alternatives such as aspirin, willow bark does not increase the danger of internal bleeding. It can be used to treat arthritis, fever, headaches, inflammation, anxiety, pain management, wounds, and ulcers, making it an essential emergency herb.

Uses for willow bark: For transdermal absorption, chew it directly from the tree or lick the bark. It can also be chewed or crushed and applied to minor incisions as a compress. In addition, it can be steeped in scalding water to create a calming tea.

Olive Oil

Garlic's potent antibacterial properties make it an indispensable herb for survival. Due to its high thiamine content, it has traditionally been used to treat infections of the ear, sinus, and throat. Allicin, an enzyme containing sulfur that operates as a natural antifungal, is present in garlic. It enhances the immune system and benefits cardiovascular health. Garlic oil can be taken orally or applied topically, but it is advised to apply a small volume of olive oil to the skin prior to use.

Cayenne Peppers

Cayenne peppers not only impart a spicy flavor to food, but also have numerous medicinal applications. They enhance heart function without increasing blood pressure and have been used to treat stomach ulcers, sore throats, congestion, bronchitis, and the common cold. Cayenne peppers' ability to staunch internal and external hemorrhaging is their most important survival benefit. This versatility, combined with the simplicity with which they can be dried and stored, makes them an essential addition to your survival kit.

Cayenne pepper can be ingested with food or applied externally as a poultice to wounds after being ground into a powder.

Feverfew

Feverfew reduces fevers and alleviates migraines, joint inflammation, and respiratory pressure. Parthenolide, its active constituent, has anti-inflammatory properties. In addition to treating migraines and relieving pain, feverfew has been used to treat menstrual problems, infertility, and labor pains. To reap its benefits, chew the flowers or ingest them in capsule form.

Valerian Root

Due to its sedative effects on the central nervous system, valerian root is commonly known as "nature's valium." It relieves pain, anxiety, muscle contractions, and insomnia, making it a valuable survival herb. Additionally, it can assist in slowing the heart rate while enhancing its vitality. Despite its pungent odor, valerian root is an essential emergency item.

Echinacea

Echinacea's immune-boosting properties are well-known. It enhances the body's ability to fend off infections by stimulating the production of white blood cells. Echinacea has been used to treat a variety of ailments, including the common cold, influenza, and respiratory infections. It is available in capsules, tinctures, and beverages, among other forms.

By including these medicinal botanicals in your emergency kit, you will have access to natural remedies for pain, infections, bleeding, and other common health issues. Remember to educate yourself on correct usage, and if necessary, consult a healthcare professional.

Chapter 4: How To Grow Your Shtf Apothecary

Creating a self-sustaining medicinal garden is essential for ensuring health and well-being in situations where access to conventional medical care may be limited. This guide will walk you through the necessary steps to establish a productive natural pharmacy at your prepper retreat or bug-in location, providing effective treatments for various illnesses and health conditions.

Objectives:
- *Self-Sufficiency:* Become your own first responder by growing and preparing natural remedies.
- *Health and Well-being:* Use natural treatments to build a stronger body and improve overall health.
- *Cost-Effectiveness:* Reduce reliance on costly over-the-counter medications by cultivating natural alternatives.

Selecting the Right Plants and Location
Choosing the right medicinal plants and their optimal location is crucial for a successful garden.
Garlic:
- *Benefits:* Garlic is a powerful antibacterial, antifungal, and antimicrobial agent.
- *Cultivation:*
  - Plant cloves pointed end up, 1-2 inches deep, 4-6 inches apart.
  - Requires full sun (6-8 hours per day) and well-drained, humus-rich soil.
  - Water every 3-5 days during growth, reduce watering as the season ends.
  - Harvest when bulbs are round and full, typically after 7-8 months.
- *Uses:* Treats cold and flu symptoms by applying garlic-infused oil to feet.

Elderberry:
- *Benefits:* Boosts immune system, soothes sore throats, and fights pathogens.
- *Cultivation:*
  - Propagate from cuttings in spring.
  - Plant in full sun or moderate shade, 6-10 feet apart.
  - Requires organically rich, well-drained soil.
  - Harvest berries in the second year of growth.
- *Uses:* Make elderberry syrup for cold and flu relief by simmering dried berries with spices and honey.

Onions:
- *Benefits:* Boosts immune system and removes pathogens.
- *Cultivation:*
  - Plant seedlings in rows 8-10 inches apart, 4-6 inches between onions.
  - Requires full sun and loose, well-drained soil with pH 6.5-6.8.
  - Water once per week, ensuring soil is hydrated but not waterlogged.
- *Uses:* Prepare natural cough syrup with honey for cold and flu relief.

Tulsi (Holy Basil):
- *Benefits:* Treats stomach ulcers, bronchitis, joint pain, eye disorders, diabetes, and malaria.
- *Cultivation:*
  - Plant in spring after frost, in well-drained, organically enriched soil.
  - Requires partial shade, keep soil consistently moist but not waterlogged.
- *Uses:* Use leaves in teas or tinctures for various health benefits.

Yarrow:
- *Benefits:* Antibacterial, anti-inflammatory, and antiviral properties.
- *Cultivation:*
  - Sow seeds in spring, in well-drained soil and full sun.
  - Water mature plants only when soil is dry.
- *Uses:* Make teas or tinctures for wound healing and treating minor cuts.

Turmeric:
- *Benefits:* Anti-inflammatory, treats sprains, strains, and various chronic conditions.
- *Cultivation:*

- o Plant rhizomes in well-drained, moist loam, in indirect light.
  - o Harvest roots when leaves fall off, typically 6-10 months.
- *Uses:* Prepare poultices for muscle pain and add to cleansers for skin health.

Echinacea:
- *Benefits:* Boosts immune system, fights infections.
- *Cultivation:*
  - o Plant seeds or seedlings in spring, in well-drained soil with morning and afternoon shade.
  - o Water as needed to keep soil moist but not waterlogged.
- *Uses:* Use leaves and roots in teas and tinctures for respiratory and urinary infections.

St. John's Wort:
- *Benefits:* Reduces inflammation, relieves tension and depression.
- *Cultivation:*
  - o Plant seeds or seedlings in spring, in well-drained soil with partial shade.
  - o Water young plants regularly until established.
- *Uses:* Apply topically for muscle pain and bruises or use in teas for calming effects.

White Willow Bark:
- *Benefits:* Natural pain relief, anti-inflammatory properties.
- *Cultivation:*
  - o Plant near a water source, in well-drained soil.
  - o Water adequately, especially during dry spells.
- *Uses:* Harvest bark from branches in spring for pain relief and fever reduction.

Ginger:
- *Benefits:* Anti-inflammatory, alleviates nausea and gastrointestinal issues.
- *Cultivation:*
  - o Plant roots in fall, in well-drained soil with partial shade.
  - o Water to keep soil moist but not waterlogged.
- *Uses:* Make ginger tea for flu relief and digestive health.

Rosehip:
- *Benefits:* High vitamin C content, boosts immunity.
- *Cultivation:*
  - o Plant in well-drained soil with full sun.
  - o Water to maintain moisture, harvest fruits after boiling for various remedies.

Aloe Vera:
- *Benefits:* Soothes burns, promotes wound healing.
- *Cultivation:*
  - o Plant offshoots in spring, in well-drained soil.
  - o Water sparingly, ensuring proper drainage.
- *Uses:* Apply gel directly to burns and wounds.

Black Walnut:
- *Benefits:* Treats poison ivy, fungal infections.
- *Cultivation:*
  - o Plant away from other crops, in deep, well-drained soil with full sun.
  - o Water generously during growing season.
- *Uses:* Use bark and leaves in poultices and ointments.

Dandelion:
- *Benefits:* Treats menopausal symptoms, menstrual cramps.
- *Cultivation:*
  - o Sow seeds in well-drained soil, in full sun or partial shade.
  - o Water regularly, harvest leaves, flowers, and roots as needed.
- *Uses:* Use in teas and remedies for various health benefits.

Lavender:
- *Benefits:* Anti-inflammatory, antiseptic, relieves anxiety and insomnia.
- *Cultivation:*
  - o Plant cuttings in well-drained soil with full sun.

- o   Water when the upper soil layer is dry.
- *Uses:* Use in teas, oils, and topical applications for various health benefits.

Calendula:
- *Benefits:* Anti-inflammatory, antibacterial, boosts immune system.
- *Cultivation:*
  - o   Sow seeds in containers or outdoors in well-drained soil.
  - o   Water moderately, ensuring soil is moist but not waterlogged.
- *Uses:* Use petals in ointments and lotions for skin health and healing.

By following this guide, you can establish a self-sustaining medicinal garden that provides natural remedies for a variety of health conditions, ensuring you are prepared for any situation where conventional medical care may not be available.

MODULE P: FIRST AID
Chapter 1: First Aid Kit

A first aid kit is essential for treating minor injuries like cuts, burns, bruises, and sprains. It should also include survival gear, emergency medical supplies, and comfort items such as anti-itch ointment and pain relievers. Having a comprehensive first aid kit is crucial for anyone who wants to be prepared for medical emergencies or catastrophes. This chapter provides a list of materials for various injuries to help you stay prepared. These items are commonly found in standard first aid kits and can be used to treat the conditions listed below. However, if you sustain a serious injury, seek immediate medical attention.

Maintaining Your First Aid Kit
Your first aid kit must always be well-organized, adequately stocked, and readily accessible. It is wise to keep a first aid kit in multiple locations, including your home, vehicle, and workplace. There are also kits that can be customized to meet particular requirements. When selecting first aid supplies for the workplace, it is recommended to consult the "First Aid in the Workplace Code of Practice" published by Safe Work Australia.

It is highly recommended that you enroll in a first aid course to acquire the knowledge and skills required to use the tools and supplies in a first aid kit effectively when assisting someone who has become abruptly ill or injured.

The Importance of First Aid
First aid is critical because it has the potential to save lives in emergency situations by providing prompt assistance. In most cases requiring emergent medical care, time is of the essence, and taking the right action at the right time is essential. In life-threatening situations, the injured or ill individual may not be able to wait until professional medical assistance arrives. Additionally, the accident site or the location of the injured person may be inaccessible or too remote for medical specialists to reach in a timely manner, necessitating additional time for assistance to arrive. If the person is surrounded by trained professionals or individuals with rudimentary life support skills or cardiopulmonary resuscitation (CPR) knowledge, they can intervene quickly to save the life of the sick or injured individual.

Pain Relief and Infection Prevention
Providing initial care also aids in pain relief. In most cases, an individual experiences pain immediately after being injured, whether in medical emergencies or traumatic events. Even in situations that are not immediately life-threatening but still require immediate medical attention due to severe pain, individuals trained in first aid can employ a variety of techniques to alleviate the suffering of the unwell or injured individual. A trained individual understands and knows how to apply specialized pain relief techniques, such as applying a cold pack to muscle injuries, using ice-cold water on burns, or rapidly administering pain relief medication to provide relief to the injured individual.

The type of first aid administered to a person following an injury, such as a cut, burn, or any other form of damage, can influence the likelihood of infection. Without adequate training and selection of the most suitable treatment for a particular injury, the situation can worsen. For example, some individuals may suggest using hydrogen peroxide instead of other methods to sterilize a wound. In practice, however, hydrogen peroxide can have the opposite effect by causing damage to the cells that promote quicker wound healing. By receiving proper education and having access to clean, sterile, and disinfected resources (such as clean bandages, antiseptic solution, detergent, and clean water), one can accelerate the healing process and reduce the likelihood of infection. This emphasizes the significance of first aid training and the need for appropriate supplies.

First Aid for Children
Children, including neonates and toddlers, are more susceptible to injuries and situations requiring immediate medical attention. Due to their inherent curiosity and propensity for hazardous play, children frequently spend time unsupervised. Accidents can occur despite vigilant parenting because children move rapidly and are easily distracted. Infants are especially susceptible to injuries that may result in long-term complications, and their risk of sustaining such injuries is significantly elevated. Seizures are relatively common among neonates, but their causes remain unknown. If parents or caregivers are trained in first aid and know how to treat minor injuries such as burns, cuts, and bruises, as well as major injuries such as seizures, it is simpler to keep children safe. Knowledge of first aid provides an additional layer of protection for children and allows for prompt and appropriate action in the event of an emergency.

Communication with Medical Professionals
After administering first aid to a sick or injured individual, you have the option to remain with them until an ambulance or emergency medical services arrive. Being present at the scene and aware of what occurred enables you to provide medical professionals with a detailed account, including the circumstances and the type of first aid administered. The injured individual may not be in the proper mental state to communicate their condition to medical personnel. Your ability to provide a detailed description of the emergency, including the sequence of events and the actions taken, is vital information for medical professionals to consider when determining the next treatment steps. Your firsthand account can contribute to a more complete understanding of the situation.

Reducing Recovery Time
In an emergency, failure to provide appropriate first aid and medical care can have fatal consequences. Even if the injured individual survives, a lack of prompt and appropriate medical care can prolong the recovery process. For instance, if a person involved in a vehicle accident is experiencing severe bleeding and does not receive immediate first aid to stop the bleeding prior to the arrival of emergency medical services, they may experience significant blood loss, low blood pressure, and an increased risk of organ failure. This delays their recuperation and exposes them to moderate to severe repercussions. If, on the other hand, someone trained in first aid is able to stop the hemorrhaging effectively, the healing process can be accelerated.

Cost Savings
First aid is always intended to prolong a person's life, but it also provides additional benefits. A timely administration of first aid can reduce the likelihood of the injured individual contracting an infection, necessitating more extensive medical care, or experiencing a deterioration in their condition. Managing minor cuts, burns, and wounds correctly can substantially reduce the likelihood of the condition worsening. Additionally, administering first aid prevents situations from escalating. Although it may still be necessary to seek additional care at a hospital or from a physician, treatment costs can be reduced. By promptly treating minor injuries, extensive medical interventions and their associated costs can be avoided. Individuals with proper first aid training, particularly in the workplace, can save a substantial amount of money by addressing minor accidents immediately and preventing them from becoming more severe.

Comprehensive Emergency Preparedness
In addition to having a well-stocked first aid kit, it is crucial to be prepared for a variety of emergency situations. This involves risk assessment and planning, building a comprehensive emergency kit, and understanding disaster-specific preparedness strategies.

Risk Assessment and Planning:
- Identify Potential Hazards: Assess the risks specific to your region and lifestyle, such as natural disasters, accidents, or health emergencies.
- Create an Emergency Plan: Develop a plan detailing how to respond to different types of emergencies, including evacuation routes and communication strategies.

Building a Comprehensive Emergency Kit:
- Essential Items: Include food, water, shelter, and tools in addition to your first aid kit.
- Regular Updates: Periodically update your kit to ensure all items are in good condition and relevant to current risks.

Disaster-Specific Preparedness Strategies:
- Natural Disasters: Tailor your preparedness for events like earthquakes, floods, hurricanes, and wildfires.
- Health Emergencies: Prepare for pandemics and personal health crises with specific supplies and plans.

Survival Psychology and Crisis Management:
- Mental Preparedness: Understand the psychological aspects of surviving a disaster and develop resilience.
- Stress Management: Techniques to manage stress and maintain calm during emergencies.

Community Emergency Response Teams:
- Forming Teams: Learn how to form or join local community response teams.
- Training and Drills: Participate in regular training and drills to stay prepared.

Essential Components of a First Aid Kit
The contents of first aid kits vary greatly depending on their intended use. For instance, a family living in the city would require a slightly different assortment of supplies in their first aid kit than a family living on a farm. The following products are crucial components of a first aid kit:

- Triangular bandages
- Variable-thickness crepe bandages, also known as conforming or elastic crepe bandages
- An assortment of non-stick, non-adhesive applications in various sizes
- Gloves made from a disposable material other than latex (sizes medium and large), if possible
- Included are a protective covering, a notepad, and a pencil
- Plastic bags in an assortment of sizes
- Adhesive tape (2.5 cm wide - preferably a permeable adhesive such as Micropore)
- Resuscitation mask or face shield
- Dressing pads with a medium combination of both (9 x 20 cm)
- Dressing pads with a large combination of both (20 x 20 cm)
- Adhesive dressing strips (bandages)
- Medium gauze dressing (7.5 x 7.5 cm)
- Saline solution in four sterile containers (minimum 10 ml)
- Metal-bladed shears
- Tweezers (or pliers)

First Aid and Emergency Response
Understanding Basic First Aid:
- Initial Steps: Learn the basic steps to take when providing first aid.
- Critical Interventions: Identify situations that require immediate attention, such as CPR or stopping severe bleeding.

Emergency Response Planning:
- Roles and Responsibilities: Assign roles and responsibilities in your emergency plan to ensure everyone knows what to do.
- Communication Plans: Develop communication strategies to stay in touch with family and emergency services.

Essential First Aid Supplies:
- Stocking Up: Ensure you have sufficient first aid supplies to last through an emergency.
- Special Needs: Consider additional supplies for special needs, such as medications or medical equipment.

Maintaining a well-stocked first aid kit and being prepared for emergencies can save lives, reduce recovery time, and mitigate medical costs. Regular training and updating your knowledge and supplies are essential for effective first aid and emergency preparedness. Remember, a little preparation can make a significant difference in an emergency situation.

Chapter 2: Medicines That Are Contained Within First-Aid Kits

Pharmaceuticals should not be included in workplace first aid supplies, per the First Aid in the Workplace Code of Practice guidelines. First aid is intended to provide immediate medical care and fundamental life support to those who are injured or ill; however, the distribution of medications is typically outside the scope of first aid. It is strongly advised that narcotics are not kept in first aid kits.

If you or a member of your family retains pain relievers such as aspirin or paracetamol, it is essential to store them safely and out of the reach of children. It is essential to properly store your emergency medical supplies. Here are some recommendations:

- _Cool and Dry Location_: Place the first aid kit in a cool and dry location.
- _Accessibility_: Ensure that it is readily accessible and that the location is known by all family members.
- _Regular Checks_: Regularly examine the expiration dates of certain products, such as solutions, and replace any components that have expired.
- _Immediate Replacement_: If an item from the first aid case is used, it should be replaced immediately so that the kit remains complete.

Proper Storage and Handling of Medicines
Proper storage and handling of medicines are crucial to maintain their effectiveness and safety.
Storage Tips:
- _Temperature Control_: Store medicines in a cool, dry place to prevent degradation.
- _Childproofing_: Use childproof containers and store medicines out of reach of children.
- _Humidity Control_: Avoid storing medicines in humid places like bathrooms.
Handling Tips:
- _Check Expiry Dates_: Regularly check the expiration dates and replace expired medicines.
- _Proper Disposal_: Dispose of expired or unused medicines safely to avoid accidental ingestion or environmental harm.
- _Labeling:_ Clearly label all medicines with their name, dosage instructions, and expiration date.

Using Medicines Effectively
Knowing how to use medicines correctly is as important as having them on hand.
Dosage and Administration:
- _Read Labels:_ Always read the labels for dosage instructions and side effects.
- _Avoid Overmedication_: Follow recommended dosages to avoid adverse effects.
- _Awareness of Interactions_: Be aware of potential interactions between different medications.
Education and Training:
- _First Aid Courses_: Enroll in first aid courses to learn how to use medicines effectively in emergencies.
- _Books and Online Resources_: Study from reputable first aid manuals and online tutorials.
- _Regular Refreshers_: Periodically refresh your skills and knowledge to stay prepared.

Comprehensive Emergency Preparedness
In addition to knowing how to store and handle medicines, it is crucial to be prepared for a variety of emergency situations that may require medical intervention.
Risk Assessment and Planning:
- _Identify Potential Hazards_: Assess the risks specific to your region and lifestyle, such as natural disasters, accidents, or health emergencies.
- _Create an Emergency Plan_: Develop a plan detailing how to respond to different types of emergencies, including evacuation routes and communication strategies.
Building a Comprehensive Emergency Kit:
- _Essential Items_: Include food, water, shelter, and tools in addition to your first aid kit.
- _Regular Updates_: Periodically update your kit to ensure all items are in good condition and relevant to current risks.

Disaster-Specific Preparedness Strategies:
- *Natural Disasters*: Tailor your preparedness for events like earthquakes, floods, hurricanes, and wildfires.
- *Health Emergencies*: Prepare for pandemics and personal health crises with specific supplies and plans.

Survival Psychology and Crisis Management:
- *Mental Preparedness*: Understand the psychological aspects of surviving a disaster and develop resilience.
- *Stress Management*: Techniques to manage stress and maintain calm during emergencies.

Community Emergency Response Teams:
- *Forming Teams*: Learn how to form or join local community response teams.
- *Training and Drills*: Participate in regular training and drills to stay prepared.

First Aid and Emergency Response

Understanding basic first aid and emergency response is critical for effective disaster management.

Understanding Basic First Aid:
- *Initial Steps:* Learn the basic steps to take when providing first aid.
- *Critical Interventions*: Identify situations that require immediate attention, such as CPR or stopping severe bleeding.

Emergency Response Planning:
- *Roles and Responsibilities*: Assign roles and responsibilities in your emergency plan to ensure everyone knows what to do.
- *Communication Plans*: Develop communication strategies to stay in touch with family and emergency services.

Essential First Aid Supplies:
- *Stocking Up:* Ensure you have sufficient first aid supplies to last through an emergency.
- *Special Needs:* Consider additional supplies for special needs, such as medications or medical equipment.

Properly storing and handling medicines in your first aid kit, along with comprehensive emergency preparedness, ensures that you are ready to respond effectively to a variety of situations. Regular training and updating your knowledge and supplies are essential for effective first aid and emergency preparedness. Remember, a well-prepared individual can make a significant difference in an emergency situation.

Chapter 3: First Aid Equipment Described

There are various types of equipment in a first aid kit, each with its specific function. Here are some examples:

- _Adhesive Strip Dressings_: Thin gauze strips adhered to an adhesive backing, used to treat superficial skin lesions and abrasions. Commonly referred to as Band-Aids, it's essential to note that some individuals may be allergic to these dressings.
- _Non-Adherent Dressings_: Ideal for safeguarding burned or abraded skin, as they do not adhere to the wound.
- _Absorbent Pads:_ These thick pads, also known as bandages, are used to stop hemorrhaging and reduce the risk of infection on wounds. They come in various sizes to treat different wound sizes.
- _Elastic Bandages_: Used to apply pressure, secure dressings, reduce edema, and offer support.
- _Triangular Bandages_: Non-elastic and versatile, these can be used to create slings, secure splints, and restrict mobility.
- _Eye Wash Solution_: Used to remove debris from the eye, such as eyelashes, insects, pollen, and sand. If an object becomes lodged in the eye, seek immediate medical attention rather than attempting to remove it yourself.
- _Stop the Bleed Kits_: Contain traumatic wound supplies such as pressure bandages, gauze, tourniquets, and latex-free gloves for stopping hemorrhaging from severe injuries like gunshot wounds. Tourniquets are used to stem blood flow from severed or crushed extremities.
- _Compressed Gauze and Abdominal Dressings_: Used to apply pressure to deep wounds to stop bleeding and prevent infection.
- _Burn Treatment Supplies_: For extensive burns, sterile water, water-based gels, and sterile gauze dressings are used to relieve pain, prevent infection, and cool the affected area.
- _Bone Fracture Stabilization Materials_: Includes various bandages, tapes, splinting materials, elastic bandages, and first aid tape. For compound fractures, sterile gauze, absorbent bandages, and compress dressings are used when the bone breaks through the skin. Immediate medical attention is required for this type of injury.

Remember that it is essential to have the appropriate knowledge and training to operate the equipment. Consider enrolling in a first aid course to learn how to utilize the items in your first aid kit effectively.

Specific Uses of First Aid Supplies

- _Minor Wounds_: Adhesive bandages, butterfly bandages, antiseptics, gauze pads, first aid tape, and gauze rolls can be used to treat minor cuts and scrapes.
- _Burns:_ Burn sprays and burn gels, created with water, are used to treat minor burns and alleviate pain. Avoid using oil, butter, and petroleum-based ointments on burns.
- _Eye Irritation_: Sterile eye irrigation treatments (eye wash) can alleviate irritation caused by dust or debris. Use a disposable eyecup and eyewash bottle for cleaning the eye.
- _Sprains:_ A quick cold compress can help reduce swelling and pain from a sprained ankle, finger, or wrist. Some injuries may require the use of elastic compression items and splinting materials, such as tongue depressors or a formable aluminum splint.
- _Eye Injuries_: Any impairment to the eye necessitates the care of a qualified medical professional. Eye coverings are frequently used when the eye must be closed or protected from further injury. Do not remove anything from the eye that you did not bring in.

Skin Care and Minor Injuries

- _Sunburns and Rashes_: Treat sunburn with burn gel and poison ivy with medicated washes and balms. Insect bites rarely result in severe medical complications and are readily treated with antihistamines or bug wipes. Severe reactions, such as those causing respiratory difficulties or swelling, require medical attention.

Essential First Aid Supplies

The essential materials that should be included in every first aid kit:

- _Adhesive Bandage Tape_: Useful for treating minor wounds.
- _Instant Cold Pack_: Provides immediate cold treatment for sprains and muscle injuries.
- _Sterile Gauze Cloth:_ For treating minor wounds.

- *First-Aid Manual:* Pocket-sized with detailed instructions for managing medical emergencies.
- *Sterile Eye Pads*: For minor eye injuries.
- *Emergency Cream*: For treating wounds; relieves pain and promotes healing.
- *Gauze Bandage*: For treating minor wounds and burns.
- *Triangular Bandage*: To secure an arm splint or head wound dressing.
- *Medical Gloves*: Latex-free gloves protect against pathogens and hazardous fluids.
- *Scissors:* For trimming first aid tape, elastic bandages, gauze, and even clothing.
- *Combination Pad:* A sterile, absorbent dressing to control bleeding and protect large incisions.
- *Adhesive Bandages*: Latex-free bandages for minor cuts.
- *Elastic Bandage Roll*: Provides wound support and secures first aid dressings.
- *Hand Disinfectant Packets*: Contain antibacterial alcohol for use in the workplace.
- *CPR Face Mask:* Protects the rescuer from hazardous body fluids during CPR.
- *Antiseptic Towelettes:* For cleaning and disinfecting minor cuts and scratches.
- *Sterile Burn Dressings*: Soaked in gel to treat minor burns.
- *Eyewash Solution*: Removes dirt or debris from the eyes and skin.
- *Antibiotic Ointment*: Used to treat and prevent skin infections following minor burns, scrapes, and abrasions.

Immediate First Aid Following a Traffic Collision

The first four minutes following an automobile accident are crucial, as most fatalities result from a lack of oxygen due to airway obstruction. It is essential to begin restoring oxygen supplies immediately. The initial hour after an accident or traumatic event, known as "the golden hour," is critical for increasing survival rates and reducing injury severity with timely and proper first aid.

First aid is the assistance given to a person suffering from an unexpected illness or injury. The primary objectives are to save lives and prevent the situation from deteriorating further. Basic first aid can save lives in life-threatening situations.

Basic First Aid Kit Contents

Every first aid kit should include:
- Plasters of various dimensions and configurations
- Sterile gauze dressings in numerous sizes
- Crepe dressings
- Safety pins
- Disposable antiseptic gloves
- Tweezers
- Scissors
- Cleansing wet swabs
- Tape
- Digitally-displayed thermometer
- Skin rash creams and moisturizers
- Analgesic spray
- Antiseptic ointment
- Sterile wound water
- Fluids for eye washes

Keeping a well-stocked first aid kit and being prepared to use it can save lives and mitigate the severity of injuries. Regularly checking and updating the contents of your first aid kit ensures you are ready to handle minor and major emergencies effectively. Training in first aid techniques is also essential to maximize the effectiveness of the equipment and supplies in your kit.

Chapter 4: Creating an Emergency Preparedness Kit

Assessing Your Needs: Tailoring the Kit to Your Circumstances
Understanding Individual Needs:
- o *Family Size and Health:* Consider the number of family members and specific health needs, such as medications for chronic conditions, infant formula, or supplies for elderly family members.
- o *Regional Risks:* Identify common natural disasters in your area, such as earthquakes, hurricanes, floods, or wildfires, and tailor your kit to address these specific risks.
- o *Personal Preferences:* Include items that cater to personal dietary preferences, comfort, and special needs.

Creating a Plan:
- o *Communication Strategy:* Develop a family communication plan that includes contact information, meeting places, and evacuation routes.
- o *Inventory Checklist:* Maintain an updated inventory checklist to ensure all necessary items are included and in good condition.
- o *Regular Drills:* Conduct regular emergency drills to familiarize all family members with the kit and the emergency plan.

Water and Filtration: Staying Hydrated in Emergencies
Water Storage:
- o *Quantity:* Store at least one gallon of water per person per day for at least three days. Increase the quantity for larger families or longer emergencies.
- o *Containers:* Use food-grade water storage containers and ensure they are properly sealed and stored in a cool, dark place.

Water Filtration and Purification:
- o *Filtration Systems:* Include portable water filters, such as straw filters or pump filters, that can remove bacteria and protozoa.
- o *Purification Tablets:* Carry water purification tablets that can kill viruses and bacteria, making water safe to drink.
- o *Boiling Water:* Include a portable stove or the means to start a fire to boil water, which is an effective method for killing most pathogens.

Food Supplies: Choosing Long-lasting Nutritious Foods
Selecting Food Items:
- o *Non-Perishable Foods:* Choose foods with long shelf lives, such as canned goods, dried fruits, nuts, and freeze-dried meals.
- o *Nutritional Balance:* Ensure a balance of proteins, carbohydrates, and fats to maintain energy levels and health.
- o *Special Dietary Needs:* Include items that cater to dietary restrictions and preferences.

Storage and Rotation:
- o *Proper Storage:* Store food in a cool, dry place to extend shelf life and prevent spoilage.
- o *Rotation System:* Implement a rotation system to regularly use and replace food items, ensuring freshness and avoiding waste.

First Aid: Building a Comprehensive First Aid Kit
Essential Components:
- o *Basic Supplies:* Include adhesive bandages, gauze pads, antiseptic wipes, and medical tape.
- o *Medications:* Store over-the-counter pain relievers, antihistamines, and any prescription medications.
- o *Advanced Equipment:* Add items like a CPR mask, tourniquet, splint, and burn dressings for more serious injuries.

Training and Maintenance:
- o *First Aid Training:* Ensure all family members are trained in basic first aid and CPR.
- o *Regular Checks:* Inspect the kit regularly to replace expired items and replenish used supplies.

Shelter and Warmth: Preparing for Adverse Weather Conditions
Emergency Shelter:
- ○ *Tents and Tarps*: Include a lightweight, waterproof tent or tarps for creating a temporary shelter.
- ○ *Emergency Blankets*: Store space blankets that provide warmth and protection from the elements.

Clothing and Bedding:
- ○ *Weather-Appropriate Clothing*: Pack extra sets of clothing suitable for various weather conditions, including rain gear and thermal layers.
- ○ *Sleeping Bags*: Choose insulated sleeping bags rated for the lowest expected temperatures in your area.

Tools and Equipment: Versatile Gear for Various Challenges
Multi-Use Tools:
- ○ *Multi-Tool*: A multi-tool with functions such as pliers, knife, screwdriver, and can opener is essential.
- ○ *Duct Tape*: Versatile and strong, duct tape can be used for repairs, creating shelter, and securing items.

Fire and Lighting:
- ○ *Fire Starters*: Include waterproof matches, lighters, and fire-starting kits.
- ○ *Lighting*: Store flashlights with extra batteries, LED lanterns, and glow sticks for illumination.

Navigation and Communication:
- ○ *Maps and Compass*: Carry topographic maps of your area and a reliable compass.
- ○ *Whistle*: A loud whistle can be used for signaling and attracting attention.

Communication Devices: Staying Connected When It Matters Most
Essential Devices:
- ○ *Cell Phones and Chargers*: Keep cell phones fully charged and include solar chargers or power banks.
- ○ *Two-Way Radios*: For communication when cell service is unavailable, include two-way radios with extra batteries.
- ○ *Emergency Radio*: A hand-crank or battery-operated radio can provide important weather updates and emergency broadcasts.

Staying Informed:
- ○ *Local Alerts*: Sign up for local emergency alerts and notifications.
- ○ *Communication Plan*: Ensure all family members know how to use the communication devices and have a plan for checking in.

Personal Protection and Self-Defense: Ensuring Your Safety
Self-Defense Tools:
- ○ *Pepper Spray*: Carry pepper spray for personal protection against potential threats.
- ○ *Personal Alarm*: A loud personal alarm can deter attackers and attract attention.

Safety Measures:
- ○ *Training*: Consider taking self-defense classes to build confidence and skills.
- ○ *Legal Considerations*: Ensure that any self-defense tools carried are legal in your area and used responsibly.

Creating a comprehensive emergency preparedness kit tailored to your specific needs and circumstances is crucial for ensuring safety and survival in various emergencies. Regularly review and update your kit, conduct drills, and educate all family members on how to use the supplies and equipment effectively. Preparedness can significantly reduce the impact of disasters and provide peace of mind knowing you are ready for the unexpected.

MODULE Q: DEFENSE SYSTEM IN YOUR HOME

Chapter 1: Bugging Out or Hunker Down?

You may be wondering, "What the heck is he talking about?" before we get too far ahead of ourselves. Let's begin by defining the term. "Bugging out" refers to the act of packing one's belongings and leaving one's residence in order to travel elsewhere. This may or may not be associated with your belief that you will never return. People who are forced to leave a city due to a natural disaster, such as a hurricane or flood, are a common example of bugging out. They board their vehicles and depart. This is one of the reasons why FEMA and other organizations recommend having a Bug-out Bag (BOB) containing 72 hours' worth of supplies so that you can leave at any time.

The opposite of Hunker Down (or Bug In) is Bug Out. When you Bug-In, you remain in one location with your supplies to weather the impending storm or chaos. Therefore, the question "Will you Bug out or Hunker down?" is posed in preparedness circles, typically in the context of political, biological, or terrorist chaos. You must first ask yourself a series of questions to determine the best option for your circumstances. The questions are straightforward and center on the following topics:

- What triggers your internal "We need to leave" button?
- This applies to both where you are and where you intend to go.
- Are you physically able to leave and potentially walk the distance?
- Dependents: Children or elderly family members. Pets?
- What is the nature of the peril against which we intend to move?
- Destination: Where do you intend to go?

Your situation can have a significant impact on whether you decide to bug out or not, and you must determine when you will actually make the decision to go. What events would cause you to flee your home and go somewhere else if you were planning an economic collapse? How bad do you believe things would have to get before you made that decision? What if you're not near your home? You'll be more concerned about getting home in this instance. What will your family do while you wait for you to arrive? Is it mid-winter, and there's two feet of snow on the ground? Do you have the means to safeguard yourself and your loved ones?

Your health is also an important consideration. Are you physically capable of standing up, strapping a backpack on your back, walking out the door, and never coming back? Are you able to evacuate if necessary? Do you require medication that must be kept refrigerated or taken on a daily basis? You may not have an option in some cases; you will be forced to Bug-In and plan accordingly.

Your family members play a crucial role as well. Do you have young children who may not travel lengthy distances? Do your children still utilize diapers or have special requirements? Even healthy children under the age of ten would have difficulty surviving a Bug-Out scenario that lasted for an extended period of time and lacked stability. You may be expecting a child. Are there any animals that you would never abandon or transport?

Your location is also an important factor in the decision-making process. Are you in a metropolitan area or a rural region with nothing to see for miles? Do you live in a location that would allow you to survive if the power went out tomorrow? I'm not disputing whether or not it would be difficult, but could you cultivate a garden, or do you reside in a Chicago skyscraper? Would you have to venture outside the city with millions of other people? Where would you go in this situation?

The threat is another factor to consider. This may be the simplest question to answer, but given the specific threat, you will most likely have more than one answer. If a flood or natural disaster is imminent and you have ample notice, you may decide to evacuate. You might stay if we're discussing a viral outbreak or mutant zombie bikers from Mars. Has your city descended into anarchy with rioting, fires, and looting mobs?

Lastly, your destination is an important factor in the decision-making process. Where do you intend to go? Do you have a location to which you can take your survival kit? If you have time and the threat is a natural calamity such as a hurricane, you can probably remain with relatives for a few days. One of the initial considerations to make is whether you will prepare your belongings, load the car, and hit the road. What are your future objectives?

Considering the aforementioned criteria, I believe that Bugging In is the best option for the average person who has nowhere to go. You won't be able to walk in the forest, kill deer and squirrels, and live like a boss. This does not occur for the "average" person. For one thing, you won't be alone. There may be millions of others with you as well. I have thought long and hard about this topic, and I know that if my life circumstances were different, I would most likely have a different answer. As it stands, my vote is for Bugging In. I have all my supplies here, and we live in a relatively rural area. I'm not naive to believe we'd be isolated from the chaos, but I think we'd have a better chance here with some shelter instead of walking through the woods sleeping under a tarp. As much as I enjoy camping, a residence is a more secure location. Might that alter tomorrow? Certainly it could. I continually evaluate my situation, and when circumstances change, so do my plans. That's why you'll find valuable guidance later in the book on Bugging Out as well. This opening headpiece introduces the topic of this chapter: home defense. If your residence will be the designated place you stay during an emergency, as well as a possible shelter option, it is your responsibility to fortify and protect it as much as possible.

Additional Considerations: Designing a Layered Home Defense System

Whether you decide to Bug Out or Hunker Down, it's crucial to consider a layered home defense system. This involves creating multiple levels of security to protect yourself and your family from potential threats. Here are some key components of a layered defense system:

1. **Perimeter Security:**
   o   Install fences and gates to establish a clear boundary around your property.
   o   Use motion sensor lights and alarms to detect any movement near the perimeter.
   o   Consider planting thorny bushes or installing barbed wire to deter intruders.
2. **Home Security Measures:**
   o   Reinforce doors and windows with security bars, locks, and shatterproof glass.
   o   Install a comprehensive security system with cameras, alarms, and sensors.
   o   Use window film or shutters to prevent easy access through windows.
3. **Interior Security:**
   o   Designate safe rooms with reinforced doors and walls.
   o   Keep emergency supplies, including food, water, and first aid kits, in multiple secure locations.
   o   Develop an emergency escape plan with multiple routes and destinations.
4. **Self-Defense Training and Weapons:**
   o   Train in self-defense techniques and ensure all family members know basic skills.
   o   Store self-defense weapons, such as pepper spray, firearms, or tasers, in accessible but secure locations.
   o   Regularly practice using these weapons and ensure they are properly maintained.

By implementing a layered defense system, you can create a more secure environment whether you choose to stay in your home or evacuate. This comprehensive approach ensures that you are prepared for various scenarios and can protect your family effectively.

Chapter 2: Life-Saving Home Fortification Tips

In the world of prepping, we categorize the topics that people wish to acquire into a few major groups. Survival is the ultimate objective of prepping and survival, but the disciplines that sustain survival can be broken down into food, water, shelter, self-defense, and first aid. Despite the fact that there are numerous other branches, this is an overly simplistic view of priorities. Home fortification designs are one of the most crucial aspects of initial survival that we can discuss. As a parent of young children, it was challenging to determine which factor was most essential to me, but I knew that home security was close to the top. The possibility of someone breaking into my home and injuring a member of my family was more frightening than any imagined armed conflict with mutant undead biker gangs in a post-apocalyptic world. In addition to providing for the overall well-being of my family, my aim as a father was to keep them safe, as break-ins occur every day.

Multiple factors make the topic of home fortification complicated. First, there are no universally applicable solutions. I am able to assume that the majority of this book's consumers reside in the United States due to the similarity of our household situations. The majority of contemporary buildings in the United States have an exterior veneer of siding for aesthetic purposes rather than structural integrity. This is followed by plywood on 2 x 4 joists, and the interior is finished with drywall. To keep our home cool during the summer and heated during the winter, we insulate 6 to 8 inches of surface area with fiberglass. Large wooden or fiberglass windows and doors, typically filled with glass, are used to seal it off. While there are exceptions, it is likely that this applies to you.

This construction preference stands in striking contrast to other countries, where houses with much thicker walls made of cinder blocks or poured concrete are the norm. There may also be exterior "fences" consisting of 10-foot-tall concrete barriers and steel doors. In the United States, fences are typically between 4 and 5 feet tall and are readily scaled by children. This is based on the preponderance of residences in the United States. It's great if you have a fortified shelter. This chapter is not for you. However, for those of us in the United States (including myself) who reside in houses with relatively weak structures, there are inexpensive methods to increase our odds of keeping intruders out.

When I contemplate home defense, I always consider the accumulation of time. When I'm not home, I want an intruder to be unable to enter my residence. If I'm at home, I'd like to have enough time to retrieve a gun and get ready to defend myself. I do not consider any of the structures I have constructed or intend to construct to be impregnable fortresses able to contain an insurgent horde or gang. A dedicated force will enter or destroy your residence while you are still inside given sufficient time.

Certainly, we can make our homes harder to break into, and this is a simple procedure, but this will not transform your home into a medieval castle. All of the measures I take to increase our security are intended to alert me that an intruder is attempting to enter and, as an added benefit, give me time to respond. How I react to someone attempting to enter depends entirely on the threat I'm facing. Again, if possible, I would prefer not to resort to home defense. This is my plan if I am forced to abandon my home to save my or my family's lives.

The nature of the peril you face is an additional factor to consider for each of the home fortification strategies covered in this chapter. Most of us will defend our homes against break-ins or invasions. Our mission is to make it difficult or, in the best-case scenario, not worth the effort for a potential intruder to target our residence. In a situation of utter anarchy, when your neighborhood HOA doesn't care about your yard or when the situation has deteriorated to the point where you don't care, I will also provide ideas for home fortification. However, we will not elaborate on the possibility of a sniper attempting to kill you through your kitchen window. Although, in a grid-down world where you have sustenance and others are starving, this is a possibility.

Designed a Layered Home Defense System
When it comes to fortifying your home, a layered defense system is essential. This involves creating multiple levels of security to protect yourself and your family from potential threats. Here are some key components of a layered home defense system:
1. **Perimeter Security:**
   o Install fences and gates to establish a clear boundary around your property.
   o Use motion sensor lights and alarms to detect any movement near the perimeter.
   o Consider planting thorny bushes or installing barbed wire to deter intruders.
2. **Home Security Measures:**
   o Reinforce doors and windows with security bars, locks, and shatterproof glass.
   o Install a comprehensive security system with cameras, alarms, and sensors.

     o   Use window film or shutters to prevent easy access through windows.

3. **Interior Security:**
    o   Designate safe rooms with reinforced doors and walls.
    o   Keep emergency supplies, including food, water, and first aid kits, in multiple secure locations.
    o   Develop an emergency escape plan with multiple routes and destinations.

4. **Physical and Electronic Security Measures:**
    o   Use electronic security systems, such as surveillance cameras and alarm systems, to monitor and protect your property.
    o   Implement physical barriers like reinforced doors, window bars, and security gates to prevent unauthorized entry.

5. **Self-Defense Weapons and Training:**
    o   Train in self-defense techniques and ensure all family members know basic skills.
    o   Store self-defense weapons, such as pepper spray, firearms, or tasers, in accessible but secure locations.
    o   Regularly practice using these weapons and ensure they are properly maintained.

6. **Perimeter Alarms and Warning Systems:**
    o   Install perimeter alarms to alert you of any breaches.
    o   Use warning systems, such as sirens or loudspeakers, to deter intruders and alert neighbors.

7. **Safe Rooms and Emergency Escape Plans:**
    o   Create safe rooms with reinforced doors and walls where your family can seek refuge during an invasion.
    o   Develop emergency escape plans that include multiple routes and destinations.
    o   Conduct regular drills to ensure everyone knows how to respond in an emergency.

By implementing these measures, you can create a robust and comprehensive home defense system that protects you and your family from a wide range of potential threats. Remember, the goal is to buy time, deter intruders, and ensure that you have the resources and plans in place to respond effectively to any situation.

Chapter 3: Why Do We Have a Problem with Home Security?

Enhancing Home Security Measures

Throughout history, humans have always sought to protect themselves and their families, from caves to modern underground bunkers. The concept of safety has evolved with time, facing threats such as thieves, rioters, gangs, and individuals with malevolent intent. The ideal home should protect against various threats, but no house is entirely impregnable. Given enough time and motivation, any home can be breached. However, there are several measures an average prepper can take to improve their home's security, both now and in a post-SHTF scenario.

In the past, homes were built with security in mind, resembling fortresses. Today, however, homes are designed to be aesthetically pleasing, energy-efficient, and environmentally friendly, often at the expense of security. Modern homes often have large windows and decorative doors that are easy to breach. This shift has left us vulnerable, relying on the police or alarm systems and assuming we are safe.

Avoid Being Discovered Without Your Pants On

Addressing both the physical and psychological aspects of home security is essential. It is crucial to maintain situational awareness and remain vigilant for potential hazards, even while at home. Recognizing the vulnerabilities of your home and devising a plan to address them is a great first step. If you have the chance to build a home from scratch, incorporating security features like reinforced doors and metal window coverings from the start is ideal.

A Layered Home Defense System

Home defense should be approached in layers, starting with securing entry points. According to ADT, the most common entry points for burglars are front doors, first-floor windows, and back doors. Strengthening these areas should be a priority. Investing in a security camera system can act as both a deterrent and a warning system. While a security camera is helpful, the door itself remains a critical point of vulnerability. Steel doors provide better security than hollow core wooden doors. Replacing a door with a steel one can significantly enhance your home's security. Adding security measures to existing doors, like longer screws that reach deep into the framing, can also make a big difference.

Window Safety

Windows are a common entry point for intruders. Ensuring they are securely locked is the first step. Installing window film can fortify glass and delay break-ins. Products like 3M Safety and Security film can add up to two minutes of delay during an intrusion, giving you crucial time to react. Window security bars are another option, providing a physical barrier to keep intruders out. These are especially useful in high-density areas or ground-floor apartments. In extreme situations, like natural disasters, plywood can be used to secure windows, although it blocks your view and requires storage space.

Detecting Outdoor Presence with Motion Sensor Lights

Motion sensor lights can help detect and deter intruders. Ensure these lights are functional and positioned to cover key areas around your home. Dogs can also serve as an early warning system, detecting unusual activity with their keen senses.

Detecting People at the Property's Edge

Securing your property's perimeter is the first line of defense. Visual detection, such as keeping an eye on your surroundings, is often the most effective method. Fences can slow down potential intruders, giving you more time to react. In extreme cases, barbed wire can enhance fence security. Reinforcing doors with steel frames and using barricades can further protect your home.

Security Lighting, Motion Detectors, and Safe Rooms

Effective outdoor lighting deters intruders by illuminating your property. Consider using infrared lighting if you have night vision equipment to remain discreet. Motion detection systems provide early warning of any movement on your property, with options like Dakota Long Range Alert systems offering extensive coverage. Safe rooms or panic rooms provide a secure place to retreat during a home invasion. While adding a safe room to an existing home can be challenging, a reinforced walk-in closet or basement room can serve this purpose. These rooms should have sturdy walls, a secure door, and essential supplies like weapons, food, and water. Implementing these security measures can significantly enhance the safety of your home. Customize these strategies to suit your needs and circumstances, ensuring you and your family are well-protected against potential threats. Regularly assess and update your security measures to stay prepared for any situation.

NO GRID SURVIVAL PROJECTS BIBLE

Chapter 4: Securing Your Residence by Strengthening Doors

In modern homes, doors are frequently the weakest site of entry, making them a common target for burglars and intruders. Reinforcing your entrances is essential for enhancing the security of your home. Despite the availability of high-end armored doors with sophisticated features, they may be prohibitively expensive for the average homeowner. However, we can still implement the door reinforcement principles to improve security without breaking the bank.

Fundamentals of Door Reinforcement
Install High-Quality Deadbolts: All exterior doors should have high-quality deadbolts as a minimum security precaution. Avoid using small, vulnerable doorknob locks, as they are easily thwarted. Deadbolts provide increased resistance to compelled entry.

Invest in Durable Doors: Invest in the most durable door that you can afford. Consider materials and construction that can resist physical assault.

Secure Adjacent Windows: Windows located close to the door, particularly if they provide access to the securing mechanism, can compromise the security of the door. Consider removing these windows or securing them with anti-theft bars or security film.

Install Peepholes or Security Cameras: Install a peephole or security camera to check who is at your door without opening it, allowing you to maintain control of the situation.

Internal Fasteners and Hinges: Ensure that the fasteners and hinges are installed on the inside of the door. If they are on the exterior, an intruder could easily deconstruct the door by removing them.

Door Reinforcement Options
Door Reinforcements: Look for products such as "door reinforcements" or "door jamb armor" that can fortify weak areas in your door jamb. These steel panels offer increased durability and can withstand common kick-in attacks. They are relatively inexpensive (less than $75) and can be installed in less than an hour with simple instruments. The Amazon-sold Door Jamb Armor, for instance, has been tested against police battering weapons.

Second Deadbolt: Consider installing a second deadbolt, also known as a single-sided/single-cylinder deadbolt, for additional protection against lock picking and unexpected entry. This results in two deadbolts: one with a key that opens from the outside and one with no key face that can only be opened from the inside. When at home, locking both deadbolts provides added security.

Security Doors: Installing a security door, which is a robust storm or hurricane-type metal door with its own deadbolt and reinforcement, can add an additional layer of security. In addition to their outward-opening design, which makes them more difficult to breach, these doors typically have a metal frame that adds to their durability. Consider your specific circumstances, as the presence of a security door may attract unwanted attention or send unintended signals.

Crossbar or Door Jammer: A crossbar is a bar in the manner of the Middle Ages that runs across the inside of a door, making entry difficult. It can be improvised with simple materials or purchased as a modern iteration on Amazon, such as Bar-Ricade. A door jammer or security bar, which is inserted between the door knob and the floor to reinforce the door, is another option. For this purpose, the Buddy Bar is the recommended steel option. While not as robust as a permanent reinforcement, they offer greater resistance than a conventional deadbolt.

By taking these measures to reinforce your doors, you can significantly increase the security of your home. Keep in mind that no security measure is failsafe, but the objective is to deter potential intruders and buy time to respond appropriately.

Additional Considerations
Layered Home Defense System
Designing a layered home defense system means having multiple lines of defense to slow down or deter intruders before they reach your main living area. This can include:

- *Perimeter Security:* Fences, gates, and surveillance systems to detect and deter intruders at the property line.
- *Yard Security:* Motion sensor lights, security cameras, and clear sightlines to spot intruders early.
- *House Security:* Reinforced doors, secure windows, and internal alarms to stop or delay intruders.

Physical and Electronic Security Measures
Combining physical barriers with electronic monitoring creates a robust security setup:

- *Physical Security*: Reinforced doors, secure windows, fences, and gates.
- *Electronic Security*: Surveillance cameras, alarm systems, and motion detectors.

Self-Defense Weapons and Training
Having self-defense weapons and knowing how to use them is crucial:
- *Weapons:* Consider non-lethal options like pepper spray, stun guns, and tasers. Firearms should only be used if you are trained and legally allowed to carry them.
- *Training:* Take self-defense classes and practice regularly with any weapons you own.

Perimeter Alarms and Warning Systems
Early detection of intruders can give you crucial time to react:
- *Alarms:* Install perimeter alarms that alert you to intruders before they reach your home.
- *Warning Systems*: Consider using loud warning systems or automated lights to scare off potential intruders.

Safe Rooms and Emergency Escape Plans
In case of a breach, having a safe room and an emergency escape plan is essential:
- *Safe Room*: Designate a secure area in your home where family members can retreat. Reinforce the room and stock it with supplies.
- *Escape Plans*: Develop and practice emergency escape plans for various scenarios. Make sure all family members know the plan.

By integrating these elements into your home security strategy, you can create a comprehensive and effective defense system that enhances the safety and security of your residence.

Chapter 5: How to Develop Your Home Defense Strategy

A well-thought-out home defense strategy is essential for preserving yourself and your family in the event of an intruder. The following stages will assist you in developing an effective plan:

Designate a Safe Room

Designate a room in your residence that can serve as a safe space in the event of an intruder. It could be a reinforced basement or any chamber with a sturdy door, preferably with a metal frame, a sturdy handle, and a reinforced deadbolt. Consider replacing the room's windows with shatterproof glass or using shatterproof window film as a cost-effective alternative.

Boost Security Measures

Boost the security of your safe room by incorporating additional features. Install a distress alarm as an extension of your existing security system within the room. This enables you to contact the authorities even if your primary alarm is not activated. Consider installing a miniature camera outside the secure room to monitor the surrounding area and provide law enforcement with visual information. If you own firearms, install a gun safe in the safe room to ensure that only you have access to them.

Response Time

In the event of an intrusion, your response time is of the utmost importance. If you are alone, you should generally remain in your safe room, lock the door, and contact law enforcement promptly. If you possess a firearm, you should prepare it for self-defense in the event that the intruder endeavors to enter your room. Even if you do not possess a weapon, verbally inform the intruder that you are armed and self-defense trained. Position yourself in a defensive position from which you can clearly see the entrance and your surroundings.

Considerations for Dependents

If you have dependent children or other family members, you may need to modify your plan. In such circumstances, you may feel compelled to exit your safe room in order to protect your family. Consider the circumstances and make decisions accordingly. If you decide to relocate, be vigilant and prioritize everyone's safety.

Preparation and Practice

Preparation and practice are essential to the successful implementation of a home defense plan. Discuss and rehearse the plan with your family members or household occupants so that everyone understands their duties and what to do in the event of an intrusion.

Close-Quarter Defense Training

Close-quarters defense training is essential for defending your home during a home invasion, particularly if you own a firearm. Important considerations for your home invasion defense plan are as follows:

Practice Your Moves

Rehearse every move you intend to make during a home incursion. Ensure that your intended route is free of obstructions and hazards, particularly in low-light conditions.

Keep a Safe Near Your Bed

Keep a secure safe nearby and easily accessible. This enables you quick access to your firearm or other self-defense tools in the event of an emergency.

Reliable Light Source

Ensure that you have access to a dependable light source before conducting any residence searches. Despite the fact that some firearms may have attached flashlights, they are typically not ideal for undertaking exhaustive searches. Consider utilizing a hand-held flashlight with adequate illumination.

Family Involvement

Ensure that all family members are included in the home invasion defense strategy. Whenever possible, labor in two groups for greater efficiency. If your family is small, you should all participate in the exercise.

Consider Children's Age

Consider your children's age and their level of comprehension. If they are of age, they should be included in the plan. However, avoid providing small children with excessive information. If they are in danger, instruct them to conceal in a designated area and wait for you to retrieve them.

Evaluate the Situation

Once you have gathered your family, evaluate the situation and determine your next course of action. This could entail remaining put and fortifying your position, or moving to a nearby safe room without being detected. Avoid returning to the area from which you departed, as it may be unpredictable and hazardous.

Keep Your Cell Phone Fully Charged

Keep your cell phone fully charged on your bedside or within easy reach. This enables you to contact law enforcement swiftly if necessary.

Avoid Attempting a "Sweep"

Unless you are evacuating your family, it is generally unwise to attempt a "sweep" or search for intruders in your home. It can be extremely dangerous, and you never know what dangers lie around corners or in other parts of your home.

Additional Considerations for a Comprehensive Home Defense Strategy

Layered Home Defense System

Designing a layered home defense system involves having multiple lines of defense to slow down or deter intruders before they reach your main living area. This can include:

- *Perimeter Security:* Fences, gates, and surveillance systems to detect and deter intruders at the property line.
- *Yard Security:* Motion sensor lights, security cameras, and clear sightlines to spot intruders early.
- *House Security:* Reinforced doors, secure windows, and internal alarms to stop or delay intruders.

Physical and Electronic Security Measures

Combining physical barriers with electronic monitoring creates a robust security setup:

- *Physical Security:* Reinforced doors, secure windows, fences, and gates.
- *Electronic Security:* Surveillance cameras, alarm systems, and motion detectors.

Self-Defense Weapons and Training

Having self-defense weapons and knowing how to use them is crucial:

- *Weapons:* Consider non-lethal options like pepper spray, stun guns, and tasers. Firearms should only be used if you are trained and legally allowed to carry them.
- *Training:* Take self-defense classes and practice regularly with any weapons you own.

Perimeter Alarms and Warning Systems

Early detection of intruders can give you crucial time to react:

- *Alarms:* Install perimeter alarms that alert you to intruders before they reach your home.
- *Warning Systems:* Consider using loud warning systems or automated lights to scare off potential intruders.

Safe Rooms and Emergency Escape Plans

In case of a breach, having a safe room and an emergency escape plan is essential:

- *Safe Room:* Designate a secure area in your home where family members can retreat. Reinforce the room and stock it with supplies.
- *Escape Plans:* Develop and practice emergency escape plans for various scenarios. Make sure all family members know the plan.

MODULE R: CANNING & PRESERVING
Chapter 1: Harvest and Preservation Techniques

Importance of Timing Harvesting Correctly
Harvesting crops at the optimal times can significantly increase yield and quality. Timing is crucial for several reasons:
- *Increased Yield*: Harvesting crops at the right time can maximize yield. Waiting too long can result in overripe or spoiled produce, while harvesting too early can reduce yields.
- *Peak Quality*: Fruits and vegetables harvested at the optimal time have the best flavor, texture, and appearance. Produce harvested too soon or too late may be immature or overripe.
- *Extended Shelf Life:* Harvesting at the right time ensures that fruits and vegetables stay fresh longer. Properly timed harvesting can maintain the freshness of produce longer than if they were harvested too early or too late.
- *Nutritional Value:* Harvest timing can affect the nutritional value of crops. Delaying harvest too long may lead to nutrient loss, while harvesting too early can diminish quality.
- *Efficiency:* Harvesting at the optimal time improves overall efficiency, ensuring that produce is picked at its peak, minimizing waste and maximizing output.

By understanding and implementing optimal harvesting times, you can maximize the quantity, quality, and nutritional value of your crops while increasing overall productivity.

Managing and Storing Perishables
Proper handling and storage of fresh produce are essential to maintain its flavor, freshness, and safety. Here are some guidelines:
- *Washing:* Thoroughly wash produce before consumption. Use a brush and clean water to scrub hard vegetables like potatoes and beets.
- *Storage:* Store produce in an appropriate cool, dry place. Apples and potatoes can be stored in a cool, dark pantry, while lettuce and berries should be refrigerated.
- *Separation*: Keep ethylene-producing fruits like apples and bananas separate from other produce. Ethylene gas can speed up the ripening process and lead to spoilage.
- *Packaging:* Proper packaging helps maintain the freshness of fruits and vegetables. Use perforated bags or breathable containers to allow adequate air circulation.
- *Labeling:* Label produce with the purchase or harvest date. This helps track freshness and prioritize consumption using the first-in, first-out (FIFO) method.
- *Rotation:* Rotate produce to ensure the oldest items are used first, reducing food waste and ensuring perishable items are consumed before spoiling.
- *Handling:* Handle produce with care to prevent bruising, as bruised produce is more likely to spoil and become contaminated.
- *Inspection*: Discard any produce that shows signs of mold or slime immediately to prevent contamination and ensure food safety.

By following these guidelines, you can extend the shelf life of fresh produce, maintain its quality, and ensure it remains safe for consumption.

Preserving Methods for Fresh Produce
There are several methods to preserve the freshness of perishable foods:
- *Refrigeration:* Cooling food slows down the growth of microorganisms that cause spoilage. Perishable items like dairy products, meat, fruits, and vegetables should be refrigerated between 34 and 39 degrees Fahrenheit (1 and 4 degrees Celsius).
- *Freezing*: Freezing is a reliable method that preserves the flavor, nutritional value, and shelf life of food. Properly packaged frozen produce can last for several months.
- *Canning:* Canning involves heating food in sealed jars to create a seal and eliminate bacteria. This method is ideal for preserving fruits, vegetables, and stews and can extend shelf life for at least a year.
- *Pickling:* Preserving food in a mixture of vinegar, water, and spices. Pickling is effective for vegetables like cucumbers, beets, and carrots. The acidity of vinegar kills microorganisms and adds a distinctive sour flavor.

- *Drying:* Removing water from fresh produce extends its shelf life significantly. Dried foods are convenient for long-term storage and can be used as snacks or meal additions.
- *Fermentation*: Fermenting food using bacteria and yeasts preserves it and adds beneficial probiotics. Vegetables like cabbage, carrots, and cucumbers can be fermented.

By using these techniques, you can extend the storage life of fresh produce while preserving its flavor, nutritional value, and reducing food waste.

Guidelines for Product Preservation

Here are some tips for preserving food for later use:
- *Meal Planning*: Create a weekly menu and shopping list based on the ingredients you'll need. This helps prevent overbuying and reduces food waste.
- *Proper Storage*: Use airtight containers or bags for food storage. Keep dry goods in a cool, dry place and refrigerate produce and other perishables.
- *FIFO Method:* Follow the FIFO (first-in, first-out) method when restocking your pantry. Use the oldest items first to prevent them from spoiling.
- *Freezing Leftovers*: Freeze leftovers that won't be consumed within a few days to preserve their freshness for longer periods.
- *Canning and Drying*: Consider canning, pickling, or drying excess produce to extend its shelf life.
- *Expiration Dates*: Always check the expiration dates on packaged foods before purchasing or consuming them. Use perishables before they expire to save money and reduce waste.
- *Donation or Composting*: If you have surplus food, consider donating it to a food bank or composting it to reduce waste and benefit the environment.

Summary of Preserving Various Types of Produce

Here is a summary of methods for preserving different types of produce:
- *Fruits:* Can be canned, frozen, dried, or made into jams and jellies. Fruits like apples, peaches, and berries can also be used to make wine.
- *Vegetables:* Can be canned, frozen, pickled, or dried. Tomatoes and peppers, for example, can be roasted before canning in oil.
- *Herbs:* Can be dried or frozen for future use. Drying herbs is simple and allows them to be stored in airtight containers for up to a year.
- *Meat:* Can be smoked, dried, or canned. Canned meats like tuna, chicken, and beef can be stored for long periods and used as needed.
- *Fish:* Can be smoked, salted, or canned. Smoking fish, particularly salmon, is a popular and flavorful preservation method.
- *Dairy Products*: Can be preserved by canning or making cheese. Dairy products like milk and cream need to be pressure-canned to kill microorganisms.
- *Eggs:* Can be pickled or coated with mineral oil to seal the shell and prevent air and pathogens from entering, allowing long-term storage.
- *Nuts and Seeds:* Can be stored in a cool, dry place. Roasting nuts and seeds and storing them in airtight containers can also extend their shelf life.

Using these methods, you can preserve a variety of fruits and vegetables for later use when their raw form may not be readily available. Utilizing perishable foods before they spoil is a great way to save money and reduce food waste.

Chapter 2: Canning Techniques

Understanding the Basics of Canning
Canning is a food preservation method involving sealing and boiling food in jars to prevent spoilage. This technique can preserve various items, including fruits, vegetables, meats, and soups.

The Basics of Canning
Choose a Canning Method:
- *Water Bath Canning*: Suitable for high-acid foods like fruits and pickles.
- *Pressure Canning:* Required for low-acid foods like meats and vegetables.

Prepare Your Ingredients:
- Wash and prepare food as directed.
- Cut fruits and vegetables into uniform sizes.
- Remove any tough parts, such as seeds or pits.

Prepare Your Jars and Lids:
- Wash jars and lids in hot soapy water and rinse well.
- Sterilize jars by boiling them in water for 10 minutes.
- Warm up jars and lids before use.

Fill Your Jars:
- Use a funnel to pack prepared food into jars, leaving recommended headspace.
- Add acid (lemon juice or vinegar) for water bath canning if necessary.

Seal the Jars:
- Wipe the rims with a moist cloth to ensure a good seal.
- Place lids on the jars and screw the bands until finger-tight.

Process the Jars:
- Place jars in boiling water and process for the specified time.
- For pressure canning, follow the manufacturer's instructions for pressure, temperature, and time.

Cool and Store the Jars:
- Remove jars from the canner and place them on a cloth to cool.
- Check the seals once cooled to ensure they are secure.
- Label jars with contents and date, and store in a cool, dry area.

Equipment Needed for Canning
Essential Tools:
- *Canning Jars*: Sturdy, heat-resistant jars like Mason or Ball jars.
- *Metal Discs and Bands*: Used to seal the jars.
- *Large Pot*: For water bath or pressure canning.
- *Jar Lifter:* For safely removing jars from boiling water.
- *Canning Funnel:* For pouring hot liquids into jars.
- *Bubble Remover Tool:* To eliminate air bubbles from jars.
- *Magnetic Lid Lifter:* For handling lids safely.
- *Thermometer:* To maintain correct processing temperature.
- *Clean Rags and Towels*: For wiping jars, lids, and bands.

Canning Methods
Water Bath Canning:
- Suitable for high-acid foods.
- Process jars in boiling water for a specified time to form a vacuum seal.

Pressure Canning:
- Required for low-acid foods.
- Process jars at a specific pressure and temperature to kill bacteria and create a vacuum seal.

Preparing Fruits and Vegetables for Canning

Guidelines:

- Choose ripe produce and avoid damaged items.
- Wash produce under cold, running water.
- Prepare according to the specific requirements (e.g., removing stems, pits, seeds, or skins).
- Pack vegetables into clean jars, leaving recommended headspace.
- Add liquid and seasonings as specified.
- Remove air bubbles, wipe rims, and seal jars.
- Use the appropriate canning method (water bath or pressure canner).
- Cool jars undisturbed for 12-24 hours.
- Check seals; refrigerate and use any jars that did not seal properly within a few days.

Step-by-Step Guide for Canning

1. *Wash and Sterilize*: Clean jars, lids, and bands in boiling, soapy water. Keep them hot.
2. *Prepare the Recipe*: Follow the recipe precisely.
3. *Heat the Water:* Bring water in the canner to 180-200°F (82-93°C), enough to submerge the jars by at least an inch.
4. *Fill the Jars:* Use the canning funnel to fill jars with hot food, leaving headspace. Remove air bubbles and adjust headspace.
5. *Seal the Jars*: Place lids using the magnetic lid lifter and screw bands finger-tight.
6. *Process the Jars:* Use the jar lifter to place jars in the canner. Process for the specified time according to the recipe and altitude.
7. *Cool the Jars*: Remove jars with the jar lifter and cool undisturbed for 12-24 hours.
8. *Check the Seals*: Press the center of lids to ensure a tight seal. Refrigerate and use any jars with faulty seals promptly.
9. *Store the Jars:* Store sealed jars in a cool, dry area and consume within the recommended time.

Safety Precautions for Canning

Key Rules:

- Use trusted recipes from reliable sources like the USDA.
- Ensure all equipment is clean and in good working condition.
- Sterilize jars and lids before use.
- Use fresh, high-quality ingredients.
- Follow the recommended processing time and temperature.
- Choose the correct canning method based on the food.
- Allow jars to cool completely without disturbing them.
- Check seals after cooling and refrigerate any jars with faulty seals.
- Store canned goods in a cool, dry area.
- Regularly inspect canned goods for signs of spoilage and discard any compromised jars.

By adhering to these guidelines, you can ensure your canned foods are safe, high-quality, and enjoyable.

Chapter 3: Freezing Techniques

Understanding the Basics of Freezing

Freezing is a common method of food preservation that involves lowering the temperature of food to below freezing to halt the growth of bacteria and other microorganisms. Here are some key aspects of freezing:

- *Versatility:* Almost any type of food, including fresh or cooked produce, meat, poultry, fish, bread, and baked goods, can be frozen.
- *Preparation:* Clean, trim, and cut food into manageable portions. Blanching certain vegetables for a few minutes helps preserve their color, texture, and flavor. Before freezing, food should be rapidly chilled to room temperature or below.
- *Containers for Freezing*: Use plastic bags, plastic containers, and freezer-safe glass containers. Label containers with the date and contents and choose ones suitable for the type of food being frozen.
- *Freezing Temperature:* Maintain freezer temperatures below zero degrees Fahrenheit (-18 degrees Celsius) for safe and effective freezing.
- *Freezing Time*: Varies depending on the quantity and composition of the food. Generally, smaller items freeze faster than larger ones. Freeze food in a single layer before stacking to prevent freezer burn.
- *Proper Thawing Methods:* Thaw food in the refrigerator, under running water, or using the defrost function of a microwave to prevent bacterial growth.
- *Storage Duration*: Frozen food can be stored for several months or even up to a year, depending on the type of food and storage conditions. Discard any food that smells off or shows signs of freezer burn to ensure safety.

By following these guidelines, you can be confident that frozen food will remain safe, high-quality, and flavorful when thawed.

Freezing Equipment and Supplies

To successfully freeze food, you will need the following equipment and supplies:

- *Freezer:* Essential for storing frozen food. The ideal temperature for a freezer is zero degrees Fahrenheit (-18 degrees Celsius).
- *Freezer-Safe Containers*: Use containers or bags specifically designed for freezing and suitable for the type of food being frozen. These containers should provide a tight seal to prevent freezer burn and leaks. Common options include plastic bags, plastic containers, and glass containers.
- *Labels and Markers:* Label each container with the contents and freezing date using a waterproof marker to prevent smudging.
- *Cutting Board and Knife*: Necessary for preparing food for freezing.
- *Wrapping Materials*: Use plastic wrap or aluminum foil to tightly wrap perishables before placing them in the freezer.
- *Vacuum Sealer:* Helps remove air from containers, creating a tight seal and preventing freezer burn.
- *Ice Cube Trays:* Can be used to freeze individual servings of herbs, sauces, or broth for future use.
- *Freezer Thermometer*: Allows you to monitor and maintain the temperature inside the freezer at or below zero degrees Fahrenheit (-18 degrees Celsius).
- *Clean Linens and Towels*: Useful for drying food and wiping containers before freezing.

With the right equipment and supplies, you can ensure successful freezing and long-term preservation of food, resulting in safe, high-quality, and delicious frozen meals.

Step-by-Step Guide for Freezing

Follow these step-by-step instructions for freezing food:

1. *Select Fresh Ingredients*: Choose the best, freshest ingredients for freezing.
2. *Prepare the Food*: Clean, trim, and cut the food into manageable portions.
3. *Blanch Vegetables*: For vegetables, blanch them in boiling water for 1-3 minutes to preserve their color and texture. After blanching, cool the vegetables in an ice bath or under cold running water.
4. *Dry Thoroughly*: Drain the food and use paper towels to thoroughly dry it.

5. *Pack the Food*: Pack the food in freezer-safe bags or containers with airtight lids, leaving room for expansion as the food freezes.
6. *Label the Containers*: Label the containers or bags with the contents and freezing date.
7. *Freeze in a Single Layer:* Freeze the containers or bags in a single layer before stacking to prevent freezer burn.
8. *Wrap Meats Securely*: For meats, securely wrap them in plastic wrap or aluminum foil before placing them in the freezer to prevent freezer burn.
9. *Use a Vacuum Sealer*: Use a vacuum sealer to remove air from containers and create a tight seal, preventing freezer burn.
10. *Freeze Individual Servings:* Freeze individual servings of herbs, sauces, or broth in ice cube trays.
11. *Thaw Safely*: When thawing frozen food, do so safely in the refrigerator, under running water, or using the defrost function of a microwave.

By following these steps, you can ensure successful freezing and long-term preservation of food. Your frozen meals will be safe, high-quality, and flavorful when thawed.

Tips for Freezing Different Types of Produce
Here are some tips for freezing various fruits and vegetables:
- **Berries:** Wash and drain the berries, then spread them in a single layer on a baking sheet and freeze until solid. Transfer the frozen berries to freezer-safe containers or bags, removing as much air as possible.
- **Apples:** Core, slice, or chop the apples into bite-sized pieces. Sprinkle them with lemon juice to prevent browning before placing them in freezer-safe bags or containers.
- **Greens:** Blanch dark greens like kale or spinach for 2 to 3 minutes, then drain and cool them before storing in freezer-safe bags or containers.
- **Corn:** Blanch the corn cob in boiling water for 4 to 6 minutes, then cool it. Remove the kernels from the cob and store them in freezer-safe containers or bags.
- **Peppers:** Clean and dice the peppers to your desired size. Blanch them for 2 to 3 minutes, then cool and store in airtight containers or bags.
- **Tomatoes:** Wash and core the tomatoes, then blanch them for 30-60 seconds. Peel off the skins and cool the tomatoes before storing them in the freezer.
- **Potatoes:** Peel and dice the potatoes, then blanch them for 2 to 3 minutes. Once cooled, place the potatoes in freezer-safe containers or bags.
- **Bananas:** Cut the bananas into pieces, peel them, and mix them with lemon juice to prevent browning. Pack the bananas in freezer-safe containers or bags.
- **Citrus Fruits:** Juice the fruits and freeze the juice in ice cube trays. Alternatively, zest the fruits and store the zest separately in the freezer for future use.

When freezing produce, it is important to follow recommended storage durations and temperatures and use fresh, high-quality ingredients. Proper planning and execution of freezing techniques will ensure successful preservation of food.

Troubleshooting Common Freezing Problems
Here are solutions to some commonly encountered freezing issues:
- **Freezer Burn:** To prevent freezer burn, use freezer-safe containers or bags that seal tightly, remove as much air as possible, and store the food in the deepest area of the freezer.
- **Ice Crystals:** Rapid freezing and minimizing temperature variations help prevent the formation of ice crystals. Freeze food as quickly as possible and avoid frequently opening the freezer door.
- **Discoloration:** Discoloration can occur due to exposure to air during freezing. Use freezer-safe containers or bags and remove as much air as possible to minimize discoloration.
- **Freezing in Clumps:** To prevent food from freezing together in clumps, freeze it in a single layer on a baking sheet before transferring to freezer-safe containers or bags.
- **Flavor Deterioration:** Some herbs and spices may lose flavor when frozen. Freeze them in ice cube trays or smaller containers and use them within a few months for optimal flavor retention.

By addressing these common freezing issues, you can prevent problems and ensure that your frozen foods maintain their quality, safety, and flavor. When freezing food, it is essential to prioritize quality and safety. By following recommended storage durations, temperatures, and best practices, you can avoid common freezing problems and ensure that your frozen meals are safe, high-quality, and delicious.

Chapter 4: PROJECT: Building a Simple Dehydrator at Home

Food dehydration is a simple and effective method of preserving food by removing moisture, which inhibits the growth of bacteria, yeast, and molds. Building a dehydrator at home allows you to create a cost-effective, eco-friendly solution for preserving fruits, vegetables, and herbs.

Materials and Tools Needed
To build a simple dehydrator at home, you will need the following materials and tools:
Materials:
- **Wooden Frame:** Plywood or repurposed wooden pallets
- **Mesh Screens:** Food-grade stainless steel or nylon mesh
- **Trays:** Wooden or metal trays to hold the food
- **Hinges and Latches:** For the dehydrator door
- **Thermometer:** To monitor the internal temperature
- **Solar Panel (optional):** For a solar-powered dehydrator
- **Reflective Material:** Aluminum foil or Mylar for insulation

Tools:
- **Saw:** For cutting wood to size
- **Drill:** For making holes and securing screws
- **Screwdriver:** For assembling parts
- **Measuring Tape:** For accurate measurements
- **Staple Gun:** For attaching mesh screens
- **Sandpaper:** For smoothing wooden surfaces

Step-by-Step Guide to Building the Dehydrator
Step 1: Build the Frame
- **Cut the Wood:** Measure and cut the plywood or wooden pallets to create the frame. You will need four pieces for the sides and additional pieces for the top, bottom, and back.
- **Assemble the Frame:** Use screws and a drill to assemble the sides, top, bottom, and back of the frame. Ensure the structure is sturdy and stable.

Step 2: Install the Mesh Screens
- **Cut the Mesh:** Cut the mesh screens to fit the openings of the trays.
- **Attach the Mesh:** Use a staple gun to secure the mesh to the trays, ensuring it is tight and secure.

Step 3: Create the Trays
- **Measure and Cut:** Measure and cut the wood to create the trays that will slide into the frame.
- **Assemble the Trays:** Use screws to assemble the trays and ensure they fit snugly into the frame.

Step 4: Install the Door
- **Cut the Door:** Measure and cut a piece of wood for the door.
- **Attach Hinges:** Attach hinges to the door and the frame, ensuring the door opens and closes smoothly.
- **Install Latches:** Install latches to keep the door securely closed.

Step 5: Add Reflective Material (Optional)
- **Line the Interior:** Line the interior of the dehydrator with reflective material such as aluminum foil or Mylar to improve heat retention.

Step 6: Add a Thermometer
- **Install the Thermometer:** Place a thermometer inside the dehydrator to monitor the internal temperature.

Step 7: Optional Solar Panel Installation
- **Install Solar Panel:** If using a solar panel, install it on the top of the dehydrator to harness solar energy for drying food.

Using the Dehydrator
Preparation:
- **Slice Food:** Slice fruits, vegetables, and herbs evenly to ensure uniform drying.
- **Arrange on Trays:** Place the sliced food on the trays in a single layer, ensuring they do not overlap.

Drying Process:
- **Load the Trays:** Slide the trays into the dehydrator.
- **Monitor Temperature:** Keep the internal temperature between 130°F and 140°F (54°C to 60°C) for optimal drying.
- **Check Regularly:** Rotate the trays periodically and check the food for dryness.

Storage:
- **Cool and Store:** Once dried, let the food cool completely before storing it in airtight containers.
- **Label and Date:** Label and date the containers for easy identification.

Fermentation: A Natural Preservation Method
Introduction to Fermentation: Fermentation is an ancient preservation method that uses beneficial bacteria, yeasts, or molds to convert sugars and starches into acids, gases, or alcohol. This process not only extends the shelf life of food but also enhances its flavor and nutritional value.

Fermented Foods and Their Health Benefits
Common Fermented Foods:
- **Sauerkraut:** Fermented cabbage rich in probiotics and vitamins.
- **Kimchi:** A spicy Korean dish made from fermented vegetables.
- **Kombucha:** A fermented tea beverage known for its probiotic content.
- **Yogurt:** Fermented milk with beneficial bacteria.
- **Pickles:** Cucumbers fermented in a brine solution.

Health Benefits:
- **Digestive Health:** Probiotics in fermented foods support gut health and improve digestion.
- **Enhanced Nutrient Absorption:** Fermentation can increase the bioavailability of nutrients.
- **Immune Support:** The beneficial bacteria in fermented foods can boost the immune system.
- **Mental Health:** Probiotics have been linked to improved mental health and reduced symptoms of anxiety and depression.

Equipment and Supplies for Fermentation
Basic Equipment:
- **Fermentation Jars:** Glass jars with airlocks or lids to hold the fermenting food.
- **Weights:** To keep the food submerged in the brine.
- **Mixing Bowls:** For preparing ingredients.
- **Cutting Board and Knife:** For chopping vegetables.

Optional Equipment:
- **Fermentation Crock:** A larger vessel for fermenting larger batches.
- **Thermometer:** To monitor the temperature during fermentation.
- **pH Strips:** To check the acidity level of the ferment.

Supplies:
- **Salt:** Non-iodized salt for making brine.
- **Water:** Filtered water free from chlorine and other chemicals.
- **Spices and Herbs:** To add flavor to the ferment.
- **Starter Cultures (Optional):** Such as whey, kefir grains, or specific bacterial cultures.

Step-by-Step Guide to Fermenting Vegetables
Preparation:
- **Clean and Sterilize:** Ensure all equipment and jars are clean and sterilized.
- **Chop Vegetables:** Chop or shred vegetables evenly.

Fermentation Process:
- **Make Brine:** Dissolve salt in water to create a brine solution.

- **Pack Vegetables:** Pack the vegetables tightly into the fermentation jars.
- **Add Brine:** Pour the brine over the vegetables, ensuring they are fully submerged.
- **Weigh Down:** Use weights to keep the vegetables submerged in the brine.
- **Seal and Store:** Seal the jars with airlocks or lids and store them in a cool, dark place.

Monitoring and Finishing:

- **Monitor Fermentation:** Check the ferment daily to ensure the vegetables remain submerged and to release any built-up gases.
- **Taste Test:** Start tasting the vegetables after a few days. The fermentation process can take anywhere from a few days to several weeks, depending on the temperature and desired flavor.
- **Store:** Once fermented to your liking, transfer the jars to the refrigerator to slow down the fermentation process.

Building a simple dehydrator at home and learning about fermentation are valuable skills for food preservation. These methods allow you to extend the shelf life of fresh produce, enhance flavors, and boost the nutritional value of your food. By understanding and utilizing these techniques, you can enjoy the benefits of preserved foods year-round.

Chapter 5: PROJECT: Building a Solar Dehydrator

The objective of this project is to build a solar dehydrator, a sustainable and energy-efficient way to preserve fruits, vegetables, and herbs. Utilizing solar energy to remove moisture from food, a solar dehydrator can help reduce waste, save money, and ensure a supply of nutritious, dried foods throughout the year.

Gathering Materials and Tools
Before starting the project, gather all necessary materials and tools to ensure a smooth construction process.
Materials:
- **Wood:** Plywood or repurposed wooden pallets for the frame and trays
- **Clear Acrylic or Glass:** For the solar collector cover
- **Mesh Screens:** Food-grade stainless steel or nylon mesh for the trays
- **Hinges and Latches:** For the doors and access panels
- **Insulation Material:** Such as foam board or reflective insulation
- **Thermometer:** To monitor the internal temperature
- **Paint:** Non-toxic black paint to absorb heat
- **Weather Stripping:** To seal the doors and prevent heat loss

Tools:
- **Saw:** For cutting wood to size
- **Drill:** For making holes and securing screws
- **Screwdriver:** For assembling parts
- **Measuring Tape:** For accurate measurements
- **Staple Gun:** For attaching mesh screens
- **Sandpaper:** For smoothing wooden surfaces
- **Paintbrush:** For applying paint

Designing the Solar Dehydrator
A well-designed solar dehydrator efficiently captures and retains heat to effectively dry food. The design includes the dehydration chamber and the solar collector.
Dehydration Chamber:
- **Size and Shape:** Decide on the dimensions based on the amount of food you plan to dry. A typical size is about 3 feet tall, 2 feet wide, and 1.5 feet deep.
- **Ventilation:** Include vents at the top and bottom to allow air circulation. The warm air will rise, drawing moisture out of the food and exiting through the top vents.

Solar Collector:
- **Placement:** Position the solar collector at an angle to maximize exposure to the sun. A 30-45 degree angle is optimal for most locations.
- **Absorber Plate:** Use a metal sheet painted black to absorb and transfer heat to the dehydration chamber.

Constructing the Dehydration Chamber
The dehydration chamber is where the food will be placed for drying.
Step-by-Step Construction:
- **Build the Frame:** Cut and assemble the wood to create a sturdy frame for the chamber.
- **Attach the Sides:** Secure the plywood or wooden pallets to the frame to form the walls, back, and bottom of the chamber.
- **Install the Trays:** Create trays using wooden frames and mesh screens. Ensure they slide easily into the chamber.
- **Add Ventilation:** Cut holes for the vents at the top and bottom of the chamber. Cover the vents with mesh to prevent insects from entering.

Setting Up the Solar Collector
The solar collector is essential for capturing solar energy and converting it into heat.

Step-by-Step Setup:
- **Construct the Frame:** Build a frame for the solar collector that will fit securely on top of the dehydration chamber.
- **Install the Absorber Plate:** Place the black-painted metal sheet inside the collector frame.
- **Cover the Collector:** Attach the clear acrylic or glass cover to the top of the collector frame to create a greenhouse effect, trapping heat inside.

Assembling the Solar Dehydrator
Combine the dehydration chamber and the solar collector to complete the solar dehydrator.
Step-by-Step Assembly:
- **Attach the Solar Collector:** Secure the solar collector to the top of the dehydration chamber, ensuring it is airtight to prevent heat loss.
- **Seal the Joints:** Use weather stripping to seal any gaps between the solar collector and the dehydration chamber.
- **Install the Door:** Attach the door to the front of the dehydration chamber using hinges and a latch. Ensure it opens and closes smoothly and seals tightly.

Testing the Efficiency of the Solar Dehydrator
Once assembled, test the solar dehydrator to ensure it works effectively.
Testing Steps:
- **Place the Thermometer:** Install a thermometer inside the dehydration chamber to monitor the temperature.
- **Load Test Food:** Place a small batch of sliced fruits or vegetables on the trays.
- **Position in Sunlight:** Place the solar dehydrator in a sunny location and monitor the internal temperature. Aim for a consistent temperature between 130°F and 140°F (54°C to 60°C).
- **Check Drying Time:** Note the time it takes for the test food to dry completely. Adjust the design or placement if necessary to improve efficiency.

Tips for Effective Dehydration and Maintenance
Maintaining your solar dehydrator and using it effectively ensures optimal performance and longevity.
Effective Dehydration Tips:
- **Slice Food Evenly:** Cut fruits and vegetables into uniform slices to ensure even drying.
- **Avoid Overlapping:** Arrange food in a single layer on the trays without overlapping.
- **Rotate Trays:** Periodically rotate the trays to ensure consistent drying throughout.
- **Monitor Progress:** Check the food regularly and remove it once it reaches the desired dryness.

Maintenance Tips:
- **Regular Cleaning:** Clean the trays and interior of the dehydrator after each use to prevent mold and bacteria buildup.
- **Inspect for Damage:** Regularly check the solar collector and dehydration chamber for any damage or wear and repair as needed.
- **Store Properly:** Store the dehydrator in a dry, sheltered location when not in use to protect it from the elements.

Building a solar dehydrator is a rewarding project that promotes sustainability and self-sufficiency. By harnessing the power of the sun, you can preserve a variety of foods, reducing waste and ensuring a steady supply of nutritious, dried foods year-round. With proper maintenance and effective use, your homemade solar dehydrator will serve you well for many seasons to come.

MODULE 5: HOW TO START A BUSINESS GROWING VEGETABLES

Chapter 1 - Market Research for Your Vegetable Business

Starting a vegetable business can be profitable for those passionate about healthy food and sustainable farming. However, conducting thorough market research before you begin is crucial to identify your target customers, understand your competitors, and assess the demand for your products. This chapter discusses the importance of market research and how to effectively conduct it for a vegetable business.

Importance of Market Research
Market research is vital for the success of any business, including those in the vegetable industry. It helps you:
- Identify your target market
- Understand customer preferences and behaviors
- Analyze your competition
- Discover market trends
- Make informed business decisions

Finding Your Target Market
Knowing your target market helps you create effective marketing campaigns, products, and sales strategies. By understanding your customers' demographics, psychographics, and dietary habits, you can better tailor your offerings to meet their needs and preferences.

Steps to Identify Your Target Audience:
1. *Define Your Target Audience:* Determine who you want to buy your produce. Are you targeting busy families, upscale restaurants, or health-conscious consumers?
2. *Gather Demographic Data:* Collect information on age, gender, income level, and education to understand your target audience better.
3. *Analyze Psychographic Data:* Learn about your clients' personality traits, values, attitudes, and interests to produce goods and marketing materials that appeal to them.
4. *Understand Customer Behavior:* Identify what your customers usually purchase, their buying frequency, and their motivations for buying. This helps you create products that meet their needs.

Methods for Gathering Data:
- *Surveys and Focus Groups:* Directly ask your target market about their preferences and opinions.
- *Online Tools:* Use tools like Google Analytics to track website traffic and customer behavior.
- *Market Reports:* Study market statistics and reports to spot trends and opportunities in your sector.

Analyzing and Interpreting Data: Once you have collected data, analyze and interpret it to make informed decisions. For example, if busy families make up most of your target market, focus on convenient, pre-packaged vegetable products. If health-conscious consumers are your target, highlight the nutritional benefits of your vegetables in your marketing communications.

Understanding Your Competitors
Understanding the competitive landscape is crucial when starting a vegetable business. By knowing your competitors, you can identify potential obstacles and opportunities and develop strategies to differentiate your products.

Types of Competitors:
- *Direct Competitors:* Businesses that offer similar goods and target the same clients. For example, if you sell organic tomatoes, other companies selling organic tomatoes are your direct competitors.
- *Indirect Competitors:* Businesses that target the same client group but offer different products. For example, a farmer's market selling various products, including organic tomatoes, would be an indirect competitor.

Conducting Competitive Analysis:
1. *Research Your Sector:* Investigate your industry and analyze the strengths and weaknesses of other companies.
2. *Evaluate Competitors' Products, Prices, and Marketing Strategies:* Identify what works and what doesn't in your business.

3. _Create a Unique Selling Proposition (USP):_ Use the information to differentiate your product from the competition.

Utilizing Online Resources:
- _Search Engines and Social Media:_ Perform online searches to learn about your competitors, the products they sell, and their marketing techniques. Observe how they interact with their audience and the type of content they post.

Analyzing Competitors' Strengths and Weaknesses: Identify your competitors' strengths and weaknesses to create strategies that emphasize your advantages while addressing theirs. For example, if your competitors sell organic tomatoes at a higher price, you might focus on offering a lower price point while maintaining quality.

Learning What Your Customers Want and Need
Market research is essential for understanding your clients' tastes, needs, and purchasing patterns. By collecting data on their preferences and behaviors, you can produce products that appeal to your target market.

Techniques to Determine Customer Preferences:
- _Surveys and Focus Groups:_ Directly question your target market about their preferences and opinions.
- _Online Behavior Analysis:_ Use tools like Google Analytics to monitor how visitors interact with your website and the search terms they use.
- _Social Media Monitoring:_ Observe social media conversations about your product or industry to spot patterns and learn what your customers say about your business.

Using Customer Insights to Create Value: Use the collected data to create products that meet your consumers' demands and exceed their expectations. Focus on providing value to your clients to develop a loyal customer base and set yourself apart from the competition.

Finding Trends
Keeping up with the latest trends and market changes is crucial in the ever-changing business environment. By performing market analysis, you can discover new trends that may impact your vegetable business's future.

Methods to Spot Trends:
- _Industry Reports and Publications:_ Analyze industry studies and publications that focus on the agricultural sector to gain insights into market trends, customer behavior, and the latest advancements.
- _Trade Shows and Industry Meetings:_ Attend these events to network with stakeholders and learn about the newest trends.
- _Online Forums and Social Media Groups:_ Monitor discussions in communities dedicated to the vegetable industry to learn about current trends and innovations.

Current Trends in the Vegetable Industry:
1. _Increased Demand for Organic and Locally Farmed Produce:_ Customers are willing to pay more for locally sourced, responsibly grown goods.
2. _Popularity of Alternative Growing Techniques:_ Hydroponics and vertical farming allow growers to cultivate vegetables in limited spaces with less water and soil, resulting in a more productive and environmentally friendly method.

Staying Ahead of Trends: By keeping up with these trends, you can make informed business decisions and set up your vegetable business for long-term success. Stay updated on industry advancements to meet changing consumer demands and remain competitive.

Chapter 2 - Developing a Business Plan

To start a vegetable business, creating a comprehensive business plan is crucial. A business plan outlines your goals, strategies, and the tools needed to ensure your business's success. Let's discuss the essential components of a business plan for a vegetable business and how to develop a plan that will guide you toward achieving your objectives.

Importance of a Business Plan
Creating a business plan is important for several reasons:
Clarity:
- *Define Objectives*: A business plan helps clarify your business objectives and goals. It forces you to think through the details and identify potential challenges and opportunities.

Strategy:
- *Roadmap to Success:* A business plan outlines the steps you need to take to reach your goals, helping you prioritize actions and allocate resources effectively.

Funding:
- *Attract Investors*: Lenders and investors often require a business plan before providing funding. A well-prepared business plan demonstrates your commitment and ability to succeed.

Components of a Business Plan
Executive Summary:
- *Overview:* The executive summary provides a concise overview of your business plan. It should explain your business concept, objectives, and strategies to achieve them. Although it appears first, it is often written last to summarize the entire plan effectively.

Business Description:
- *Detailed Overview:* This section gives a detailed description of your business, including the products or services you offer, your target market, and your unique value proposition. Explain what makes your business stand out from competitors.

Market Analysis:
- *Target Market*: Analyze your target market, including demographics, trends, and opportunities. Identify your customers' needs and preferences, and explain how your business will meet them.
- *Competitive Analysis:* Evaluate your competitors, highlighting their strengths and weaknesses. Describe how your business will compete effectively in the market.

Marketing and Sales Strategy:
- *Marketing Plan*: Outline how you plan to market your products. Include information about your target audience, pricing strategy, distribution methods, and promotional activities.
- *Sales Strategy*: Detail your sales approach, including sales tactics, customer service policies, and sales goals. Explain how you will attract and retain customers.

Operations Plan:
- *Daily Operations*: Describe how you will run your business daily. Include information about production processes, inventory management, and staffing requirements.
- *Supply Chain:* Outline your supply chain, from sourcing raw materials to delivering finished products to customers. Highlight any unique aspects of your operations that give you a competitive edge.

Financial Plan:
- *Financial Projections*: Provide detailed financial projections, including income statements, balance sheets, and cash flow statements. These projections should cover at least the first three to five years of your business.
- *Funding Requirements:* If you need funding, specify how much you need and how you will use it. Include a repayment plan and a timeline for reaching financial milestones.

Risk Management Plan:
- *Identify Risks*: List potential risks that could affect your business, such as market fluctuations, supply chain disruptions, or regulatory changes.
- *Mitigation Strategies*: Describe how you plan to mitigate these risks. This could include diversification, contingency planning, or securing insurance.

Steps to Developing a Business Plan

1. Research and Analysis:
- Conduct thorough research on your market, industry trends, and competitors. Gather data to support your assumptions and projections.

2. Define Your Vision:
- Clarify your business vision, mission, and core values. These will guide your decision-making and help align your team with your goals.

3. Set SMART Goals:
- Establish specific, measurable, achievable, relevant, and time-bound (SMART) goals. These provide clear targets for your business to aim for.

4. Develop Strategies:
- Outline strategies for marketing, sales, operations, and finance. Ensure these strategies are aligned with your goals and supported by your research.

5. Write the Plan:
- Organize your information into a clear, structured document. Use headings and subheadings to make it easy to navigate.

6. Review and Revise:
- Review your business plan thoroughly, and seek feedback from trusted advisors or mentors. Make necessary revisions to improve clarity and completeness.

7. Implement and Monitor:
- Once your plan is finalized, start implementing your strategies. Regularly monitor your progress and adjust your plan as needed to stay on track.

Developing a business plan for your vegetable business is a critical step toward success. A well-crafted plan provides clarity, strategy, and a roadmap for achieving your goals. By including detailed sections on your business description, market analysis, marketing and sales strategy, operations plan, financial projections, and risk management, you can create a comprehensive guide to launching and growing your vegetable business. Remember, a business plan is a living document that should be reviewed and updated regularly to reflect changes in your business and market conditions.

Chapter 3 - Legal and Financial Considerations

Starting a vegetable business can be both fun and profitable. However, several legal and financial considerations must be addressed before you begin. This chapter will discuss these essential considerations and provide advice on managing them effectively.

Legal Considerations
Business Structure
- *Types of Structures*: When starting a vegetable business, you need to choose an appropriate business structure. The most common types are sole proprietorships, partnerships, limited liability companies (LLCs), and corporations. Each structure has its pros and cons regarding liability, taxes, and management.
- *Consult Professionals*: It's important to consult a lawyer or accountant to determine the best structure for your business. They can help you understand the implications of each structure and ensure your business is set up correctly from a legal standpoint.

Licenses and Permits
- *Required Licenses*: Depending on your location and the nature of your business, you may need various licenses and permits. These can include a business license, food handling permits, and health department approvals.
- *Local Regulations*: Check with your local government to understand the specific licenses and permits required to operate legally in your area. Compliance with these regulations is crucial to avoid fines and legal issues.

Zoning and Land Use Rules
- *Agricultural Zoning*: Ensure that your land is zoned for agricultural use before you start growing vegetables. Different areas have different zoning laws, so it's important to verify that your intended use complies with local regulations.
- *Land Use Compliance*: Contact your local zoning office to find out about any land use restrictions or requirements that might affect your business.

Contracts and Agreements
- *Written Agreements*: Establishing written contracts and agreements with suppliers, distributors, and clients is important. These documents should outline the terms and conditions of your business relationships, including payment terms, delivery schedules, and quality standards.
- *Legal Counsel*: Work with a lawyer to draft these agreements to ensure they are legally binding and protect your interests.

Financial Considerations
Budgeting and Cash Flow Management
- *Create a Budget*: Developing a detailed budget is essential for managing your finances. Your budget should include all production, marketing, and overhead costs.
- *Cash Flow Plan*: A cash flow plan will help you track your income and expenses over time. This is critical for ensuring that you have enough funds to cover your costs and sustain your business.

Pricing Strategy
- *Set Prices Wisely*: Your pricing strategy should reflect your production costs, market demand, and competition. It's important to price your vegetables competitively while ensuring a reasonable profit margin.
- *Adjust Prices as Needed:* Be prepared to adjust your prices based on changes in costs or market conditions. Regularly review your pricing strategy to remain competitive.

Taxes
- *Understand Tax Obligations*: As a business owner, you will need to pay various taxes, including income tax, self-employment tax, and sales tax.
- *Consult a Tax Professional*: Work with a tax expert to ensure you meet all your tax obligations and take advantage of any available deductions. Proper tax planning can save you money and prevent legal issues.

Tips for Success
Get Professional Help

- *Seek Expert Advice*: Starting a vegetable business can be complex, so seeking professional help is important. Consider hiring a lawyer, accountant, or business consultant to guide you through the legal and financial aspects of your business.

Keep Accurate Records
- *Track Finances*: Maintaining accurate records of your expenses, income, and transactions is essential for effective financial management.
- *Use Accounting Tools*: Use accounting software or hire an accountant to help you keep track of your finances and prepare financial statements.

Stay Legal
- *Compliance*: Ensure that your business complies with all relevant laws and regulations. Failure to comply can result in fines, legal action, or damage to your reputation.

Stay Flexible
- *Adapt to Changes*: Be prepared to adapt your business as market conditions and customer preferences change. Flexibility is key to staying competitive and meeting the evolving needs of your customers.

Starting a vegetable business requires careful planning and consideration of legal and financial factors. By understanding these key considerations and taking steps to manage your finances effectively, you can set your business up for success. Always seek professional advice when needed, keep accurate records, ensure compliance with laws and regulations, and stay flexible to adapt to market changes. With the right approach, your vegetable business can thrive and grow.

Chapter 4 - Marketing Your Vegetable Business

Once you've created a solid business plan and addressed the legal and financial aspects of your vegetable business, it's time to focus on marketing. Building a customer base, establishing your brand, and increasing sales depend on how effectively you market your business. Let's explore how to market your vegetable business successfully.

Know Your Target Audience
To market your vegetable business effectively, you need to know your target audience. Consider demographics such as age, location, lifestyle, and buying behavior. By understanding your target audience, you can create marketing messages that resonate with them and increase your sales.

Develop a Brand Identity
Your brand identity is what makes your business memorable and sets you apart from your competitors. Develop a brand that reflects your values, mission, and unique selling points. This includes your company logo, website, advertising materials, and packaging. Consistent branding helps build trust and recognition among your customers.

Use Social Media
Social media is a powerful tool for promoting your vegetable business. Create accounts on popular platforms like Facebook, Instagram, and Twitter. Post engaging content such as recipes, gardening tips, and visually appealing photos of your produce. Use social media to interact with your customers, respond to their inquiries, and build a community around your brand.

Participate in Farmer's Markets and Community Events
Farmer's markets and community events are excellent opportunities to meet potential customers and promote your business. Set up a booth, offer free samples, and distribute flyers or business cards. These events provide a platform to showcase your products and connect with your local community.

Partner with Local Restaurants and Grocers
Collaborating with local restaurants and grocery stores can expand your reach and increase your sales. Approach local businesses and offer to supply them with fresh, locally grown vegetables. Emphasize the quality and freshness of your products to attract these partners.

Offer a CSA Program
A Community-Supported Agriculture (CSA) program allows customers to subscribe for weekly or monthly deliveries of fresh vegetables. This model helps build a loyal customer base and ensures a steady income. Offer various subscription options and highlight the benefits of eating fresh, locally grown food to attract subscribers.

Use Email Marketing
Email marketing is an affordable way to reach your customers and promote your business. Collect email addresses from customers and potential buyers and send them regular newsletters or promotional offers. Include appealing photos and information about the freshness and quality of your products to engage your audience.

Create a Referral Program
Referral programs encourage your current customers to recommend your business to their friends and family. Offer discounts, free products, or special deals for referrals. This can help you attract new customers and retain existing ones.

Attend Trade Shows and Conferences
Attending trade shows and conferences can help you network with industry professionals, learn about new trends and technologies, and promote your business. Bring samples, flyers, and business cards to share with potential buyers and partners.

Monitor and Measure Your Results

It's crucial to monitor and measure the results of your marketing efforts to understand what's working and what isn't. Use tools like Google Analytics to track website traffic, social media engagement, and email open rates. This data can help you refine your marketing strategies and improve your results over time. Marketing your vegetable business is essential for building a customer base, establishing your brand, and increasing sales. By understanding your target audience, developing a strong brand identity, leveraging social media, participating in community events, and using various marketing strategies, you can effectively promote your business and achieve your goals. Regularly monitor and measure your results, and be willing to adjust your strategies to ensure continued success.

MODULE T: OFF-GRID HEATING AND COOLING

Chapter 1: Introduction to Off-Grid Temperature Control

Maintaining comfortable living conditions is crucial for any off-grid home, but doing so without conventional power sources poses unique challenges. Off-grid temperature control requires innovative solutions tailored to the specific environment and available resources. This chapter introduces the fundamental principles of off-grid temperature control, explaining how to manage your home's climate in a sustainable and energy-efficient way. Whether you're living in a hot desert or a cold northern climate, temperature control is essential for comfort, survival, and efficiency.

The Importance of Temperature Control in Off-Grid Living
Temperature control is more than just a comfort issue—it's a critical factor in health and safety. Extreme temperatures can pose severe risks, including heat exhaustion, dehydration, or hypothermia, especially in an off-grid setting where access to conventional heating and cooling systems is limited.

Why Temperature Control is Critical:
- **Survival**: Extreme heat or cold can threaten health and safety, especially without traditional heating or cooling systems.
- **Food and Water Preservation**: Maintaining safe temperatures for food and water is essential, particularly when refrigeration is limited.
- **Energy Efficiency**: Efficient temperature control is vital in off-grid living, where energy resources are limited. Using energy wisely ensures your home can be heated and cooled effectively with renewable resources like solar, wind, or hydroelectric power.

Understanding Passive and Active Temperature Control
Off-grid temperature control methods can be categorized into passive and active systems. A combination of both is often the most effective way to create a comfortable living environment.

Passive Temperature Control
Passive temperature control relies on natural techniques to manage your home's internal climate without using electricity. These methods utilize the home's design, orientation, and materials.
- **Passive Solar Design**: This strategy uses the sun's energy to heat or cool a building. In winter, south-facing windows collect heat, while shades or overhangs prevent overheating in summer. Insulation is key to maintaining stable temperatures.
- **Thermal Mass**: Materials like concrete, stone, and brick absorb heat during the day and release it slowly at night, helping to regulate indoor temperatures naturally.
- **Natural Ventilation**: Cross-ventilation, using windows or vents, allows cool air to enter and warm air to exit, providing a natural cooling effect without mechanical fans.

Active Temperature Control
Active temperature control systems mechanically heat or cool your home. In off-grid homes, these systems are often powered by renewable energy sources like solar, wind, or biomass.
- **Solar Heating and Cooling**: Solar thermal panels capture heat for space heating, while photovoltaic (PV) panels can power fans or air conditioning units.
- **Wood Stoves**: A traditional off-grid heating method, wood stoves use renewable biomass to generate heat for living spaces and water.
- **Heat Pumps**: Powered by renewable energy, heat pumps transfer heat from the ground, air, or water into your home for both heating and cooling.
- **Hydronic Systems**: These systems use water heated by solar panels or wood-fired boilers to distribute heat through radiators or underfloor heating.

The Role of Insulation and Building Materials

Good insulation and the right building materials are essential for regulating indoor temperatures, especially in off-grid homes where energy efficiency is crucial. Effective insulation minimizes heat loss in cold weather and prevents heat gain in hot weather, reducing reliance on active systems.

Insulation for Heating and Cooling

- **R-Value**: Insulation effectiveness is measured by its R-value—the higher the R-value, the better the insulation's ability to resist heat flow. Homes in cold climates require higher R-values in walls, floors, and ceilings to retain heat.
- **Natural Insulation Materials**: Eco-friendly materials like straw bales, wool, cellulose, and cork are sustainable and effective options for insulating off-grid homes, with the added benefit of being renewable and environmentally friendly.

Building Materials

The materials used to construct an off-grid home have a significant impact on its temperature regulation.

- **Stone and Brick**: These materials have high thermal mass, meaning they absorb heat during the day and release it at night, making them ideal for passive temperature control.
- **Wood**: While wood doesn't store heat as effectively as stone, it provides excellent insulation and is a renewable resource.
- **Earth Sheltering**: Building homes partially underground or using earth walls provides natural insulation, helping to maintain stable indoor temperatures in extreme climates.

Climate-Specific Strategies for Off-Grid Temperature Control

Tailoring your temperature control strategy to your specific climate is essential for creating an energy-efficient off-grid home. Whether dealing with hot, cold, or temperate environments, different techniques are required to manage indoor temperatures effectively.

Hot Climates

In hot climates, the focus is on minimizing heat gain and encouraging airflow.

- **Shade and Overhangs**: Roof overhangs, shade trees, or external shades block direct sunlight, preventing overheating.
- **Ventilation and Airflow**: Cross-ventilation and solar-powered fans can move air through the home, while the chimney effect (where warm air rises and exits through higher vents) helps cool the interior.
- **Reflective Roofing and Light Colors**: Roofs and walls made of reflective materials or painted in light colors reduce heat absorption, keeping the home cooler.

Cold Climates

In cold climates, the primary focus is retaining heat. A combination of proper insulation and efficient heating systems is necessary.

- **South-Facing Windows**: Large windows facing south (in the Northern Hemisphere) capture sunlight to heat the home, and thermal curtains help retain heat at night.
- **Wood or Pellet Stoves**: Wood-burning or pellet stoves provide reliable, renewable heat, especially when using locally sourced fuel.
- **Thermal Mass and Insulation**: Thick stone or earth walls and high-quality insulation in the roof and walls help prevent heat loss.

Temperate Climates

In temperate regions, a balanced approach is required, combining passive and active methods.

- **Seasonal Adaptation**: Use passive solar heating in colder months and switch to natural ventilation and shading in warmer months to maintain comfort without excessive energy use.
- **Flexible Insulation**: Moderate insulation is necessary to balance heating and cooling needs without trapping excess heat during summer.

Energy Sources for Off-Grid Heating and Cooling

Off-grid homes typically rely on renewable and alternative energy sources to power active temperature control systems. The best energy source for heating and cooling depends on your location, available resources, and personal preferences.

Solar Power

Solar energy is one of the most versatile and accessible renewable energy sources for off-grid homes.

- **Solar Thermal Systems**: These systems use solar collectors to heat water, which is circulated through radiators or underfloor heating systems.
- **Solar Air Heaters**: Solar air heaters capture sunlight to warm air, which is then circulated through the home, providing heat with minimal energy input.

Biomass Energy

Biomass, particularly in the form of wood or pellets, is a common and renewable heating source for off-grid homes, especially in colder regions.

- **Wood Stoves**: Efficient and affordable, wood stoves are a reliable heating method for off-grid living.
- **Pellet Stoves**: Pellet stoves burn compressed wood or biomass pellets, providing consistent, easily regulated heat.

Wind Power

In areas with consistent wind, wind turbines can generate electricity to power heating and cooling systems. Wind energy is especially useful in colder months when solar power may be less effective.

Geothermal Energy

Geothermal systems use the earth's stable underground temperature to provide heating in the winter and cooling in the summer. Geothermal heat pumps, powered by solar or wind energy, offer an efficient, long-term solution for off-grid homes. By understanding the principles of passive and active temperature control and selecting the right materials and energy sources, off-grid homeowners can maintain a comfortable living environment year-round. Whether facing intense heat or extreme cold, innovative solutions and thoughtful design are key to successful off-grid temperature management.

Chapter 2: Solar Heating and Cooling Systems

Harnessing the sun's energy for heating and cooling is one of the most efficient ways to maintain comfort in an off-grid home. Solar power is a renewable, sustainable resource that can provide both heat and cooling with minimal environmental impact and low long-term costs. This chapter explores various solar heating and cooling systems, how they work, and how to implement them to maintain a comfortable temperature in your off-grid home year-round.

How Solar Heating Works

Solar heating systems capture the sun's energy and convert it into heat for warming living spaces or providing hot water. There are two primary types of solar heating systems: active and passive.

Active Solar Heating Systems

Active solar heating systems use mechanical components like pumps, fans, and controllers to distribute heat throughout your home. These systems rely on solar collectors to absorb sunlight and transfer heat to your home or a water storage system.

Solar Thermal Collectors: These solar panels absorb sunlight and convert it into heat, typically mounted on roofs for maximum sun exposure.

- **Flat-Plate Collectors**: The most common type, consisting of a flat, insulated box with a dark absorber plate. The plate heats up as it absorbs sunlight, and this heat is transferred to a circulating fluid.
- **Evacuated Tube Collectors**: More efficient in colder climates, these collectors consist of rows of glass tubes containing heat-absorbing fluid. Their vacuum-sealed design helps retain more heat, making them ideal for cold environments.

Heat Transfer and Storage: In active systems, heat is transferred to a fluid (water or antifreeze) that circulates through pipes into a storage tank. This heated fluid can be used for space heating or domestic hot water.

- **Hydronic Heating**: This method circulates heated fluid through radiators or underfloor heating systems, warming the home efficiently.
- **Hot Water Storage**: Excess heat is stored in an insulated tank and can be used later when the sun isn't shining.

Passive Solar Heating Systems

Passive solar heating uses the design of the home itself to collect, store, and distribute heat, without mechanical systems. Homes are designed to maximize sunlight, naturally heating the space during the day and releasing heat at night.

- **South-Facing Windows**: Large windows on the south side of the home allow sunlight to penetrate deeply, heating interior surfaces like floors and walls. These surfaces absorb heat during the day and release it slowly at night.
- **Thermal Mass**: Materials with high thermal mass, such as stone, brick, or concrete, store heat and gradually release it as temperatures drop.
- **Overhangs and Shades**: Roof overhangs or external shades block the summer sun to prevent overheating while allowing sunlight in during winter when the sun is lower in the sky.

Solar Cooling Systems

Solar cooling systems use the sun's energy to reduce indoor temperatures, making hot climates more bearable.

Solar-Powered Air Conditioning

Solar-powered air conditioning systems use photovoltaic (PV) panels to generate electricity, powering conventional air conditioning units. These systems are ideal for homes with enough solar capacity to run air conditioners during the hottest parts of the day.

- **DC-Powered Air Conditioners**: Some systems use direct current (DC) from solar panels, eliminating the need for inverters and improving efficiency.
- **Hybrid Systems**: These systems can switch between solar power and grid power or batteries. During sunny days, the system runs on solar energy, and during cloudy weather or at night, it uses stored or grid power.

Solar Absorption Cooling

Solar absorption cooling uses solar heat to power a cooling system, making it highly efficient in sunny, hot climates.

- **How It Works**: Solar absorption systems use solar thermal collectors to drive an absorption cycle. Solar heat evaporates a refrigerant, which absorbs heat from inside the building, cooling the air.
- **Common Types**: Solar absorption chillers and evaporative coolers are popular in dry, hot climates where they efficiently convert solar heat into cooling power.

Solar-Powered Fans and Ventilation
Natural ventilation can be enhanced with solar-powered fans, which help circulate air and exhaust hot air from attics or living spaces. These fans are ideal for off-grid homes, running only when the sun is shining.
- **Attic Fans**: Installed on the roof, these fans help remove hot air from the attic, reducing the overall home temperature and lowering air conditioning needs.
- **Ventilation Fans**: Solar-powered ventilation fans circulate air in living areas, helping cool the home without relying on the grid.

Key Components of Solar Heating and Cooling Systems
To function effectively, solar heating and cooling systems rely on specific components. Here are the key parts:

Solar Collectors
Solar collectors absorb sunlight and convert it into heat. Proper sizing of collectors—whether flat-plate or evacuated tube—is essential for meeting your home's heating needs.

Photovoltaic Panels (PV)
In solar cooling systems that use electric-powered air conditioners or fans, PV panels convert sunlight into electricity. A well-sized solar array is crucial to generating enough power to run cooling systems during peak sun hours.

Inverters and Controllers
In solar-powered air conditioning or fan systems, inverters convert the DC electricity from solar panels into AC electricity for conventional appliances. Controllers optimize and regulate the system for efficient energy use.

Storage Tanks and Heat Exchangers
In solar thermal systems, storage tanks hold heated water or air until it's needed. Heat exchangers efficiently transfer the heat from collectors to the storage medium.

Sizing and Installing a Solar Heating and Cooling System
Proper sizing is crucial for solar heating and cooling systems to meet your home's energy demands. Oversized systems waste energy, while undersized systems may fail to provide adequate comfort.

Determining Heating and Cooling Needs
- **Heating Requirements**: Calculate the amount of heat required to warm your home during the coldest months, considering home size, insulation, and climate zone.
- **Cooling Requirements**: Estimate your cooling needs based on home size and sun exposure in the hottest parts of the year.

Installing Solar Collectors and Panels
Install solar collectors or panels in locations with maximum sun exposure—typically on a south-facing roof in the Northern Hemisphere or a north-facing roof in the Southern Hemisphere. Ensure there are no obstructions like trees or buildings casting shadows.

Maintaining Your System
Solar systems are low-maintenance, but periodic inspections are necessary to ensure efficiency. Clean panels or collectors regularly, check for leaks in piping or storage tanks, and ensure mechanical components are working properly.

Advantages and Challenges of Solar Heating and Cooling
Advantages
- **Renewable and Sustainable**: Solar energy is abundant and eco-friendly, making it an excellent option for off-grid homes.
- **Low Operating Costs**: Once installed, solar systems have minimal operational costs since they rely on free solar energy.
- **Reduced Grid Dependence**: Using solar for both heating and cooling significantly reduces or eliminates reliance on traditional energy sources.

Challenges
- **Initial Investment**: Solar heating and cooling systems can have high upfront costs, though they offer long-term savings.
- **Weather Dependency**: Solar systems rely on sunlight, so they may be less effective during cloudy or rainy periods. Backup systems may be necessary for year-round reliability.
- **Space Requirements**: Solar panels and collectors require sufficient space for installation, which may be limited on smaller properties.

By implementing solar heating and cooling systems, off-grid homeowners can enjoy a sustainable, low-cost way to maintain a comfortable indoor environment. With careful planning and installation, these systems can provide reliable, year-round comfort while reducing energy consumption and reliance on traditional power sources.

Chapter 3: DIY Geothermal Heating for Your Homestead

Geothermal heating is one of the most efficient and sustainable methods for maintaining a comfortable indoor temperature, making it ideal for off-grid homes and homesteads. Unlike solar or wind power, geothermal systems harness the constant temperature beneath the earth's surface to provide consistent heating in the winter and cooling in the summer. This chapter explores the basics of geothermal heating, the different system types, and how you can set up a DIY geothermal heating system for your off-grid homestead.

What is Geothermal Heating?

Geothermal heating uses the stable temperature found just a few feet below the earth's surface. Ground temperature remains relatively constant year-round, typically between 45°F and 75°F (7°C to 24°C), depending on location. A geothermal system transfers this heat into your home during the winter and reverses the process for cooling in the summer.

How Geothermal Heating Works:

- **Heat Transfer**: Geothermal systems use a heat pump to transfer heat from the ground into your home. In winter, the pump pulls heat from the ground and distributes it via air ducts, radiant floor heating, or water-based systems.
- **Cooling Function**: In summer, the process is reversed, with the pump removing heat from your home and transferring it into the cooler ground.
- **Efficiency**: Geothermal systems use much less energy than traditional heating and cooling methods, making them an ideal choice for off-grid living.

Types of Geothermal Heating Systems

Several geothermal systems exist, each suited to different climates, budgets, and installation conditions. The two most common systems are **closed-loop** and **open-loop** systems.

Closed-Loop Systems

In a closed-loop system, a network of pipes is buried underground and filled with a heat-transfer fluid (usually a water-antifreeze mixture). This fluid circulates through the pipes, absorbing or releasing heat to the ground based on the season.

- **Horizontal Closed-Loop**: Pipes are laid horizontally in trenches dug across your yard. This is the most common type for residential applications but requires a large land area.
- **Vertical Closed-Loop**: Pipes are installed vertically in deep boreholes, making this system ideal for properties with limited space. Vertical systems are more expensive due to the drilling required.
- **Pond/Lake Closed-Loop**: If you have access to a pond or lake, pipes can be submerged in the water, where they absorb or release heat. This method is cost-effective but requires proximity to a suitable water source.

Open-Loop Systems

Open-loop systems use water from a nearby well, pond, or lake as the heat-transfer medium. Water circulates through the heat pump and is then discharged back into the water source.

- **Pros**: Open-loop systems are generally cheaper to install since they don't require extensive piping.
- **Cons**: They rely on a reliable water source, and water quality and temperature can affect the system's performance.

Planning Your DIY Geothermal Heating System

Careful planning is essential before starting a DIY geothermal installation. Assess your property, choose the right system, and determine if your site can support geothermal heat exchange.

Assessing Your Property

Your property's size and layout will dictate which type of geothermal system is best suited for your homestead.

- **Land Area**: A large yard allows for a horizontal closed-loop system, which is more cost-effective. Smaller properties may require a vertical system due to space constraints.
- **Soil Conditions**: The type of soil, rock, or bedrock beneath your property affects system efficiency. Sandy or loose soil transfers heat well, while rocky soil may require more extensive excavation.
- **Water Source**: If you have a well, pond, or lake nearby, you can consider an open-loop system, provided the water source is reliable year-round.

Climate Considerations

Geothermal systems work well in a wide range of climates, but their efficiency may be impacted by extreme conditions. In colder climates, a deeper or more extensive loop may be required to pull sufficient heat from the ground. In warmer climates, the system must effectively dissipate heat during summer.

Materials and Tools for DIY Geothermal Installation

Installing a geothermal system requires specific materials and tools. While professional assistance may be needed for tasks like vertical drilling, much of the work can be done independently.

Materials:
- Piping (polyethylene or copper) for the heat exchange loop
- Heat-transfer fluid (water and antifreeze)
- Geothermal heat pump (appropriately sized for your home)
- Insulation for piping
- Ground loop manifolds
- Trencher or backhoe for digging trenches (for horizontal systems) or drilling equipment (for vertical systems)
- Cement or sand for backfilling trenches

Tools:
- Pipe cutters
- Wrenches and screwdrivers
- Shovels and digging equipment
- Measuring tape
- Heat pump installation guide and wiring tools

Step-by-Step Guide to Installing a Geothermal Heating System

Step 1: Design the System
Determine the size of the system you need based on your home's heating and cooling requirements. You can use a professional assessment or online calculator to figure out the size of the heat pump and the length of piping required for maximum efficiency.

Step 2: Dig the Trenches or Drill the Wells
For a horizontal system, dig trenches 4–6 feet deep and 100–300 feet long, depending on the system's size. For vertical systems, drill boreholes to a depth of 100–400 feet. For pond or lake systems, submerge the pipes 8–10 feet below the water surface.

Step 3: Install the Ground Loop
Lay the pipes into the trenches or boreholes. In horizontal systems, loop the piping at the trench ends to create a continuous flow. For vertical systems, connect the pipes at the borehole bottom using U-bends or manifolds.

Step 4: Connect the Ground Loop to the Heat Pump
Run the pipes from the ground loop into your home, connecting them to the geothermal heat pump, which should be centrally located for even heat distribution. The pump can be connected to your existing ductwork or a radiant heating system.

Step 5: Fill the System with Heat-Transfer Fluid
Fill the loop with a mixture of water and antifreeze to prevent freezing. The system must be pressurized and tested for leaks before sealing and burying the pipes.

Step 6: Backfill and Insulate
After testing, backfill the trenches or boreholes with soil or sand to insulate and protect the pipes. Vertical systems should be backfilled with cement or bentonite to ensure efficient heat transfer.

Step 7: Start Up and Monitor the System
Once the system is installed, start the geothermal heat pump and monitor performance. It may take a few days for the ground loop to reach its optimal temperature. Regularly check for leaks and monitor temperature readings to ensure efficient operation.

Costs and Savings of a DIY Geothermal System

Initial Investment
DIY geothermal systems have a significant upfront cost, especially for vertical systems that require professional drilling. However, a well-designed system will quickly pay for itself through energy savings.

- **Horizontal Systems**: Typically cost between $10,000 and $20,000, with most expenses coming from the heat pump and trenching.
- **Vertical Systems**: More expensive due to drilling, with costs ranging from $20,000 to $35,000 or more, depending on depth and location.

Long-Term Savings
Geothermal systems are highly efficient, often reducing heating and cooling costs by up to 70%. Their reliance on the earth's stable temperature allows for lower energy consumption compared to traditional HVAC systems, making them ideal for off-grid setups using renewable energy.

Maintenance and Longevity
One of the key benefits of geothermal systems is their low maintenance. Underground components typically last 50+ years, while the heat pump can last up to 25 years with proper care.

Routine Maintenance
- **Check the Heat Pump**: Annual inspections ensure optimal performance. Filters should be cleaned or replaced regularly to maintain proper airflow.
- **Monitor Fluid Levels**: Periodically check the heat-transfer fluid levels to ensure the system is properly pressurized and free of leaks.
- **Inspect the Ground Loop**: While underground components rarely require maintenance, monitor the system for signs of decreased efficiency or leaks.

Geothermal heating is an efficient and sustainable solution for off-grid homes. With proper planning, materials, and knowledge, a DIY geothermal system can significantly reduce energy consumption and provide reliable, year-round comfort. While the initial investment may be high, the long-term savings and environmental benefits make it an excellent choice for homesteaders looking to reduce reliance on external energy sources.

Chapter 4: Using Passive Solar Design to Heat and Cool Your Home

Passive solar design is a sustainable, energy-efficient way to heat and cool a home by harnessing the sun's energy without relying on mechanical systems. By carefully considering factors like orientation, materials, and insulation, passive solar strategies can help maintain comfortable indoor temperatures, capturing and storing solar energy in the winter while minimizing heat gain during the summer. For off-grid living, passive solar design is particularly beneficial as it reduces dependence on external energy sources, making your home more self-sufficient. This chapter explores the principles of passive solar design and how to implement them for an energy-efficient, naturally controlled home environment.

What is Passive Solar Design?
Passive solar design focuses on utilizing natural sunlight and heat to maintain indoor temperatures, reduce energy consumption, and improve comfort. Unlike active solar systems that require mechanical equipment, passive systems rely on the home's architecture to manage solar energy effectively.

Key Elements of Passive Solar Design:
- **Solar Gain**: Capturing sunlight to heat the home during colder months.
- **Thermal Mass**: Using materials that absorb, store, and gradually release heat.
- **Insulation**: Preventing heat loss in winter and limiting heat gain in summer.
- **Ventilation**: Managing natural airflow to maintain cool indoor temperatures, particularly during warm months.

Benefits of Passive Solar Design in Off-Grid Living
The advantages of passive solar design go beyond energy savings. When properly implemented, it enhances indoor comfort, reduces dependence on external power sources, and strengthens a home's resilience in off-grid settings.
- **Energy Efficiency**: Passive solar design cuts down on the need for heating in winter and cooling in summer, lowering energy consumption.
- **Minimal Maintenance**: Passive solar systems require little to no maintenance, unlike mechanical systems that may need regular upkeep.
- **Eco-Friendly**: This design approach lowers your carbon footprint by utilizing clean, renewable solar energy.
- **Cost Savings**: Over time, passive solar design can lead to substantial savings on energy costs, especially in off-grid homes relying on alternative energy sources like solar or wind power.

Key Principles of Passive Solar Design
To create a home that is naturally heated and cooled by the sun, several important principles must be followed. Success in passive solar design depends on proper orientation, the right materials, and smart architectural decisions.

Orientation
The orientation of your home is crucial for maximizing solar energy in winter and minimizing heat gain in summer.
- **South-Facing Windows**: In the Northern Hemisphere, most windows should face south to capture the maximum amount of sunlight in winter. In the Southern Hemisphere, windows should face north for the same effect.
- **Shading Devices**: Roof overhangs, pergolas, or deciduous trees can block excess sunlight during summer to keep the home cooler.
- **Building Shape**: Compact buildings with fewer exterior walls reduce heat loss, while an elongated design along the east-west axis allows for more south-facing windows, enhancing solar gain.

Thermal Mass
Thermal mass materials absorb and store heat from sunlight, gradually releasing it when temperatures cool, helping to maintain a stable indoor temperature.
- **Best Materials for Thermal Mass**: Concrete, brick, stone, and tile are ideal due to their high heat storage capacity. These materials should be placed in areas with direct sunlight for optimal heat absorption.
- **Thermal Mass in Summer**: In hot climates, thermal mass can also help cool the home by absorbing excess heat during the day and releasing it at night, when temperatures drop and natural ventilation can cool the house.

Insulation

Proper insulation prevents heat loss during winter and blocks heat gain in summer. Using materials with a high R-value (which measures thermal resistance) ensures efficient temperature regulation.

- **Types of Insulation**: Fiberglass, cellulose, spray foam, and natural materials like wool or straw bales are commonly used in off-grid homes for maintaining consistent indoor temperatures.
- **Double-Glazed Windows**: Windows are a major source of heat transfer, so double or triple-glazed windows reduce heat loss in winter and prevent excessive heat gain in summer.

Natural Ventilation

Ventilation is key to passive cooling, especially in warm climates. Natural airflow can be used to cool homes without the need for air conditioning.

- **Cross-Ventilation**: Positioning windows or vents to allow cool air to enter from one side and warm air to exit from the other helps cool the home naturally.
- **Chimney Effect**: Hot air rises, so installing vents or windows high on walls or roofs allows warm air to escape, drawing in cooler air from below. This method is effective when combined with thermal mass and shading strategies.

Design Techniques for Passive Solar Heating
Sunspaces and Greenhouses

Sunspaces and attached greenhouses capture solar heat, which can be used to warm the home.

- **How It Works**: A sunspace has large south-facing windows that collect sunlight, warming the air. This warm air can then be circulated into the main living areas through vents or fans. At night, insulating the windows prevents heat loss.
- **Benefits**: In addition to providing heat, sunspaces can serve as living areas, growing spaces for plants, or places to dry clothes and store supplies.

Trombe Walls

A Trombe wall is a thick, dark-colored wall made of thermal mass materials like concrete or stone, placed behind a layer of glass. It absorbs heat from the sun during the day and radiates it into the home at night.

- **How It Works**: The sun heats the wall, which stores and releases the heat slowly. Vents at the top and bottom of the wall can help circulate warm air into the home.
- **Advantages**: Trombe walls provide consistent heating without moving parts or mechanical systems, making them highly durable and low maintenance.

Clerestory Windows

Clerestory windows are narrow windows placed high on walls to allow sunlight to reach deeper parts of the home.

   Benefits: These windows provide natural light and heat while maintaining privacy. They also aid in ventilation by allowing hot air to escape through higher openings.

Design Techniques for Passive Solar Cooling

In warmer climates, cooling strategies are essential. Several passive solar design techniques can help keep homes cool during the hot months.

Shading and Overhangs

Properly designed overhangs and shading devices prevent excessive heat from entering the home.

- **Fixed Overhangs**: Designed to block the high summer sun while allowing lower winter sun to enter, fixed overhangs help regulate temperature throughout the year.
- **Pergolas and Vegetation**: Pergolas covered in climbing plants provide shade while allowing air circulation. Deciduous trees can also block sunlight in summer but let it through in winter after leaves fall.

Earth Sheltering

Earth-sheltered homes are built into the ground or surrounded by earth, which acts as a natural insulator.

   Benefits: Earth-sheltered homes maintain stable temperatures year-round, reducing the need for heating and cooling systems. They also offer protection from extreme weather conditions.

Light Colors and Reflective Materials

Exterior surfaces painted in light colors or covered with reflective materials help reflect sunlight and prevent heat absorption.

Roofing and Walls: Using light-colored or reflective materials on roofs, walls, and paving surfaces significantly reduces the amount of heat entering the home.

Combining Passive Solar Design with Renewable Energy Systems

While passive solar design reduces the need for mechanical heating and cooling systems, it can also be integrated with renewable energy sources like solar photovoltaic panels or wind turbines for even greater efficiency.

Solar and Passive Synergy

Combining passive solar techniques with active systems like solar PV panels allows you to maximize energy savings. For example, solar panels can power ventilation fans or provide backup energy on cloudy days when passive solar heat gain is reduced.

Hybrid Heating Systems

A hybrid system might combine passive solar heating with a small, efficient backup system like a wood stove or biomass heater. This ensures the home remains warm even during periods of minimal sunlight.

Retrofitting Existing Homes for Passive Solar

Many passive solar design principles can be applied to existing homes through retrofitting. Adding insulation, upgrading windows, or installing overhangs can improve energy efficiency without a full rebuild.

- **Window Upgrades**: Replacing single-pane windows with double or triple-glazed ones reduces heat loss in winter and heat gain in summer.
- **Insulating Walls and Roofs**: Adding insulation to walls, attics, and basements keeps temperatures stable.
- **Thermal Mass Additions**: Adding materials like stone or concrete to areas exposed to sunlight can create additional thermal mass, helping stabilize indoor temperatures.

By employing passive solar design techniques, you can create an off-grid home that stays comfortable year-round with minimal energy use. These strategies harness the power of the sun to heat and cool your home naturally, reducing the need for mechanical systems and lowering overall energy consumption.

Chapter 5: Insulation Strategies for Energy Efficiency

Proper insulation is the cornerstone of any energy-efficient home, especially in off-grid living where maintaining a stable indoor temperature with minimal energy use is crucial. Insulation helps prevent heat loss in the winter and heat gain in the summer, significantly reducing the need for active heating and cooling systems. This chapter explores various insulation strategies, materials, and techniques for creating a well-insulated, energy-efficient home, allowing you to conserve energy, lower costs, and increase comfort year-round.

Why Insulation is Critical for Off-Grid Homes

In an off-grid home, insulation plays a critical role in reducing the need for external energy to heat or cool your living space. Without access to the conventional energy grid, off-grid systems rely on renewable energy sources like solar panels, wind turbines, or wood stoves, which can be expensive or require significant management. Good insulation maximizes the efficiency of these energy sources by minimizing energy loss.

Benefits of Proper Insulation:

- **Energy Conservation**: Insulation reduces heat transfer, keeping warm air inside during the winter and blocking heat from entering in the summer, cutting down on heating and cooling energy needs.
- **Lower Costs**: A well-insulated home reduces reliance on costly fuel or energy inputs, such as firewood, propane, or solar energy storage systems.
- **Increased Comfort**: Insulation helps maintain a stable indoor temperature, preventing uncomfortable drafts, cold spots, or overheating.
- **Environmental Impact**: By reducing energy consumption, insulation lowers your carbon footprint and helps preserve natural resources.

Understanding R-Value and Its Importance

R-value measures an insulation material's resistance to heat flow. The higher the R-value, the better the insulation's performance. Choosing the right R-value depends on your climate, the area of the home being insulated, and whether the goal is to block heat in summer or retain warmth in winter.

R-Value by Climate:

- **Cold Climates**: In regions with cold winters, higher R-values (R-38 or higher for ceilings, R-20 or higher for walls) are recommended to prevent heat loss.
- **Mild Climates**: In milder climates, lower R-values (R-30 for ceilings, R-13 for walls) may be sufficient for maintaining comfortable temperatures.
- **Hot Climates**: Insulating for hot climates focuses on blocking heat gain, with R-30 or higher for ceilings and R-13 to R-20 for walls.

R-Value by Area:

- **Attics and Roofs**: Attics and roofs are critical areas to insulate, as heat rises. They generally require higher R-values (R-30 to R-60).
- **Walls**: Exterior walls should be insulated to R-13 to R-21, depending on climate and building materials.
- **Floors and Basements**: Insulating floors and basements prevents heat loss to the ground, with R-values of R-19 to R-30 recommended.

Types of Insulation Materials

Various insulation materials are suited for different areas of the home, each offering unique advantages in terms of R-value, sustainability, ease of installation, and cost. Natural and sustainable materials are often favored in off-grid homes for their low environmental impact.

Fiberglass Insulation

Fiberglass insulation is affordable and widely used. It is available in batts or loose-fill form, providing a good balance between cost and performance.

- **R-Value**: R-2.2 to R-4.3 per inch

- **Best Use**: Walls, ceilings, attics
- **Advantages**: Inexpensive, widely available, easy to install
- **Disadvantages**: Can irritate skin and lungs; proper installation is needed to avoid air leaks.

Spray Foam Insulation

Spray foam insulation expands to fill gaps, creating an airtight seal. It is ideal for hard-to-reach or irregular spaces.
- **R-Value**: R-3.5 to R-6.5 per inch (open-cell vs. closed-cell foam)
- **Best Use**: Walls, ceilings, crawlspaces
- **Advantages**: Excellent air sealing, high R-value, moisture-resistant
- **Disadvantages**: Expensive, requires professional installation, not as eco-friendly.

Cellulose Insulation

Made from recycled paper, cellulose insulation is an eco-friendly option treated with fire-retardant chemicals.
- **R-Value**: R-3.2 to R-3.8 per inch
- **Best Use**: Walls, attics
- **Advantages**: Environmentally friendly, good for filling irregular spaces, affordable
- **Disadvantages**: Can settle over time, reducing its insulating value.

Wool Insulation

Sheep's wool is a natural, renewable insulation material offering excellent thermal performance and moisture regulation.
- **R-Value**: R-3.5 per inch
- **Best Use**: Walls, roofs, attics
- **Advantages**: Renewable, non-toxic, moisture-regulating
- **Disadvantages**: More expensive than synthetic options, requires pest resistance treatment.

Straw Bale Insulation

Straw bales offer high R-values and can be used as insulation or as structural elements in eco-friendly construction.
- **R-Value**: R-1.3 to R-2.0 per inch (whole bales can reach R-30 to R-35)
- **Best Use**: Exterior walls
- **Advantages**: Sustainable, natural, good soundproofing
- **Disadvantages**: Requires thick walls and moisture protection to prevent rot.

Cork Insulation

Cork is a renewable, moisture-resistant, and fire-resistant natural insulation material made from cork tree bark.
- **R-Value**: R-3.0 to R-4.0 per inch
- **Best Use**: Walls, floors, roofs
- **Advantages**: Renewable, non-toxic, moisture-resistant
- **Disadvantages**: Expensive, limited availability.

Key Areas for Insulation in Off-Grid Homes

To create an energy-efficient home, insulation should be applied strategically to prevent heat loss or gain.

Attics and Roofs

Attics are prime areas for heat loss in winter and heat gain in summer due to their exposure to external temperatures.
- **Strategies**: Blown-in cellulose or fiberglass batts are effective for insulating attic spaces. Insulating the roof deck in addition to the attic floor provides maximum efficiency.
- **Radiant Barriers**: In hot climates, radiant barriers installed under the roof can reflect heat away from the home, reducing cooling needs.

Exterior Walls

Properly insulated walls prevent heat from escaping in cold climates and keep cool air inside during summer.
- **Strategies**: In new construction, materials like straw bales, insulated concrete forms (ICFs), or structural insulated panels (SIPs) offer excellent insulation. For retrofits, spray foam or blown-in cellulose are ideal.
- **Thermal Breaks**: A thermal break, an additional layer of insulation, prevents heat transfer between exterior and interior walls.

Floors and Foundations

Insulating floors and foundations helps prevent heat loss to the ground, crucial for homes with crawlspaces or basements.

Strategies: Rigid foam board or spray foam insulation beneath floors is effective. For basements, insulating walls and floors helps prevent both heat loss and moisture buildup.

Windows and Doors

Windows and doors are often weak points in a home's insulation envelope. Proper sealing and upgrading to energy-efficient models are critical.

Strategies: Use double or triple-glazed windows with low-emissivity (low-E) coatings to reduce heat transfer. Weatherstrip doors and windows to seal gaps and opt for insulated doors.

Natural and Sustainable Insulation Solutions

For off-grid homes prioritizing sustainability, natural insulation materials are excellent alternatives to synthetic options. These materials are renewable, biodegradable, and non-toxic.

Straw Bale Construction

Straw bale construction offers excellent thermal mass and insulation, making it a popular choice for eco-conscious homeowners.

- **Advantages**: Affordable, high R-values, and soundproofing capabilities, with the added benefit of being locally sourced in many areas.
- **Challenges**: Straw bales need to be well-protected from moisture to prevent rot, requiring proper plastering or cladding.

Rammed Earth

Rammed earth construction involves compressing layers of earth to create dense walls with excellent thermal mass properties.

- **Advantages**: Natural, abundant, and highly sustainable, rammed earth walls regulate indoor temperatures effectively.
- **Challenges**: Requires specialized knowledge and equipment, making it labor-intensive but highly efficient for off-grid homes.

Hempcrete

Hempcrete is a biocomposite material made from hemp fibers and lime. It provides insulation and thermal mass, making it ideal for sustainable homes.

- **Advantages**: Renewable, carbon-negative, non-toxic, and pest-resistant, hempcrete is environmentally friendly and offers sound insulation.
- **Challenges**: Lower R-value than other insulation materials, requiring thicker walls for optimal thermal performance.

Air Sealing for Maximum Efficiency

Even with proper insulation, air leaks can undermine a home's efficiency. Sealing air leaks ensures insulation performs at its best by preventing conditioned air from escaping.

Common Air Leaks

- **Windows and Doors**: Weatherstripping and caulking gaps around windows and doors prevent drafts.
- **Attic and Basement**: Unsealed hatches, plumbing gaps, and cracks in foundation walls allow air to escape. Seal these with spray foam or caulking.
- **Electrical Outlets**: Install foam gaskets behind electrical outlets and light switches to prevent drafts.

Blower Door Test

A blower door test can identify areas where air leaks from your home. This test uses a fan to depressurize the house, revealing leaks that need to be sealed for maximum insulation efficiency.

Retrofitting an Existing Home with Insulation

For off-grid homes not initially built for energy efficiency, retrofitting insulation is a cost-effective way to improve comfort and reduce energy consumption.

- **Blown-In Insulation**: Blown-in cellulose or fiberglass is an easy way to add insulation to walls and attics without major renovations.
- **Spray Foam**: Closed-cell spray foam can be applied to walls, ceilings, and floors for an airtight seal.
- **Reflective Insulation**: In hot climates, reflective insulation (like radiant barriers) can be added to attics and walls to reflect heat away from the home.

Effective insulation is one of the most important investments you can make for your off-grid home. By selecting the right materials, insulating key areas, and sealing air leaks, you can create a more energy-efficient and comfortable living environment that reduces reliance on external energy sources. Whether building a new home or retrofitting an existing one, proper insulation will improve the sustainability and resilience of your off-grid lifestyle.

Chapter 6: Building a Wood-Fired Heating System

Wood-fired heating systems have been used for centuries to provide warmth and comfort in off-grid homes. They offer a reliable and sustainable way to heat your living space, especially in regions where firewood is abundant. Building and maintaining a wood-fired heating system not only reduces dependence on external energy sources but also fosters a sense of self-sufficiency. In this chapter, we will explore different types of wood-fired heating systems, guide you on how to build one, and discuss key considerations for efficiency and safety.

Why Choose a Wood-Fired Heating System?

For off-grid living, wood-fired heating is an excellent option due to its simplicity, sustainability, and affordability. Wood is a renewable resource that, when harvested and burned responsibly, provides consistent heat during the cold months.

Benefits of Wood-Fired Heating:

- **Sustainability**: Wood is a renewable fuel source that can be harvested locally, reducing transportation costs and emissions.
- **Self-Sufficiency**: Wood-fired heating systems can operate independently of electricity, providing reliable heat during power outages or when other energy sources are unavailable.
- **Cost-Effective**: Although initial investments are required to build or purchase a wood stove or furnace, long-term heating costs are generally lower than propane, oil, or electricity.
- **Dual Functionality**: Many wood-fired systems can also be used for cooking or heating water, adding extra value in an off-grid home.

Types of Wood-Fired Heating Systems

Several types of wood-fired systems can heat off-grid homes, each with unique advantages depending on heating needs, available space, and wood supply.

Wood Stoves

Wood stoves are the most common and straightforward wood-fired heating systems. They burn wood in a firebox and radiate heat into surrounding spaces. Modern wood stoves are highly efficient and can heat small to medium-sized homes effectively.

- **Key Features**: Airtight fireboxes, glass doors to monitor the fire, and adjustable air vents to control burn rate.
- **Installation**: Requires a chimney or flue for proper ventilation, which must comply with safety regulations to prevent carbon monoxide buildup.
- **Heat Output**: Varies from 5,000 to 100,000 BTUs (British Thermal Units), depending on the size of the stove.

Masonry Heaters

Masonry heaters, also known as thermal mass heaters, use a large mass of stone, brick, or concrete to absorb and slowly release heat into the home over time. They are highly efficient and can store heat for up to 24 hours after the fire has gone out.

- **Key Features**: Large thermal mass, high efficiency, long-lasting heat, and even heat distribution.
- **Installation**: Requires a solid foundation due to its weight and is usually built as a permanent fixture in the home.
- **Heat Output**: Provides steady, radiant heat, making it ideal for cold climates, though it takes longer to heat up initially.

Wood-Fired Furnaces and Boilers

Wood-fired furnaces and boilers are larger systems designed to heat entire homes by distributing hot air or water through ducts or pipes. They are more complex but ideal for larger homes or multiple rooms.

- **Wood Furnaces**: Burn wood to heat air, which is distributed through ducts, and can often be connected to existing ductwork if upgrading from conventional furnaces.
- **Wood Boilers**: Heat water that is circulated through radiators or underfloor heating systems. Outdoor wood boilers are available, keeping the fire outside the home.
- **Heat Output**: Often exceeding 100,000 BTUs, wood-fired boilers and furnaces can heat larger homes effectively.

Planning Your Wood-Fired Heating System
Careful planning is essential for building or installing a wood-fired heating system that meets your needs, adheres to safety standards, and integrates well with your off-grid lifestyle.

Sizing the System
The size of the wood-fired system depends on the size of your home, climate, and insulation. Oversized systems can waste wood and overheat your space, while undersized systems may struggle to meet heating demands.
- **Heat Load Calculation**: The heat load, measured in BTUs, is determined by factors such as insulation, window area, and local climate.
- **Example Calculation**: For a well-insulated home in a cold climate, around 20–30 BTUs per square foot may be required. Multiply by your home's square footage to estimate heat output.

Fuel Supply and Storage
A steady supply of wood is critical for a wood-fired heating system. You will need to store and season wood properly for efficient burning.
- **Types of Wood**: Hardwoods like oak, maple, and hickory burn longer and hotter than softwoods like pine or fir. A mix of hardwoods and softwoods can help start fires quickly and maintain long-lasting heat.
- **Wood Storage**: Store wood in a dry, ventilated area to season it. Properly seasoned wood, with a moisture content below 20%, burns efficiently and reduces creosote buildup in the chimney.
- **Quantity of Wood**: For a small home, 3 to 5 cords of wood may be needed for the winter, while larger homes or colder climates could require 8 to 12 cords.

Placement and Ventilation
Choosing the right location is important for distributing heat evenly and ensuring safety.
- **Central Location**: A wood stove positioned centrally heats the home more evenly, while a furnace or boiler should be placed where it can connect to ducts or radiators easily.
- **Chimney and Ventilation**: Proper ventilation removes smoke and gases. Chimneys should meet building codes and be positioned with appropriate clearances from flammable materials.

Step-by-Step Guide to Building a Wood-Fired Heating System
If you're planning a DIY wood-fired heating system, follow these steps for a safe and efficient build.
Step 1: Choose the Right System
Choose a system based on your home size, heating needs, and available materials—whether it's a simple wood stove, a masonry heater, or a more complex wood furnace.
Step 2: Prepare the Installation Site
- **Clearances**: Ensure safety clearances (usually 36 inches) from walls and combustible materials.
- **Floor Protection**: Place a non-combustible hearth pad (stone, brick, or metal) under the stove.
- **Chimney/Flue Installation**: Install a chimney or flue following local codes. Stainless steel chimneys are commonly used for durability.
Step 3: Install the Heating System
- **Wood Stove**: Follow the manufacturer's instructions. Secure the stove and connect the chimney or flue.
- **Masonry Heater**: Build on a solid foundation following construction plans. Professional help may be needed for this more complex installation.
- **Wood Boiler/Furnace**: Connect to ductwork or radiators. Outdoor boilers will require underground piping for heated water.
Step 4: Test the System
Test the system with a small fire, monitoring for proper airflow, heat output, and safety.
- **Monitor Airflow**: Ensure air vents are working properly. Adjust them to control the fire's burn rate.
- **Check for Smoke**: If smoke leaks into the room, inspect the chimney or flue for blockages or leaks.

Efficient Operation and Maintenance
Proper operation and maintenance are key to getting the most out of your wood-fired heating system. Regular cleaning and good burning techniques maximize efficiency, safety, and heat output.

Burn Wood Efficiently
- **Use Seasoned Wood**: Burn only dry, seasoned wood to increase heat output and minimize creosote buildup.
- **Control Air Intake**: Adjust vents to regulate the fire. Too much air makes the fire too hot, while too little leads to smoldering.
- **Avoid Overloading**: Do not overfill the firebox, as this reduces efficiency and increases smoke production.

Regular Maintenance
- **Chimney Cleaning**: Clean the chimney annually to prevent creosote buildup, which can lead to chimney fires.
- **Inspect for Cracks/Leaks**: Regularly check for any damage in the stove, boiler, or furnace.
- **Replace Worn Parts**: Over time, gaskets, air vents, or glass doors may need replacement to maintain efficient operation.

Safety Considerations for Wood-Fired Systems
Safety is paramount when using wood-fired systems, as they can pose fire hazards or lead to carbon monoxide poisoning if not properly maintained.
- **Smoke Detectors and Carbon Monoxide Alarms**: Install alarms near the wood stove or boiler to detect potential dangers.
- **Chimney Fires**: Regular cleaning prevents dangerous chimney fires caused by creosote buildup.
- **Fire Safety**: Always keep a fire extinguisher nearby, and store kindling and wood away from the stove or heater to reduce the risk of accidental fires.

Building a wood-fired heating system is an effective way to stay warm in an off-grid home, offering reliability, cost savings, and self-sufficiency. With proper planning, installation, and maintenance, a wood-fired system can provide heat for many years, making it a valuable investment for any off-grid homestead. By following the steps and safety precautions outlined in this chapter, you can enjoy the benefits of renewable, wood-fired heat while ensuring the safety and efficiency of your system.

Chapter 7: Project: DIY Rocket Mass Heater

A rocket mass heater (RMH) is an efficient and sustainable way to heat an off-grid home, combining the benefits of a wood stove with the heat-retaining properties of thermal mass. It burns wood at high efficiency, storing heat in a mass structure such as cob or stone, which radiates warmth long after the fire has gone out. This chapter provides a step-by-step guide to building your own DIY rocket mass heater, covering design principles, materials, and construction methods to create an energy-efficient heating system for your off-grid home.

What is a Rocket Mass Heater?

A rocket mass heater operates by burning small amounts of wood in a highly efficient combustion chamber that produces minimal smoke and maximizes heat output. The heat is stored in a thermal mass—such as a cob bench or masonry structure—which slowly radiates warmth throughout the living space.

Key Features of a Rocket Mass Heater:

- **Efficient Combustion**: RMHs burn fuel completely, resulting in little smoke and ash.
- **Low Fuel Usage**: RMHs use less wood than traditional wood stoves, making them ideal for homesteads with limited wood supplies.
- **Thermal Mass Storage**: The thermal mass stores heat from the exhaust gases, slowly releasing it over time.
- **Versatility**: RMHs can be used for heating, cooking, and even water heating with the right setup.

Advantages of a Rocket Mass Heater

Rocket mass heaters are popular among off-grid enthusiasts and homesteaders due to their numerous benefits:

- **Fuel Efficiency**: RMHs use 50–80% less wood than traditional stoves, reducing the need for constant wood collection.
- **Low Emissions**: High-efficiency combustion results in minimal smoke and ash, making RMHs eco-friendly.
- **Cost-Effective**: RMHs can be built with inexpensive, locally sourced materials like clay, sand, and bricks, lowering the overall cost.
- **Extended Heating**: The thermal mass continues radiating heat for hours after the fire has gone out.

Design and Components of a Rocket Mass Heater

An RMH consists of several key components, each crucial for its efficiency and functionality.

The Feed Tube

This is where wood is loaded into the system. The wood is placed vertically in the feed tube and pulled into the combustion chamber by gravity as it burns.

  Design Tip: Insulate the feed tube to keep the combustion chamber hot, ensuring complete combustion.

The Burn Tunnel

The burn tunnel is a horizontal chamber connecting the feed tube to the heat riser, where wood burns and hot gases flow toward the next stage of combustion.

  Design Tip: Keep the burn tunnel as short as possible to reduce heat loss.

The Heat Riser

The heat riser is an insulated vertical chamber that intensifies combustion, ensuring the gases reach a high temperature. It creates the draft needed to circulate the hot gases through the system.

  Design Tip: Insulate the heat riser with materials like perlite or vermiculite to retain heat and maximize efficiency.

The Thermal Mass

The thermal mass absorbs heat from the exhaust gases, storing and releasing it slowly. Common materials for the mass include cob, stone, or masonry, often shaped into a bench for seating.

  Design Tip: A larger thermal mass stores more heat. Design the mass size according to your home's heating needs.

The Exhaust System

Unlike traditional wood stoves, RMHs direct exhaust gases through the thermal mass before venting outside. This allows maximum heat extraction before the gases exit.

  Design Tip: Ensure the exhaust pipe has a gentle slope to maintain airflow and prevent blockages.

Materials and Tools Needed for Building a Rocket Mass Heater

A rocket mass heater requires basic construction materials, many of which can be sourced locally or repurposed.

Materials:

- Fire bricks for the combustion chamber and burn tunnel.
- Clay and sand for cob and insulation.
- A 55-gallon steel drum for capturing and directing heat.
- Perlite or vermiculite for insulating the heat riser.
- Metal ducting for the exhaust system.
- Chimney pipe for venting the exhaust outside.
- Gravel or stone for the foundation.

Tools:

- Shovels and wheelbarrows for mixing cob.
- Trowels for shaping cob.
- Angle grinder or saw for cutting metal pipes.
- Hammer and masonry tools for working with bricks.
- Level and measuring tape for accurate construction.

Step-by-Step Guide to Building a Rocket Mass Heater

Follow these steps to build your own rocket mass heater.

Step 1: Prepare the Foundation

Select a central location in your home to distribute heat evenly. Build a solid, heat-resistant foundation using gravel, stone, or bricks. Ensure the foundation is level and can support the weight of the heater and thermal mass.

Step 2: Build the Combustion Chamber

Construct the feed tube, burn tunnel, and heat riser using fire bricks arranged in a U-shape. Ensure all connections are airtight.

> **Tip**: Use high-temperature mortar to bind the fire bricks and ensure durability.

Step 3: Install the Metal Barrel

Place the metal drum over the heat riser. The drum captures the heat and directs it into the thermal mass. Cut a hole in the drum's top to fit snugly over the heat riser.

> **Tip**: Allow airflow between the heat riser and the barrel for proper draft.

Step 4: Construct the Thermal Mass

Using a clay-sand mix, form the thermal mass around the exhaust pipes. Shape the mass into a bench, wall, or other structure that suits your space. Ensure the exhaust pipes slope slightly for proper gas flow.

Step 5: Install the Exhaust System

Connect the exhaust pipes to a chimney or vertical flue to vent gases outside. Ensure all joints are sealed.

> **Tip**: Add a cleanout port for easy maintenance.

Step 6: Test the System

Light a small fire in the feed tube and check for proper airflow and heat transfer. Adjust the burn chamber or exhaust if needed.

> **Tip**: If the fire doesn't draw properly, check the diameter of the heat riser and improve insulation around the burn chamber.

Maintaining Your Rocket Mass Heater

Proper maintenance ensures that your RMH operates efficiently and safely over time.

Cleaning the Exhaust System

Annually clean out any ash or debris from the exhaust system to prevent blockages and maintain airflow.

> **Tip**: A cleanout port simplifies the cleaning process.

Inspecting the Cob

Check the cob structure regularly for cracks. Repair any damage using a fresh clay-sand mixture.

> **Tip**: Add straw to the cob for reinforcement and crack prevention.

Improving Efficiency and Performance

To maximize the performance of your RMH, consider the following tips:

Use Well-Seasoned Wood

Burn well-seasoned wood with a moisture content below 20% to improve efficiency and reduce smoke.

Insulate the Heat Riser

Ensure the heat riser is fully insulated to maintain a high combustion temperature, promoting better fuel efficiency and fewer emissions.

Optimize Airflow

If the fire is weak, check airflow through the feed tube and ensure there are no blockages in the system.

Building a rocket mass heater is an ideal DIY project for off-grid homes seeking a low-cost, efficient, and sustainable heating solution. Following the steps in this guide, you can create a system that provides long-lasting warmth, reduces wood consumption, and minimizes environmental impact. With proper care and maintenance, your rocket mass heater will be a reliable and efficient source of heat for years to come.

MODULE U: OFF-GRID TRANSPORTATION

Chapter 1: Alternative Transportation in a Grid-Down World

In a world where access to conventional transportation is disrupted—whether due to a natural disaster, a breakdown of societal infrastructure, or a long-term grid-down scenario—having alternative modes of transportation is essential. Without access to gasoline, public transit systems, or even electricity to charge electric vehicles, reliance on traditional cars and trucks becomes impractical.

We will cover sustainable, low-tech methods, human-powered transport, and vehicles that run on alternative fuels. With the right planning and the use of alternative transportation methods, you can maintain mobility even when conventional systems fail.

The Importance of Mobility in a Grid-Down Scenario

Mobility is crucial for survival in a grid-down world. Whether you need to relocate to a safer area, transport supplies, or maintain connections with other off-grid communities, having reliable transportation is key. In such scenarios, gasoline shortages, lack of infrastructure, and limited repair options make most modern vehicles impractical.

Key Reasons Mobility is Essential

- **Access to Resources**: Mobility allows you to gather essential resources such as food, water, and medical supplies from a wider range of locations.
- **Evacuation and Relocation**: In dangerous situations, having transportation allows you to evacuate or relocate quickly.
- **Community and Trade**: Mobility enables you to maintain contact with other off-grid communities, fostering trade and resource sharing.

Challenges in a Grid-Down World

Without gasoline, functioning roads, or vehicle maintenance, many forms of modern transportation become obsolete. Roads may be impassable due to weather, infrastructure collapse, or a lack of upkeep, making traditional vehicles ineffective. Alternative, non-fuel-based transportation options are essential for ensuring long-term mobility.

Human-Powered Transportation

Human-powered transportation is one of the most reliable and sustainable ways to stay mobile in a grid-down world. Without the need for fuel, electricity, or complex machinery, human-powered transport helps you navigate your environment effectively.

Bicycles

Bicycles are practical and versatile, requiring no fuel and little maintenance. They are invaluable for short- and medium-distance travel.

- **Advantages**: Easy to maintain, low-cost, efficient, and capable of carrying small loads. Bicycles can traverse roads, paths, and even off-road terrain.
- **Challenges**: Limited carrying capacity, not ideal for rough terrain, and requires physical stamina.

Key Gear for Bicycle Transportation:

- **Trailers or Cargo Attachments**: Increases the load you can transport, such as food or water.
- **Spare Parts and Repair Tools**: Essential tools include spare tires, tubes, chains, and a repair kit.

Walking and Hiking

Walking is the most basic and reliable form of transportation. Though slower than other options, walking allows you to navigate nearly any terrain.

- **Advantages**: Requires no equipment, allows flexible routes, and is highly reliable.
- **Challenges**: Slow and physically demanding, especially when carrying heavy loads over long distances.

Key Gear for Walking and Hiking:
- **Backpack with Load-Bearing System**: Distributes weight evenly to help carry supplies long distances.
- **Hiking Poles**: Provides stability on rough terrain and reduces fatigue.

Canoes and Kayaks

In regions with waterways, canoes and kayaks offer low-tech, fuel-free transportation. They allow you to travel long distances across lakes, rivers, and coastal waters.
- **Advantages**: Efficient on water, ideal for areas with many waterways. Can carry substantial supplies.
- **Challenges**: Limited to water routes and can be physically demanding.

Key Gear for Watercraft Transportation:
- **Paddles and Spare Paddles**: Having spare paddles ensures you're prepared in case of damage.
- **Waterproof Storage**: Protect your supplies from water damage with dry bags or waterproof containers.

Animal-Powered Transportation

Animal-powered transportation, such as horses, mules, or even dogs, provides mobility without reliance on fuel or electricity. This form of transport is particularly effective for long-distance travel and carrying heavy loads.

Horses and Mules

Horses and mules are highly effective for carrying heavy loads and navigating rough terrain.
- **Advantages**: High endurance, capable of carrying supplies over long distances.
- **Challenges**: Requires feed, water, and regular care, and access to veterinary care may be limited.

Key Gear for Horse or Mule Transportation:
- **Saddle and Saddlebags**: Ensures comfort and allows for supply transport.
- **Hoof Care Tools**: Hoof picks and other tools help maintain hoof health on long journeys.

Dog Sleds

In cold, snowy environments, dog sleds offer fast, efficient transportation. Trained sled dogs can pull heavy loads over long distances.
- **Advantages**: Ideal for snowy terrain and long-distance travel.
- **Challenges**: Requires well-trained dogs and regular care. Limited to cold climates.

Key Gear for Dog Sledding:
- **Sled Harnesses**: Ensures weight distribution across the dog team, reducing injury.
- **Dog Food and Supplies**: High-calorie food and essential care items are necessary for maintaining the dogs' energy.

Alternative Fuel-Powered Transportation

For those who prefer motorized transport, alternative fuel-powered vehicles can offer speed and capacity while relying on sustainable fuel sources.

Biodiesel Vehicles

Biodiesel can be produced from vegetable oils or animal fats, making it a sustainable alternative to traditional diesel.
- **Advantages**: Renewable fuel source with long-range capabilities.
- **Challenges**: Requires raw materials and a setup for processing biodiesel.

Wood Gasification Vehicles

Wood gasification converts wood into gas that powers combustion engines, making it ideal when gasoline is unavailable.
- **Advantages**: Wood is widely available, and gasification is relatively simple.
- **Challenges**: Requires regular maintenance and specialized knowledge.

Electric Vehicles with Solar Charging

Solar-powered electric vehicles (EVs) are a sustainable option if paired with off-grid solar charging systems.
- **Advantages**: Low maintenance and renewable energy source.
- **Challenges**: Upfront investment is significant, and solar efficiency depends on weather conditions.

Planning for Long-Term Mobility

To ensure reliable transportation in a grid-down scenario, planning is essential. Whether you're relying on human power, animals, or alternative fuels, consider your environment, distance, and available resources.

Creating a Transportation Plan

When creating your transportation plan, consider the following steps:

- **Evaluate Your Environment**: What type of terrain will you be traversing? Consider rivers, mountains, or forests that may affect your routes.
- **Assess Fuel and Feed Availability**: If using animals, ensure there are grazing areas or enough feed along your route. For biodiesel or wood gas vehicles, plan for fuel production or wood availability.
- **Plan for Emergencies**: Have backup options ready in case your primary mode of transport fails, such as preparing to walk if a vehicle breaks down.

Stocking Spare Parts and Tools

Maintaining long-term mobility requires spare parts and repair tools.

- **Bicycles**: Keep spare tires, tubes, chain lubricant, and a repair kit.
- **Animal-Powered**: Carry extra saddles, harnesses, and hoof care tools.
- **Alternative Fuel Vehicles**: Stock spare filters, raw materials for fuel production, and basic engine repair tools.

In a grid-down world, maintaining reliable transportation is key to survival. From bicycles and walking to animal-powered and alternative fuel vehicles, having mobility without reliance on gasoline or electricity is achievable. By understanding your environment and selecting the right transportation methods, you can remain mobile even in the most challenging conditions.

Chapter 2: Maintaining Bicycles for Long-Term Use

In a grid-down scenario, bicycles become one of the most reliable and accessible modes of transportation. They don't require fuel, are simple to maintain, and can travel over various terrains with minimal effort. However, to ensure that your bicycle remains a long-term transportation solution, proper maintenance is critical. Regular maintenance helps prevent breakdowns, prolongs the life of your bike, and ensures it remains functional even when spare parts or professional repairs are hard to come by.

Why Bicycle Maintenance is Crucial in a Grid-Down World

In any off-grid or emergency scenario, access to repair shops and new parts will be severely limited. A well-maintained bicycle can offer years of reliable use if properly cared for. Failing to maintain your bicycle can lead to premature wear, preventable breakdowns, and a lack of mobility when you need it most.

Advantages of Regular Maintenance

- **Prevents Major Breakdowns**: Regular inspections help catch small issues before they escalate, such as fraying brake cables or loose chains.
- **Extends Lifespan**: Cleaning and lubricating moving parts ensures your bicycle's components last longer, reducing the need for replacements.
- **Maintains Efficiency**: A well-maintained bike runs smoothly and efficiently, allowing you to travel farther with less effort.

Essential Bicycle Maintenance Tasks

Key maintenance tasks should be performed regularly to keep your bicycle in good working order. These tasks focus on cleaning, lubricating, adjusting, and inspecting the main components of the bike.

Tire Maintenance

Your tires are your bike's connection to the ground. Keeping them in good condition is essential for safe and efficient riding.

Check Tire Pressure Regularly: Proper tire pressure reduces flats and improves performance. Under-inflated tires make riding harder and wear out faster.

> **Tip**: A small hand pump and pressure gauge are essential tools. Most bikes have recommended tire pressure listed on the side of the tire.

Inspect for Wear and Damage: Regularly check for cracks or punctures. Worn treads increase the risk of flats and reduce traction.

> **Repairing Flats**: Carry a tire patch kit and spare inner tubes. Learn how to quickly patch or replace a tube for long-distance travel.

Chain Care and Lubrication

The chain transfers power from the pedals to the wheels, making it essential to keep clean and lubricated to avoid rust and wear.

- **Clean the Chain Regularly**: Dirt buildup accelerates wear and makes pedaling harder. Clean the chain with a brush or rag and a degreaser every few weeks.
- **Lubricate the Chain**: After cleaning, apply bike-specific lubricant and wipe off excess oil to prevent attracting dirt.
  > **Tip**: In wet or muddy conditions, clean and lubricate more frequently to maintain performance.

Brakes

Reliable brakes are essential for safety, especially in rough terrain or downhill travel. Whether your bike has rim or disc brakes, maintaining them ensures stopping power.

- **Inspect Brake Pads**: Pads wear down over time and should be replaced when thin or worn to avoid damaging rims or rotors.
- **Adjust Brake Cables**: Loose or ineffective brakes may need cable adjustments. This can often be done with the barrel adjuster located on the brake lever.

> **Tip**: Keep spare brake pads and cables in your kit for easy replacements.

Wheel Alignment (Truing)

A misaligned wheel causes wobbling, affects steering, and can damage tires.

Check for Wobbling: Lift the bike and spin the wheels. If they wobble side-to-side, adjust the tension of the spokes with a spoke wrench.

Tip: Carry a spoke wrench and learn basic wheel truing to prevent long-term damage.

Lubricating Moving Parts

Lubricate other moving parts like the derailleur and gear mechanism, headset, and pedals regularly to prevent stiffness or malfunction.

- **Lubricate the Derailleur**: This mechanism allows smooth shifting but needs regular attention.
- **Grease the Headset and Pedals**: Clean and grease to avoid stiffness or seizing.

Inspect and Tighten Bolts

Vibrations from riding can loosen bolts, especially on rough terrain.

Regularly Check All Bolts: Inspect bolts on the frame, seat, handlebars, and pedals, and tighten any loose ones with the appropriate tools.

Long-Term Bicycle Maintenance: Stocking Spare Parts

In a grid-down scenario, spare parts may be hard to come by. It's essential to stockpile critical parts and learn basic repairs.

Essential Spare Parts to Keep

- **Inner Tubes and Tire Patch Kits**: Flats are inevitable, so keep extra tubes and patch kits.
- **Brake Pads and Cables**: Brake components wear down over time, so always have spares.
- **Chain Links or Spare Chain**: Chains stretch and wear out. Carry a spare chain or links with a chain tool for quick repairs.
- **Spokes**: A broken spoke weakens the wheel, so carry spares and a spoke wrench.

Basic Tools for Bicycle Maintenance

- **Multi-Tool**: Includes hex wrenches, screwdrivers, and a chain breaker for on-the-go adjustments.
- **Tire Levers**: Necessary for removing tires when fixing a flat.
- **Hand Pump**: Allows you to reinflate tires after repairs.
- **Chain Tool**: Breaks and reassembles chains for quick repairs.

Advanced Tools for Home Repairs

- **Truing Stand**: For extensive wheel repairs at home.
- **Pedal Wrench**: For replacing or adjusting pedals.
- **Spoke Tension Meter**: Useful for ensuring even tension during wheel truing.

Building a Bicycle Repair and Maintenance Kit

Your repair kit should be portable for rides but comprehensive for more extensive home repairs.

Basic On-the-Go Kit

This kit includes essential tools for fixing common issues during a ride:

- Spare Inner Tubes
- Tire Patch Kit
- Hand Pump
- Multi-Tool
- Tire Levers
- Spoke Wrench

Home Repair Kit

For more extensive at-home repairs, your kit should include:

- Chain Tool and Spare Chain Links
- Spare Spokes and Wrench
- Pedal Wrench
- Brake Pads and Cables
- Degreaser and Lubricant

Preventing and Handling Common Bicycle Issues

Despite regular maintenance, issues may arise, especially in rugged environments. Knowing how to address common problems ensures long-term mobility.

Handling a Flat Tire
Flat tires are common but easy to fix if you're prepared.
Steps:
- o   Use tire levers to remove the tire from the rim.
- o   Replace the inner tube or patch the puncture.
- o   Reinstall the tire and inflate it with a hand pump.

Dealing with Chain Issues
A broken or worn chain can be a major issue without proper knowledge.
Steps:
- o   Use a chain tool to remove the damaged section.
- o   Insert a replacement link or reassemble the chain.
- o   Ensure smooth operation through the derailleur.

Adjusting Misaligned Brakes
Misaligned brakes can reduce stopping power and cause uneven wear.
Steps:
- o   Align the brake pads with the rim or disc.
- o   Adjust the brake cable tension with the barrel adjuster.
- o   Test for smooth stopping power.

Bicycles are a reliable, fuel-free transportation option in a grid-down scenario, but their utility depends on regular maintenance and repair skills. By performing routine checks, stocking essential spare parts, and building a repair kit, you can ensure that your bicycle remains a long-term transportation solution. In the next chapter, we will explore human-powered transportation alternatives beyond bicycles, including walking, hiking, and watercraft.

Chapter 3: Electric Bikes and Solar-Powered Vehicles

Electric bikes (e-bikes) and solar-powered vehicles offer modern, sustainable transportation solutions that don't rely on fossil fuels. In a grid-down world, these alternatives can provide reliable mobility, especially when combined with off-grid power systems like solar charging. This chapter explores the benefits, limitations, and essential maintenance of electric bikes and solar-powered vehicles, as well as how to create a solar charging setup to keep these vehicles operational even when the electrical grid is down.

The Role of Electric Bikes and Solar-Powered Vehicles in Off-Grid Transportation

Electric bikes and solar-powered vehicles are increasingly popular for off-grid living due to their combination of modern efficiency and renewable energy. E-bikes provide a blend of human-powered and electric-assisted transport, making them suitable for short and long-distance travel.

Advantages of Electric Bikes

Electric bikes are an excellent alternative in a grid-down scenario, allowing riders to travel further with less physical effort.

- **Reduced Physical Strain**: E-bikes assist with pedaling, reducing fatigue on long trips or when carrying heavy loads.
- **Increased Speed and Range**: E-bikes enable faster travel, crucial when mobility is limited due to fuel shortages.
- **Dual-Power Flexibility**: Even if the battery runs out, e-bikes can still be pedaled manually, ensuring transportation even without solar charging.

Solar-Powered Vehicles

Solar-powered vehicles use energy stored in batteries charged by solar panels, making them highly sustainable for off-grid living.

- **Clean and Renewable**: They eliminate reliance on fossil fuels, essential during long-term grid-down scenarios.
- **Ideal for Off-Grid Living**: Solar-powered vehicles can be charged indefinitely if paired with a proper solar system.
- **Low Maintenance**: Fewer moving parts than gas vehicles mean fewer breakdowns and repairs.

Electric Bikes: Functionality, Maintenance, and Battery Management

Electric bikes (e-bikes) are equipped with a motor and battery to assist pedaling, increasing efficiency and reducing physical strain. Regular maintenance is key to keeping them operational for the long term.

How Electric Bikes Work

E-bikes feature an electric motor and a rechargeable battery. There are two types: **pedal-assist models**, where the motor activates as you pedal, and **throttle-based models**, where the motor can be engaged independently of pedaling.

- **Motor Types**: Hub motors (in the wheel) are simpler, while mid-drive motors (near the pedals) are better for hills and rough terrain.
- **Battery Pack**: Typically lithium-ion, which is efficient and long-lasting.

Maintaining Electric Bikes

Maintaining an e-bike involves caring for both its mechanical and electrical components.

- **Battery Care**: Charge regularly and avoid letting the battery discharge completely.
  - **Tip**: Store the battery at about 50% charge if not in use for long periods.
- **Chain and Gears**: Clean and lubricate the chain to prevent wear. The extra weight of the motor makes chain maintenance even more crucial.
- **Motor and Brakes**: Check motor wiring for wear and ensure brakes are in good condition, as e-bikes are heavier and faster than standard bikes.

Managing E-Bike Batteries Off-Grid

In a grid-down world, keeping your e-bike charged requires a solar charging setup.

> **Solar Charging**: A portable 100-200W solar panel can efficiently charge an e-bike battery.
> > **Tip**: Use a charge controller to prevent overcharging and damaging the battery.

Solar-Powered Vehicles: Feasibility and Off-Grid Sustainability

Solar-powered vehicles are fueled by solar energy, making them ideal for long-term off-grid transportation. A well-designed solar charging station can keep them operational even when the grid is down.

Types of Solar-Powered Vehicles

Solar Electric Vehicles (SEVs): Compact, solar-charged electric vehicles ideal for short trips in off-grid environments.

DIY Solar Conversions: Traditional electric vehicles can be converted to run on solar power by adding solar panels and batteries.

Solar Charging Systems for Vehicles

A robust solar charging system is essential to power electric vehicles in a grid-down scenario.

Solar Panel Size and Output: A 100-200W panel may suffice for e-bikes, while larger vehicles may need a 1,000W array.

> **Tip**: Position panels in open, sunlit areas for maximum efficiency.

Battery Storage: A battery bank stores energy for cloudy days when sunlight is limited.

> **Tip**: Use deep-cycle batteries, which are built for repeated charging and discharging.

Solar-Powered Vehicle Maintenance

Solar-powered vehicles require less frequent maintenance compared to gas-powered vehicles.

Battery Management: Avoid deep discharges and charge regularly with solar power.

Solar Panel Care: Keep panels clean and free from dust or snow to ensure optimal power generation.

Tire and Mechanical Components: Regularly inspect tires, brakes, and other mechanical parts to ensure a smooth ride.

Limitations of Electric and Solar-Powered Vehicles

While electric bikes and solar-powered vehicles offer numerous advantages, they also have limitations in off-grid scenarios.

Range and Battery Life

The range of electric and solar-powered vehicles is limited by the battery's capacity. Extended trips may require additional solar charging time.

> **Tip**: Carry a portable solar panel or backup battery to extend range.

Weather Dependence

Solar-powered vehicles rely on sunlight, meaning their efficiency decreases in cloudy or rainy conditions.

> **Tip**: In less sunny areas, consider increasing your solar panel capacity to store more energy during sunny periods.

Upfront Cost

The initial investment in electric bikes and solar-powered vehicles can be high, but over time, the elimination of fuel costs makes them cost-effective for off-grid living.

Electric bikes and solar-powered vehicles are excellent transportation options for grid-down scenarios. Their reliance on renewable energy and low maintenance requirements make them sustainable solutions for long-term use. Proper maintenance, careful battery management, and solar charging systems are key to keeping these vehicles operational. In the next chapter, we will explore another vital mode of off-grid transportation: animal-powered vehicles and how to care for them.

Chapter 4: Using Horses and Livestock for Transport

Before motorized vehicles, horses and livestock were essential for transportation, and in a grid-down scenario, they again become invaluable. These animals require no fuel, can traverse rugged terrain, and carry heavy loads, making them ideal for off-grid transportation. However, using animals for transport requires proper care, training, and equipment. This chapter covers the advantages, care, essential gear, and training needed to use horses and livestock for long-term transport.

The Role of Horses and Livestock in Off-Grid Transportation
In a grid-down scenario, horses and livestock provide reliable, fuel-free transportation over short and long distances.

Benefits of Animal-Powered Transportation
- **Fuel-Free Mobility**: Horses, mules, and livestock need only food and water to function, making them an excellent fuel-independent solution.
- **Versatility in Terrain**: They can navigate rough terrain that would be impassable to vehicles, such as mountains, forests, and riverbanks.
- **Carrying Capacity**: Horses, donkeys, and mules can carry significant loads or pull carts, allowing for efficient transport of supplies or people.

Challenges of Using Livestock for Transport
- **Care and Feeding**: Animals require regular feeding, water, and medical attention, making their upkeep more involved than motor vehicles.
- **Training and Handling**: Animals need proper training for load-bearing and obedience, which requires time and experience.
- **Limited Speed**: Horses travel at around 4-6 mph, slower than motor vehicles, limiting their speed over long distances.

Choosing the Right Animals for Transportation
Different animals excel in different transportation roles, based on their strength, endurance, and temperament.

Horses
Horses are versatile, capable of carrying riders, pulling carts, and carrying loads.
- **Advantages**: Horses are fast, strong, and can cover long distances. They can carry loads of 20-25% of their body weight.
- **Challenges**: Horses require substantial food, water, and medical care and are prone to injuries.
- **Breeds for Work**: Draft horses like Clydesdales are ideal for heavy pulling, while lighter breeds like Arabians are better suited for long-distance riding.

Donkeys and Mules
Mules and donkeys are known for their endurance, strength, and resilience, making them ideal for long-distance transport.
- **Advantages**: Mules are strong and require less food and water than horses. They handle harsh terrain better than horses.
- **Challenges**: Mules and donkeys are slower and can be more stubborn, requiring patience during training.
- **Best Uses**: Perfect for pack animals and pulling carts, especially in mountainous or arid environments.

xen
Oxen are cattle trained to pull heavy loads and are ideal for slow, heavy-duty work like hauling large carts or plowing fields.
- **Advantages**: Oxen are incredibly strong and hardy, requiring less specialized care.
- **Challenges**: Oxen are much slower and are generally used for pulling rather than riding or carrying loads directly.

Essential Gear for Animal-Powered Transport
Proper gear ensures the safety and efficiency of using animals for transportation, preventing injuries and maximizing load capacity.

Saddles and Bridles
Riding animals like horses and mules requires properly fitted saddles and bridles to ensure comfort and control.

- **Saddles**: A sturdy, well-padded saddle such as a Western or endurance saddle ensures weight is distributed evenly across the animal's back.
- **Bridles**: The bridle, along with a bit, allows for effective control of the animal. Make sure it fits well to avoid discomfort or injury.

Packs and Saddlebags

For pack animals, saddlebags and pack saddles allow for the even distribution of cargo.

- **Pack Saddles**: Specially designed saddles for carrying goods, ensuring that the load is balanced and doesn't strain the animal's back.
- **Saddlebags and Panniers**: Bags made of durable materials like leather or canvas to carry supplies, food, or tools.

Harnesses and Carts

To pull carts or wagons, animals need well-fitted harnesses to distribute the weight of the load.

- **Harnesses**: Use draft harnesses for heavy loads to ensure the animal can pull carts without injury.
- **Carts and Wagons**: Ensure carts are balanced and sturdy, with wheels capable of handling rough terrain.

Caring for Your Animals: Nutrition, Health, and Shelter

Proper care, including feeding, hydration, medical attention, and shelter, is crucial to maintain the health of transportation animals.

Feeding and Hydration

Animals used for transport need adequate food and water to sustain energy and health.

Forage and Feed: Grazing animals need access to grass and hay, supplemented with grains for high-energy work.

Tip: Carry high-energy feed like oats or barley during long trips to maintain stamina.

Water Needs: Horses may drink up to 20 gallons a day, so ensure access to fresh water.

Veterinary Care and Hoof Maintenance

Regular veterinary care is essential, especially in grid-down situations where outside help may be limited.

First Aid: Carry a basic animal first aid kit including bandages, antiseptics, and medications.

Hoof Care: Regularly clean and inspect hooves to prevent injury or lameness. Learning basic hoof trimming is essential.

Shelter and Rest

Providing shelter and regular rest for your animals ensures their longevity and performance.

Shelters: Portable shelters like tarps can provide protection in the field, while a stable or barn is necessary for longer-term housing.

Rest: Plan regular breaks for your animals during long journeys to prevent exhaustion.

Training Animals for Transportation

Training is critical for getting animals to reliably carry or pull loads, respond to commands, and navigate difficult terrain.

Basic Commands for Riding and Driving

Animals need to understand basic commands to be effectively controlled during transport.

Voice Commands: Train your animals to respond to simple voice commands like "walk," "trot," and "whoa" for easier navigation.

Rein Control: For riding or pulling carts, ensure the animal is trained to respond to reins or harness tension for direction and speed.

Training for Load Bearing

Animals should be gradually conditioned to carry or pull loads, starting light and increasing as their strength builds.

Tip: Practice with lighter loads before embarking on long or difficult journeys to build strength and confidence.

Acclimating to Terrain

Expose your animals to different terrains early in their training to build their confidence and ability to navigate difficult environments.

Chapter 5: Building Your Own DIY Electric Vehicle

In a world where fuel shortages and infrastructure collapse are real possibilities, building your own DIY electric vehicle (EV) offers a sustainable and practical alternative for transportation. While commercial electric vehicles are common, creating your own allows you to customize it for off-grid living, making it efficient, affordable, and tailored to your specific needs. This chapter will guide you through the process of building a DIY electric vehicle, from selecting the right components to managing solar power systems that keep your vehicle operational even when the electrical grid is down.

Why Build a DIY Electric Vehicle?
Building your own electric vehicle gives you complete control over the design, functionality, and energy source of your transportation, making it ideal for off-grid living. A DIY EV can be powered by renewable energy sources like solar, offering energy independence in a grid-down scenario.

Advantages of a DIY Electric Vehicle
- **Customizable**: Tailor the vehicle's size, range, and features to meet your specific transportation needs, whether for short trips or longer journeys.
- **Fuel Independence**: Paired with solar panels or wind energy, your DIY EV can become completely independent of fossil fuels.
- **Simpler Mechanics**: Electric vehicles have fewer moving parts than gas-powered cars, making them easier to maintain and repair in a survival situation.
- **Cost-Effective**: Building your own EV can be more affordable than buying a commercial one, especially when using recycled parts or a pre-existing vehicle chassis.

Challenges of DIY Electric Vehicle Construction
- **Technical Knowledge**: Building an EV requires a basic understanding of electronics, batteries, and vehicle mechanics.
- **Upfront Costs**: The initial investment in batteries, motors, and charging systems can be significant, though DIY builds tend to be cheaper than commercial EVs in the long term.
- **Range Limitations**: DIY EVs may have limited range compared to commercial models, depending on the size of the battery and motor used.

Planning and Designing Your DIY Electric Vehicle
Before building your electric vehicle, careful planning is essential. Decide on the vehicle's intended use, the type of chassis or donor vehicle, and the key components like the motor, battery, and controller.

Defining the Purpose of Your EV
Determine the purpose of your EV to guide your design decisions. For example:
- **Short-Range vs. Long-Range**: For local use, a smaller, lower-capacity battery will suffice, while long-range travel requires larger batteries and more powerful motors.
- **Passenger vs. Cargo**: A vehicle intended to carry heavy loads may need a more robust design compared to one focused on transporting passengers.

Choosing a Chassis or Donor Vehicle
Choosing the right chassis is a key first step. You can convert an existing vehicle or build a new frame.
- **Lightweight Vehicles**: Bikes, scooters, or golf carts are great for short-range EV conversions due to their low weight and energy requirements.
- **Standard Vehicle Conversion**: Converting small cars or SUVs is common for DIY EV builders. Focus on vehicles with a strong, lightweight frame as the engine and transmission will be removed.

Components of a DIY Electric Vehicle
The three main components of any electric vehicle are the **electric motor**, **battery pack**, and **controller**:
- **Electric Motor**: DC motors are commonly used due to their simplicity, though AC motors are more efficient. Used motors from forklifts, golf carts, or older EVs are affordable options.
- **Battery Pack**: Lithium-ion batteries are ideal due to their high energy density, but lead-acid batteries can be used for budget builds. The size of the battery pack will determine the vehicle's range and power.

Controller: The controller regulates electricity flow from the battery to the motor, allowing you to control speed and acceleration. Ensure compatibility between the motor, battery, and controller.

Building Your DIY Electric Vehicle
Once your design is ready and components selected, you can start assembling the vehicle.

Stripping the Donor Vehicle
If converting an existing vehicle, the first step is to remove unnecessary parts like the engine, exhaust system, and fuel tank. This reduces weight and makes room for the electric motor and battery pack.

> **Tip**: Retain the transmission if possible, as it can improve efficiency, especially on hilly terrain.

Installing the Electric Motor
Mount the electric motor in place of the combustion engine. It can be directly attached to the drivetrain or connected through the transmission.

> **Direct Drive vs. Transmission**: A direct drive offers simplicity, while using the transmission allows for better torque management.

Installing the Battery Pack
Mount the battery pack securely in areas like the engine bay, trunk, or under the seats, ensuring proper weight distribution.

> **Wiring**: Use appropriately sized cables for high-current connections between the battery, motor, and controller.

Wiring the Controller
The controller connects the battery pack to the motor, regulating power flow. Install the controller in a secure, dry location and wire it to the throttle system, which controls acceleration.

Powering Your Electric Vehicle Off-Grid with Solar Energy
One of the primary advantages of an electric vehicle is its ability to be charged using renewable energy. A solar charging setup allows you to recharge your vehicle without relying on external power.

Solar Charging Setup
To power your EV off-grid, you'll need a solar panel array capable of generating enough electricity to recharge the batteries.

- **Solar Panels**: A 1,000-2,000-watt solar array is typically sufficient for charging small DIY EVs. Panels can be mounted on a roof, a portable stand, or even on the vehicle itself for small setups.
- **Charge Controller**: The charge controller regulates electricity flow from the panels to the battery pack, preventing overcharging.
- **Inverter**: If using an AC motor, an inverter will convert the DC power generated by the solar panels into AC for the motor.

Managing Solar Energy Storage
Inconsistencies in sunlight can be mitigated by using a battery storage system to save excess solar power for later use.

> **Deep-Cycle Batteries**: These are ideal for storing solar energy, as they can withstand frequent charging and discharging.

Charging Cycles and Efficiency
Optimize your vehicle's charging by monitoring solar output and managing your driving patterns. Charge during peak sunlight hours and plan for cloudy days by reducing vehicle usage or using backup power.

Maintaining and Troubleshooting Your DIY Electric Vehicle
Regular maintenance of the motor, battery, and electrical systems will keep your DIY electric vehicle running smoothly.

Battery Maintenance
Batteries require careful management to ensure long life.

> **Charging Cycles**: Avoid full discharges; instead, keep the charge between 20% and 80%.
> **Temperature Control**: Extreme temperatures can degrade battery performance, so protect them from excessive heat or cold.

Motor and Controller Maintenance
While electric motors require little upkeep, routine checks will prevent issues.

> **Wiring Inspections**: Check for loose or damaged wires and ensure connections are clean and secure.
> **Cooling**: Some motors and controllers use cooling systems to prevent overheating, so ensure these are functioning properly.

Troubleshooting Common Issues

Power Loss: Check the battery charge and wiring. If the issue persists, inspect the motor and controller for signs of failure.

Overheating: Ensure proper ventilation and cooling. Overheating can result from overloading or poor maintenance. Building a DIY electric vehicle offers a path to sustainable, off-grid transportation, especially when combined with renewable energy sources like solar power. With the right components, design, and maintenance, you can create a reliable vehicle that operates independently of fossil fuels or grid power.

Chapter 6: Project: DIY Solar-Powered Bicycle Charger

Electric bikes (e-bikes) are an excellent solution for off-grid transportation due to their efficiency, speed, and ease of use. However, one of the main challenges of using an e-bike off the grid is maintaining a reliable power source for recharging the battery. In a grid-down scenario, relying on traditional electrical outlets is not an option, which makes a solar-powered charging system a sustainable and practical alternative. In this chapter, we will guide you through building your own DIY solar-powered charger for an electric bicycle, allowing you to keep your e-bike operational without the need for external power sources.

Why Build a Solar-Powered Bicycle Charger?

A solar-powered bicycle charger allows you to maintain the independence and mobility of your electric bike without being reliant on the grid. By harnessing solar energy, you can recharge your e-bike battery even in remote locations, ensuring that your transportation remains sustainable and reliable.

Benefits of Solar-Powered Charging

- **Energy Independence**: Solar energy provides a renewable and endless power source, making it ideal for off-grid living or emergency situations where the electrical grid is unavailable.
- **Cost-Effective**: After the initial setup cost, solar energy is free, which can significantly reduce your reliance on traditional fuel or paid electricity.
- **Eco-Friendly**: Solar energy is a clean and renewable resource, meaning that you are reducing your carbon footprint while maintaining a functional mode of transportation.

Challenges of Solar Charging

- **Weather-Dependent**: Solar charging is dependent on sunlight, which means that cloudy days, rainy weather, or winter months with less daylight can impact your ability to recharge the battery efficiently.
- **Initial Setup Costs**: The cost of solar panels, charge controllers, and batteries can be high upfront, although the long-term savings make it worthwhile.

Planning Your Solar Bicycle Charger System

Before diving into the construction of your solar-powered charger, you need to carefully plan the system to ensure it meets your specific needs. The most important factors to consider are the power requirements of your electric bike, the type of solar panels you'll use, and how you'll store excess energy.

Understanding Your E-Bike's Power Needs

The first step in designing your solar charging system is to understand your e-bike's power requirements. Most e-bike batteries operate at either 36V, 48V, or 52V, and the size of the battery (in watt-hours or amp-hours) will determine how much energy is needed for a full recharge.

- **Battery Voltage**: Confirm the voltage of your e-bike's battery to ensure that your solar system can provide the correct output. For example, a 48V battery will need a solar setup that can output at least 48V.
- **Battery Capacity**: The capacity of the battery is measured in watt-hours (Wh) or amp-hours (Ah). For example, if your battery is rated at 500Wh, you'll need a solar setup capable of providing at least 500 watt-hours of energy to fully charge the battery.

Choosing Solar Panels

The type and size of your solar panels will determine how much energy you can generate to charge your e-bike. Ideally, you'll want portable, high-efficiency solar panels that can easily be transported or mounted when needed.

- **Panel Wattage**: For a reliable charging system, aim for solar panels with a total output of 100W-300W, depending on your battery size. The higher the wattage, the faster your battery will charge.
- **Portability**: For off-grid mobility, portable and foldable solar panels are ideal. They are lightweight, easy to carry, and can be set up quickly when you need to charge your e-bike on the go.

Solar Charge Controller

A solar charge controller is necessary to regulate the energy flowing from the solar panels to the e-bike's battery. It ensures that the battery is charged safely and efficiently, preventing overcharging or overheating.

- **MPPT vs. PWM Controllers**: Maximum Power Point Tracking (MPPT) controllers are more efficient and can extract more power from the solar panels, especially in varying sunlight conditions. Pulse Width Modulation (PWM) controllers are simpler and cheaper but less efficient.
- **Voltage Compatibility**: Make sure the charge controller matches the voltage of your e-bike battery. For a 48V battery, you'll need a 48V charge controller to prevent overvoltage or damage to the battery.

Battery Storage for Backup Power

If you plan to charge your e-bike in areas with inconsistent sunlight, it's a good idea to include a backup battery storage system. This allows you to store excess energy generated by the solar panels during peak sunlight hours, which can then be used later to charge your e-bike when the sun isn't shining.

- **Deep-Cycle Batteries**: Choose deep-cycle batteries for your backup storage, as they are designed to handle frequent charging and discharging cycles.
- **Inverter (if necessary)**: If your e-bike runs on AC power, you may need an inverter to convert the DC power from the solar panels or backup batteries into AC power.

Building the DIY Solar-Powered Bicycle Charger

Now that you've planned your system, it's time to begin constructing the solar-powered charger. This section outlines the step-by-step process for building your charger and ensuring it works properly with your electric bike.

Gathering Materials

Here's a list of materials you'll need to build your DIY solar-powered charger:

- Solar Panels (100W-300W, portable or foldable panels recommended)
- Solar Charge Controller (MPPT recommended for efficiency)
- Cables and Connectors (appropriate gauge for your solar setup and e-bike battery)
- Deep-Cycle Battery (optional, for backup power storage)
- Inverter (if necessary, for AC charging)
- Mounting Equipment (for solar panels, if you plan to mount them on a bike trailer or other structure)

Assembling the Solar Charger System

Follow these steps to set up your solar-powered bicycle charger:

- **Install the Solar Panels**: If you are using portable solar panels, simply position them in an area with maximum sunlight exposure. If you plan to mount the panels on a bike trailer or frame, securely attach them using mounting brackets. Ensure the panels are angled correctly to capture the most sunlight throughout the day.
- **Connect the Solar Panels to the Charge Controller**: Using the appropriate cables, connect the positive and negative terminals of the solar panels to the input ports of the solar charge controller. The charge controller will regulate the energy output from the panels to match the voltage requirements of your e-bike battery.
- **Connect the Charge Controller to the E-Bike Battery**: Using another set of cables, connect the output terminals of the charge controller to the battery's input ports. Ensure that the voltage and polarity are correct to avoid damaging the battery.
- **Test the System**: Once everything is connected, turn on the solar charge controller and check the charging status of your e-bike battery. The charge controller should display the current charge level and indicate that the battery is charging.

Incorporating Backup Battery Storage

If you are using a backup battery system, follow these additional steps:

- **Connect the Backup Battery to the Charge Controller**: Use cables to connect the backup battery to the charge controller's output terminals. This allows the solar panels to charge both your e-bike battery and the backup battery when there is excess energy.
- **Install an Inverter (if needed)**: If your e-bike uses AC power, install an inverter between the backup battery and the e-bike battery. This will convert the stored DC energy into AC for charging your e-bike.

Monitor Energy Levels: Use the charge controller's display to monitor both the e-bike battery and the backup battery levels. Charge the e-bike from the backup battery when the solar panels are not generating enough energy (such as during nighttime or cloudy weather).

Testing and Optimizing the Solar Charger
Once your solar charger is set up, it's important to test the system to ensure everything is functioning as expected. You should also optimize the setup to maximize charging efficiency based on your location and sunlight conditions.

Testing the Charging System
Start by testing the system during peak sunlight hours, when solar generation is highest. Check the following:

- **Charge Controller**: Ensure the charge controller is regulating the voltage correctly and displaying charging progress.
- **Battery Charging**: Monitor the e-bike battery to see how quickly it charges. You may need to adjust the placement of the solar panels to get maximum sunlight exposure.
- **Backup Battery (if applicable)**: If using a backup battery, check that it is also being charged by the solar panels.

Optimizing Solar Panel Placement
Maximizing sunlight exposure is key to efficient solar charging. Here are some tips for optimizing your solar panel placement:

- **Adjust the Angle**: Angle the panels toward the sun based on your geographic location and the time of year. In general, solar panels should be tilted at an angle equal to your latitude for maximum efficiency.
- **Avoid Shaded Areas**: Ensure the solar panels are placed in areas without shade from trees, buildings, or other obstructions that could block sunlight.
- **Portable Panels**: If using portable panels, move them periodically throughout the day to track the sun's movement and capture the most energy possible.

Maintaining Your Solar Charging System
To ensure your solar-powered bicycle charger remains functional for the long term, regular maintenance is necessary. This includes keeping the solar panels clean, checking connections, and monitoring the performance of the charge controller and battery.

Cleaning and Inspecting Solar Panels
Dust, dirt, and debris can reduce the efficiency of solar panels, so it's important to clean them regularly. Use a soft cloth or sponge and water to wipe down the surface of the panels. Avoid using abrasive materials that could scratch the panels.

Monitoring Battery Health
Regularly check the charge levels of your e-bike battery and backup battery (if applicable) to ensure they are holding a charge properly. Batteries degrade over time, so monitoring their performance can help you detect issues early.

Checking Connections
Periodically inspect the wiring and connections between the solar panels, charge controller, and battery. Loose or corroded connections can reduce the efficiency of the system and lead to power loss.

Building your own DIY solar-powered bicycle charger is an empowering project that provides you with a sustainable, off-grid solution for keeping your electric bike operational. By harnessing the power of the sun, you can travel long distances, even in a grid-down scenario, without worrying about fuel or electricity availability. With proper planning, setup, and maintenance, your solar charging system will ensure your e-bike remains a reliable mode of transportation.

MODULE V: OFF-GRID POWER TOOLS AND HAND TOOLS:

Chapter 1: Essential Hand Tools for Off-Grid Living

Living off the grid means becoming more self-sufficient in almost every aspect of life. Without access to modern conveniences like electricity or professional repair services, hand tools become invaluable for building, repairing, and maintaining everything from shelters to furniture. While power tools are convenient, hand tools provide reliability and independence from fuel and electricity. In this chapter, we will explore the essential hand tools needed for off-grid living and their various applications in daily tasks, from construction to gardening and general repairs.

Why Hand Tools are Crucial in Off-Grid Living

Hand tools offer numerous advantages for off-grid living. They do not require electricity or fuel, making them dependable in any situation. Furthermore, hand tools are often more durable, portable, and versatile than their powered counterparts. In an off-grid world, where self-reliance is key, mastering the use of hand tools is essential.

Advantages of Hand Tools

- **No Power Required**: Hand tools function independently of electricity, fuel, or batteries, making them ideal for off-grid situations where access to power may be unreliable.
- **Long-Lasting**: With proper care and maintenance, high-quality hand tools can last for generations.
- **Versatility**: Many hand tools are multi-functional and can be used for a wide range of tasks, from building structures to making furniture or performing repairs.
- **Quiet and Environmentally Friendly**: Unlike power tools, hand tools produce no noise pollution or harmful emissions, making them both quiet and eco-friendly.

Hand Tools for Construction and Building

In an off-grid scenario, having the ability to build your own structures or make repairs to existing ones is critical. The following hand tools are essential for general construction, carpentry, and repairs around your homestead.

Hammers and Mallets

A reliable hammer is a foundational tool for any off-grid project, from driving nails into wood to breaking down materials.

- **Claw Hammer**: The claw hammer is perfect for driving and removing nails. It's versatile and can be used for both construction and minor repairs.
- **Sledgehammer**: A sledgehammer is ideal for heavy-duty tasks such as breaking concrete or driving stakes into the ground.
- **Wood Mallet**: A wood mallet is useful for striking chisels and performing fine carpentry work without damaging the tools or the material.

Saws

While power saws are fast, hand saws are indispensable for off-grid projects. They are essential for cutting wood, trimming logs, or preparing firewood.

- **Crosscut Saw**: The crosscut saw is designed for cutting across the grain of wood, making it ideal for cutting boards, logs, and beams during construction.
- **Rip Saw**: This type of saw is used for cutting along the grain of the wood, making it useful for ripping boards and preparing lumber.
- **Bow Saw**: The bow saw is excellent for cutting both green wood and dry wood. It's perfect for gathering firewood or cutting larger logs for construction.

Chisels

Chisels are essential for woodworking projects, as they allow for precise cuts, carving, and shaping of wood.

- **Wood Chisel Set**: A set of wood chisels in various sizes will help you with detailed carpentry work, such as fitting joints, trimming wood, and creating decorative details.

- **Mortise Chisel**: A mortise chisel is specifically designed for cutting square holes, or mortises, in wood, which are commonly used in traditional joinery techniques.

Measuring and Marking Tools
Accurate measurements are critical in construction and woodworking. The right measuring and marking tools help ensure your projects are precise and properly aligned.
- **Tape Measure**: A reliable tape measure allows you to measure lengths and distances accurately, which is crucial for all construction and repair tasks.
- **Speed Square**: This tool is used for marking right angles and making quick measurements, especially in carpentry.
- **Chalk Line**: A chalk line is used for marking long, straight lines on surfaces, which helps when cutting or aligning materials.

Planes
Hand planes are used for smoothing and shaping wood, removing rough edges, and achieving a fine finish on woodworking projects.
- **Block Plane**: A block plane is a small, versatile tool used for smoothing the ends of boards or trimming edges. It's particularly useful for fine carpentry and cabinet making.
- **Jack Plane**: This larger plane is designed for removing larger amounts of material and leveling boards. It's a workhorse tool for preparing rough lumber for use in construction.

Hand Tools for Gardening and Land Management
Maintaining a garden or small farm is a key part of off-grid living, providing food security and sustainability. These hand tools are essential for managing land, cultivating crops, and maintaining gardens without relying on fuel-powered machinery.

Shovels and Spades
Shovels and spades are used for digging, planting, and moving soil or compost. A well-made shovel is a multipurpose tool that can help with everything from digging garden beds to creating drainage ditches.
- **Digging Shovel**: A sturdy digging shovel is essential for breaking ground, moving soil, and digging trenches.
- **Spade**: A spade is used for edging garden beds, digging straight-sided holes, and transplanting shrubs or trees.

Hoes
A hoe is one of the most versatile tools in the garden, used for breaking up soil, weeding, and cultivating crops.
- **Draw Hoe**: This classic hoe is great for chopping through weeds, breaking up soil, and shaping garden beds.
- **Scuffle Hoe**: A scuffle hoe is designed for shallow weeding without disturbing the soil too much, making it perfect for maintaining crops and vegetable gardens.

Rakes
Rakes are used for leveling soil, removing debris, and spreading mulch or compost. They are essential for preparing garden beds and keeping your homestead clean and organized.
- **Garden Rake**: This rake is designed for leveling soil, spreading compost, and preparing garden beds.
- **Leaf Rake**: A leaf rake is used for clearing leaves and light debris from lawns or garden areas.

Axes and Hatchets
Axes and hatchets are crucial for cutting wood, chopping firewood, and clearing brush. These tools are indispensable for managing land and preparing timber for construction or fuel.
- **Felling Axe**: A large felling axe is used for cutting down trees and splitting logs into firewood.
- **Hatchet**: A hatchet is a smaller version of the axe, useful for lighter tasks like chopping kindling, trimming branches, or carving wood.

Hand Tools for Repairs and Maintenance
Beyond construction and gardening, hand tools are essential for making repairs and maintaining your homestead. These tools allow you to fix equipment, mend structures, and perform routine upkeep without the need for electricity or complex machinery.

Screwdrivers
A set of high-quality screwdrivers is indispensable for assembling furniture, repairing machines, and general maintenance

tasks.

> **Flathead and Phillips Screwdrivers**: Having both flathead and Phillips screwdrivers in various sizes ensures you can work with a wide range of fasteners and hardware.

Wrenches and Pliers

Wrenches and pliers allow you to grip, turn, and manipulate nuts, bolts, and other small components. They are essential for fixing mechanical equipment, plumbing, and basic repairs.

- **Adjustable Wrench**: An adjustable wrench is versatile and can be used for turning nuts and bolts of different sizes.
- **Needle-Nose Pliers**: Needle-nose pliers are perfect for gripping small parts, bending wire, and performing delicate tasks.
- **Channel-Lock Pliers**: These pliers are adjustable and can grip larger objects, making them ideal for plumbing or mechanical repairs.

Files and Rasps

Files and rasps are used for smoothing rough edges, shaping metal or wood, and making fine adjustments to parts.

> **Flat File**: A flat file is used for smoothing and shaping metal, sharpening tools, and finishing metal surfaces.
> **Wood Rasp**: A wood rasp is useful for shaping wood and smoothing rough edges on carpentry projects.

Caring for and Maintaining Hand Tools

Hand tools can last for generations if properly cared for. Regular maintenance not only extends the lifespan of your tools but also ensures they remain functional and efficient for off-grid tasks.

Cleaning and Oiling

After each use, clean your tools to remove dirt, rust, or sap that can cause corrosion. Use a wire brush to remove debris, and apply a light coat of oil to metal parts to prevent rust.

> **Tip**: For wooden handles, periodically apply linseed oil to prevent cracking and to extend the life of the wood.

Sharpening Blades

Tools like axes, knives, chisels, and planes need regular sharpening to function properly. Dull tools require more effort to use and can be dangerous.

> **Sharpening Stones**: Use a sharpening stone to maintain a sharp edge on blades. Ensure you use the correct grit for your tool—coarse for sharpening, fine for honing.

Storing Tools Properly

Proper storage is essential to prevent rust, damage, or wear to your tools. Keep your tools in a dry, protected space, such as a tool shed or storage box.

> **Tool Racks**: Store tools on racks or hooks to keep them off the ground and prevent moisture damage.
> **Toolboxes**: For smaller hand tools, use a toolbox with compartments to keep everything organized and protected from the elements.

Regular Inspections

Periodically inspect your tools for signs of wear or damage. Check wooden handles for cracks and replace them if necessary. For metal tools, look for signs of rust or damage to the blades and repair or replace as needed. Regular inspections will help you catch small issues before they turn into bigger problems, ensuring your tools remain reliable and safe to use.

Hand tools are the backbone of off-grid living, providing reliable, fuel-free solutions for building, repairing, gardening, and maintaining your homestead. By selecting high-quality tools and caring for them properly, you can ensure that these essential items last for many years, allowing you to remain self-sufficient even in the most challenging conditions. In the following chapters, we will explore power tools and how to adapt them for off-grid use through alternative energy sources like solar or manual power.

Chapter 2: Solar-Powered Power Tools: How to Choose and Use

While hand tools are indispensable for off-grid living, power tools can greatly enhance your ability to tackle larger, more complex tasks efficiently. However, without access to the electrical grid, using power tools presents a challenge. Solar energy offers a sustainable and renewable solution to power your tools, allowing you to maintain the convenience and efficiency of modern power tools while living off the grid. This chapter will guide you through choosing the right solar-powered power tools, setting up a solar charging system, and using these tools effectively in an off-grid environment.

Why Solar-Powered Power Tools are Ideal for Off-Grid Living
Solar-powered power tools provide a reliable way to increase productivity on your off-grid homestead while reducing dependency on fossil fuels or traditional power sources. By utilizing solar energy to charge batteries for your tools, you can continue to perform construction, repairs, and maintenance without worrying about the availability of electricity.

Benefits of Solar-Powered Tools
- **Energy Independence**: Solar power allows you to charge your tools without needing a connection to the electrical grid, making it ideal for remote locations.
- **Sustainability**: Solar energy is renewable and eco-friendly, reducing your reliance on gasoline generators or fossil fuels for powering tools.
- **Versatility**: Solar-powered power tools can be used for various tasks, from construction to gardening, helping you complete projects faster and with less physical effort than hand tools.

Challenges of Solar-Powered Tools
- **Weather Dependence**: Solar-powered systems rely on sunlight, so cloudy or rainy days may reduce the efficiency of your charging system.
- **Initial Costs**: Setting up a solar power system involves upfront costs for panels, batteries, and charge controllers, although these investments often pay off over time.

Choosing Solar-Compatible Power Tools
Not all power tools are equally suited for off-grid living. When selecting tools for your solar-powered system, it's important to prioritize those that are battery-operated and energy-efficient. The goal is to balance the power demands of your tools with the output of your solar setup.

Battery-Powered vs. Corded Tools
Battery-powered tools are the best choice for solar charging because they offer flexibility and portability. Most modern cordless power tools run on rechargeable batteries, which can be easily recharged using a solar system.
- **Battery-Powered Tools**: These tools operate on rechargeable lithium-ion or nickel-metal hydride (NiMH) batteries. They are ideal for off-grid use as they can be recharged via solar power and do not require a constant power source.
- **Corded Tools**: Corded tools require continuous access to electricity, making them less practical for off-grid living. If needed, they will require a solar-powered generator or inverter to function.

Tool Efficiency and Power Requirements
When choosing power tools for off-grid use, consider their energy efficiency and power consumption. Tools that use less power will allow you to maximize your solar energy, enabling longer periods of use between charges.
- **Energy-Efficient Tools**: Opt for tools with high-efficiency brushless motors. These use less power than traditional brushed motors but offer similar performance. While more expensive initially, they provide better battery life and efficiency over time.
- **Low-Power Tools**: For lighter tasks, use lower-powered tools that draw less energy. For instance, a 12V drill consumes less energy than an 18V or 24V drill, making it more practical for long-term off-grid use.

Choosing the Right Battery System
Power tools come with various battery voltages, ranging from 12V to 60V, and battery types. When selecting tools for solar charging, choose those that use the same battery platform to simplify charging and maintenance.

- **Lithium-Ion Batteries**: Lithium-ion batteries are ideal for off-grid power tools because of their high energy density, long lifespan, and lightweight design. They are also more efficient with solar recharging compared to older technologies like lead-acid batteries.
- **Universal Battery Platforms**: Many tool brands offer a universal battery system that allows a single type of battery to power multiple tools. This streamlines your charging process, eliminating the need for different voltage requirements across multiple tools.

Setting Up a Solar Power System for Charging Tools

To keep your power tools charged, you'll need a solar power system that generates enough energy to meet your daily tool usage. The key components of this system include solar panels, a charge controller, batteries for energy storage, and an inverter (if necessary).

Solar Panel Selection

The size and type of solar panels you choose will determine how quickly you can recharge your tools and how many tools you can charge simultaneously.

- **Panel Size and Output**: For charging multiple power tools, a solar panel array with a total output of 200W to 500W is typically sufficient. The larger the array, the faster your battery will charge, especially on sunny days.
- **Portable Panels**: For portability, consider foldable or portable solar panels that you can reposition to maximize sunlight exposure throughout the day.

Solar Charge Controllers

A solar charge controller regulates the voltage and current from the solar panels, ensuring safe charging of your tool batteries.

- **MPPT vs. PWM**: Maximum Power Point Tracking (MPPT) controllers are more efficient and help you get the most energy from your solar panels. Pulse Width Modulation (PWM) controllers are more affordable but less efficient.
- **Voltage Matching**: Ensure that your charge controller matches the voltage of your tool batteries (e.g., 12V, 18V, 24V) to avoid overcharging or damaging the battery.

Battery Storage and Backup Power

A deep-cycle battery storage system is essential for maintaining a consistent power supply, especially during cloudy days or high-demand periods.

- **Deep-Cycle Batteries**: Designed for repeated charging and discharging, deep-cycle batteries are perfect for storing solar energy.
- **Battery Capacity**: Choose a battery that can store enough energy for a full day's work. For instance, a 100Ah battery can store enough energy to charge several tool batteries multiple times.

Inverters (for AC Tools)

If you need to power corded tools that run on AC power, an inverter will convert the DC power generated by the solar panels into AC power.

- **Inverter Size**: Choose an inverter capable of handling the wattage of your tools. A 500W inverter can power light tools, while a 1500W inverter is better for heavy-duty tools.
- **Pure Sine Wave Inverters**: Opt for pure sine wave inverters for sensitive electronics or tools, as they provide a stable power output similar to the electrical grid.

Using Solar-Powered Power Tools Effectively

Once your solar-powered tool system is set up, there are ways to maximize efficiency and ensure you have enough power for all your projects.

Work During Peak Sunlight Hours

Plan your work during peak sunlight hours (10 AM to 3 PM) to ensure your solar panels are generating maximum energy. This allows direct charging of batteries and replenishing storage batteries.

    Tip: Charge extra batteries during peak hours so you have reserves for later use or cloudy days.

Rotate Battery Use

Rotate your batteries if your tools share a common battery platform. Use one battery while others charge, ensuring a continuous workflow.

    Tip: Invest in several backup batteries to avoid downtime.

Prioritize Energy-Efficient Tools

On days with limited sunlight, prioritize energy-efficient tools for tasks that require less power. For example, use a manual saw for small cuts and save your circular saw for more demanding work.

Maintenance of Solar Panels and Batteries

Regular maintenance is key to keeping your solar-powered system running efficiently.

Cleaning Solar Panels: Keep them clean and free from debris to maximize efficiency. Use a soft cloth or sponge with water to clean the panels.

Battery Care: Charge lithium-ion batteries regularly and avoid extreme temperatures to prolong their lifespan.

Solar Generators as a Backup Power Source

In addition to your dedicated solar-powered charging system, consider using a solar generator as a backup. Solar generators combine panels, batteries, and an inverter into a portable unit for powering tools, lights, and other appliances.

Benefits of a Solar Generator

- **Portability**: Solar generators are portable, making them ideal for remote off-grid projects where a flexible power source is needed.
- **Versatility**: They can power a variety of devices, from power tools to electronic gadgets, making them useful in many off-grid scenarios.

Choosing the Right Solar Generator

When choosing a solar generator, consider its wattage output and battery capacity.

- **Wattage Output**: Ensure the generator can handle the wattage of your tools. For example, if your tools require 800W, choose a generator with at least 1000W output to allow for peak use.
- **Battery Capacity**: Select a generator with a battery large enough to store energy for multiple tool charges, especially if you plan to work through periods without sunlight.

Solar-powered power tools offer a sustainable, efficient solution for off-grid living. By selecting the right tools, setting up a solar charging system, and using your tools effectively, you can maintain the convenience of modern power tools without relying on the grid. Proper planning and maintenance will enable you to complete a wide range of projects while remaining energy independent.

Chapter 3: Building a Solar-Powered Workshop

Creating a fully functional off-grid workshop powered by solar energy allows you to complete projects, repairs, and build items essential for self-sufficient living. A solar-powered workshop can support a variety of power tools and provide lighting, all without relying on grid electricity. This chapter will guide you through designing and constructing a solar-powered workshop, from selecting the right location to planning the solar setup that will provide enough power for your daily tasks.

Planning Your Solar-Powered Workshop
Building a solar-powered workshop starts with careful planning. Consider factors such as the location, size, solar power needs, and intended use of the space. The goal is to create an efficient, well-lit workspace where you can reliably use power tools while maintaining energy independence.

Choosing the Right Location
The location of your workshop is crucial for both its functionality and solar power efficiency.
- **Sunlight Exposure**: Choose a location with maximum sunlight exposure, especially during peak sunlight hours. South-facing locations (in the northern hemisphere) or north-facing (in the southern hemisphere) ensure optimal solar energy collection.
- **Proximity to Work Areas**: Position the workshop close to where you'll need access to tools or repairs, such as near your homestead, garden, or other outbuildings. This minimizes the need to transport materials long distances.
- **Ventilation and Insulation**: Good ventilation helps keep the workshop cool during hot summer days when solar energy is abundant. Consider insulating the building if you're working during colder months to conserve heat and reduce energy needs for heating.

Designing the Layout
The layout of your workshop should be practical, providing enough space for both power tools and hand tools, while ensuring a comfortable and efficient workflow.
- **Workbenches and Tool Storage**: Organize the workshop with sturdy workbenches for assembly and repair tasks. Install shelving or pegboards for easy access to hand tools and frequently used items.
- **Power Tool Stations**: Designate specific areas for power tools such as saws, drills, sanders, and grinders. Make sure these stations are placed near electrical outlets for easy charging and use of tools.
- **Lighting**: Include overhead LED lighting for bright, energy-efficient illumination during evening or cloudy day projects.

Solar Power System Requirements for the Workshop
The power demands of a workshop depend on the number of tools you plan to use, their wattage, and how often you'll need to run them. You'll need a well-sized solar system that provides enough electricity to run your workshop efficiently.

Estimating Power Consumption
Begin by calculating the total energy requirements of your workshop, based on the tools you'll use and how frequently they will be running.
- **Tool Wattage**: Each power tool has a specific wattage rating that determines its energy consumption. For example, a power drill might use 500W, while a table saw could use 1,500W or more. Multiply the wattage by the hours you plan to use each tool to estimate daily energy consumption.
- **Lighting and Accessories**: Don't forget to account for lighting, chargers, and other accessories such as air compressors or battery backups. Energy-efficient LED lighting typically uses minimal power but must be factored into your overall system capacity.

Selecting Solar Panels
Once you've estimated your power consumption, choose solar panels with enough capacity to meet the energy needs of your workshop.
- **Panel Output**: Aim for a solar panel array that can generate enough electricity to handle your estimated daily power consumption. For example, if your tools and lighting require 3,000W of power per day, you'll need solar panels with at least 1kW-3kW of capacity, depending on your local sunlight hours.

- **Monocrystalline vs. Polycrystalline**: Monocrystalline solar panels are more efficient and produce more energy per square foot, making them ideal if you have limited roof space. Polycrystalline panels are slightly less efficient but often more affordable.

Battery Storage

To ensure your workshop remains operational even on cloudy days or during times when solar generation is low, you'll need a battery storage system to store excess energy.

- **Battery Capacity**: Choose deep-cycle batteries with enough capacity to store at least a day's worth of energy usage. For a workshop that uses 3kWh per day, you'll want batteries capable of storing at least 3kWh to 6kWh to account for overcast days or increased demand.
- **Lithium-Ion vs. Lead-Acid Batteries**: Lithium-ion batteries are lighter, more efficient, and have a longer lifespan than lead-acid batteries, making them ideal for a solar-powered workshop. However, lead-acid batteries are less expensive and can still be a viable option if budget is a concern.

Charge Controllers and Inverters

To manage the energy flow from the solar panels to your workshop, you'll need both a charge controller and an inverter.

- **Charge Controller**: An MPPT (Maximum Power Point Tracking) charge controller is recommended for efficiently converting solar energy into usable power for your battery bank. It ensures that your batteries are charged safely and maximizes the efficiency of your solar panels.
- **Inverter**: If your tools run on AC power, you'll need an inverter to convert the DC energy stored in your batteries to AC power. Choose an inverter with enough wattage capacity to handle the simultaneous use of your most power-hungry tools.

Building and Installing the Solar System

With the components selected, the next step is to install the solar power system that will supply electricity to your workshop. This section covers the installation of solar panels, battery storage, and the wiring required to power your tools and lighting.

Mounting the Solar Panels

The solar panels should be installed in an area that receives maximum sunlight exposure, either on the roof of the workshop or mounted on a nearby stand.

- **Roof-Mounted Panels**: If your workshop's roof has sufficient space and is angled toward the sun, mounting the panels directly on the roof is a convenient option. Ensure the roof can support the weight of the panels and that they are angled to capture the most sunlight throughout the day.
- **Ground-Mounted Panels**: If the roof is not ideal for solar panels, consider ground-mounted panels. These panels can be placed on a fixed or adjustable stand that allows you to adjust the angle throughout the year for optimal solar energy capture.

Wiring the Solar System

Once the solar panels are installed, they need to be wired to the charge controller, battery bank, and inverter.

- **Wiring the Panels to the Charge Controller**: Connect the positive and negative terminals of the solar panels to the input terminals of the charge controller using appropriately gauged wiring. Ensure all connections are secure to prevent power loss.
- **Connecting the Battery Bank**: From the charge controller, wire the batteries to store the excess solar energy. Use a fuse or circuit breaker between the charge controller and the battery bank to protect against overloads.
- **Inverter Setup**: Wire the batteries to the inverter, which will convert the stored DC power into usable AC power for your tools. The inverter should then be wired into the workshop's electrical system, supplying power to outlets and lighting.

Installing Outlets and Lighting

With the inverter supplying AC power, you can now install electrical outlets and lighting in the workshop.

- **Outlets**: Install enough outlets around the workshop to accommodate your power tools. Make sure outlets are spaced conveniently near tool stations and workbenches.
- **Lighting**: Install LED lights in the workshop to provide bright, energy-efficient lighting. LEDs consume far less energy than incandescent bulbs, allowing you to illuminate your workspace without significantly draining your solar power system.

Optimizing and Maintaining Your Solar Workshop

To get the most out of your solar-powered workshop, it's essential to optimize your energy use and perform regular maintenance on the system. This ensures long-term reliability and efficiency.

Maximizing Solar Energy Production

To optimize your solar system's efficiency, ensure that the solar panels are always positioned to receive the maximum amount of sunlight.

- **Panel Cleaning**: Dust, dirt, and debris can reduce the efficiency of your solar panels. Regularly clean them with a soft brush or cloth to maintain their optimal performance.
- **Angle Adjustments**: Depending on your location, you may need to adjust the angle of the panels to capture the most sunlight throughout the year. Adjustable mounts make this process easier.

Monitoring Battery Performance

Keep an eye on the performance of your battery bank to ensure it's holding a charge properly.

- **Battery Maintenance**: For lead-acid batteries, check the water levels and top off with distilled water as needed. Lithium-ion batteries generally require less maintenance but should be monitored for charge capacity over time.
- **Battery Temperature**: Keep your battery bank in a temperature-controlled environment to prevent overheating in the summer or freezing in the winter, both of which can reduce battery lifespan.

Tool Use Efficiency

To maximize the efficiency of your power tools, consider the following:

- **Charge Tools in Batches**: Charge your tool batteries during peak sunlight hours when solar production is at its highest, ensuring you always have fully charged batteries on hand.
- **Use High-Efficiency Tools**: Opt for brushless motor tools, which are more energy-efficient and provide longer runtimes on a single charge.

Building a solar-powered workshop is a major step toward off-grid self-sufficiency. By creating a workspace that can support a wide range of power tools and other electrical needs, you ensure that you can tackle large projects, repairs, and maintenance with minimal reliance on external power sources. With the right solar system in place, your workshop will be a reliable, energy-efficient hub for all your off-grid projects. In the next chapter, we will explore specific off-grid projects you can complete using the tools in your solar-powered workshop.

Chapter 4: Maintaining and Sharpening Hand Tools

Hand tools are invaluable in off-grid living, offering reliability without the need for electricity or fuel. However, to ensure their effectiveness and longevity, proper maintenance and sharpening are essential. Well-maintained tools not only work more efficiently but also reduce the risk of injury and improve the quality of your work. This chapter will guide you through the best practices for cleaning, storing, and sharpening hand tools, ensuring they remain in peak condition for years to come.

Why Tool Maintenance is Critical for Off-Grid Living
In an off-grid setting, hand tools are a vital part of daily life, whether you are building, repairing, or working in the garden. Without regular maintenance, tools can degrade quickly due to rust, wear, and dullness. Maintaining and sharpening your tools ensures they remain reliable and effective, minimizing downtime and the need for replacements.

Benefits of Proper Tool Maintenance
- **Longevity**: Proper care significantly extends the lifespan of your tools, reducing the need for replacements in an off-grid scenario where access to new tools may be limited.
- **Efficiency**: A well-maintained, sharp tool requires less effort to use, making tasks easier and quicker.
- **Safety**: Dull or damaged tools are more dangerous, as they require more force to use and are prone to slipping or breaking, potentially causing injury.

Common Issues Caused by Poor Maintenance
- **Rust and Corrosion**: Rust can weaken the tool's structure, making it more prone to breaking. It also reduces the effectiveness of blades and cutting edges.
- **Dullness**: A dull blade or edge requires significantly more effort to use and can result in uneven or damaged work.
- **Loose Handles or Parts**: Wooden handles can crack or loosen over time, causing tools to be unsafe or uncomfortable to use.

Cleaning and Maintaining Hand Tools
Regular cleaning and maintenance are the foundation of keeping your hand tools in top condition. Dirt, moisture, and grime can cause rust and wear, so it's important to clean tools after each use and store them properly.

Cleaning Tools After Use
After each use, clean your tools to remove dirt, debris, and moisture. This prevents rust from forming and keeps moving parts in good working order.
- **Wipe Down Metal Surfaces**: Use a dry cloth to wipe down the metal parts of tools to remove moisture and debris. For tools exposed to sap or stubborn dirt, use a small amount of mineral spirits on a cloth to clean the surface.
- **Scrub Tough Grime**: For tools with heavy buildup, use a wire brush or steel wool to scrub away dirt, rust, or grime. Be careful not to damage the tool's surface, especially on cutting edges.

Oiling and Protecting Metal Parts
Applying a light coat of oil to metal surfaces helps protect them from rust and corrosion. This is especially important for tools stored in humid or damp environments.
- **Use Linseed Oil for Wood Handles**: For tools with wooden handles, apply linseed oil to keep the wood from drying out and cracking. This helps preserve the handle's strength and comfort.
- **Apply Lubricating Oil**: For metal parts, use a light machine oil or a rust-preventive oil to coat the tool's surface. Rub the oil in with a cloth, making sure to cover all exposed metal areas.

Storing Tools Properly
Proper storage prevents tools from being exposed to moisture, dirt, or temperature extremes, all of which can damage them over time.
- **Tool Racks or Pegboards**: Store tools on a tool rack or pegboard to keep them off the ground and in an organized manner. Hanging tools allows air to circulate and prevents moisture buildup.
- **Toolboxes**: For smaller tools, a toolbox with individual compartments helps keep everything organized and protected. Make sure the toolbox is stored in a dry, sheltered location.

- **Dry, Ventilated Storage Area**: Store your tools in a dry, well-ventilated space to prevent rust and deterioration, especially for metal tools. Avoid storing tools on concrete floors, as they can attract moisture.

Sharpening Hand Tools

Sharp tools are essential for efficient and safe work. Whether it's a saw, chisel, axe, or knife, sharpening your tools regularly ensures they perform at their best. This section covers the tools and techniques needed to keep your hand tools sharp and ready for use.

Tools for Sharpening

To sharpen your hand tools effectively, you'll need a few essential sharpening tools:

- **Sharpening Stones**: These are used to sharpen blades and edges. Oil stones, water stones, and diamond stones are the most common types.
- **Files**: Flat files and round files are used to sharpen saw blades, axes, and other tools with large cutting edges.
- **Honing Guides**: These guides help maintain the correct angle when sharpening chisels, plane blades, and other precision tools.
- **Sharpening Jigs**: Jigs hold tools securely at the correct angle while you sharpen them, ensuring consistent results.
- **Leather Strop**: A leather strop is used for final honing and polishing of blades to remove burrs and create a razor-sharp edge.

Sharpening Techniques

Different types of tools require different sharpening techniques. The key is to maintain the correct sharpening angle for each tool to ensure optimal performance.

- **Chisels and Planes**: Use a sharpening stone with a honing guide to maintain a consistent bevel angle (typically 25 to 30 degrees). Start with a coarse grit to remove nicks and dullness, then move to finer grits to polish the edge.
  - **Tip**: Finish with a leather strop to remove any remaining burrs and achieve a razor-sharp edge.
- **Saws**: Use a flat file to sharpen saw teeth. For crosscut saws, file each tooth at an angle to create a sharp cutting edge. For rip saws, file the teeth straight across. A saw set tool may be needed to adjust the angle of the teeth.
- **Axes and Hatchets**: Sharpen an axe using a file or sharpening stone. Hold the tool securely and file or stone the edge in smooth, even strokes, maintaining the original bevel angle (typically around 20 to 25 degrees).
- **Knives**: Sharpen knives using a sharpening stone, starting with a coarse grit and finishing with a fine grit. Maintain a sharpening angle of 20 degrees for general-purpose knives and a slightly lower angle for finer blades. Use a leather strop to finish and polish the edge.

Frequency of Sharpening

How often you need to sharpen your tools depends on their use. Frequent use on hard materials dulls blades more quickly, while softer tasks may allow for longer intervals between sharpening.

- **Daily Use Tools**: Tools used daily, such as chisels, knives, or saws, should be sharpened regularly—ideally after every few uses or when you notice a drop in performance.
- **Heavy-Duty Tools**: Tools like axes, which are used for chopping wood or clearing brush, should be sharpened after every few uses or whenever the blade begins to dull.
- **Fine Precision Tools**: Tools like planes and fine carving tools should be sharpened before each use to ensure a clean, smooth cut.

Repairing Damaged Tools

Over time, even well-maintained tools can develop cracks, chips, or broken handles. Knowing how to repair these issues extends the life of your tools and ensures they continue to perform reliably.

Replacing Tool Handles

Wooden handles on hammers, axes, and other tools can crack or break from wear. Replacing a handle is a straightforward process that restores the tool to full functionality.

Step 1: Remove the broken handle by cutting it off near the tool head. Use a punch or hammer to drive out the remaining wood from the tool's eye.

Step 2: Insert the new handle into the tool head, making sure it fits snugly.

Step 3: Secure the handle with wedges or epoxy to ensure it doesn't loosen during use.

Writing this book has been an incredible adventure for me, and it's my deepest wish that the pages you've read have sparked new ideas, inspired you to take action, and empowered you with the knowledge to thrive off the grid.

At this point, you should have discovered some powerful tools and strategies for living more independently. Now it's the time for you to have full access to your free bonuses.

🔥 HERE IS YOU FREE GIFT! 🔥
👇 SCAN THE QR CODE 👇

Conclusion

Congratulations on completing "No Grid Survival Projects Bible – 22 in 1"! I hope you have found this book to be a valuable resource in your journey towards self-sufficiency and off-grid security.

Throughout these pages, you have explored a vast world of DIY projects and innovative ideas, all designed to help you live independently and securely, even in times of uncertainty. You have learned how to harness alternative energies, ensure food security, protect your home, and secure a reliable water supply. You have acquired essential survival skills and learned how to manage emergency situations.

But remember, your journey towards self-sufficiency doesn't end here. Use what you have learned as a foundation for further exploration and experimentation. Continue to enhance your skills, adapting and customizing projects to fit your specific needs. Share your knowledge with others and inspire those who seek to embrace a more sustainable and resilient lifestyle.

Always remember that self-sufficiency is not just about survival, but about freedom and self-determination. With the knowledge and skills you have acquired, you have the power to take control of your future and become a protagonist in your life.

As an independent author, I rely on the support of readers like you to continue creating content that makes a difference. If you've enjoyed the book and feel it's made an impact, I kindly ask you to share your thoughts in a review on Amazon. Your review not only helps me but also allows other readers to find this book and start their own journey toward off-grid living.

I'm honored to have shared this knowledge with you, and I look forward to continuing this adventure together. Prepare yourself for a world of endless possibilities and adventure. Remember, the power to live off the grid is in your hands.

Good luck and safe travels!

Sincerely,

Max Maverick

THANK YOU

Dear reader, this book has come to an end. I would take this opportunity to thank you for going through this pages together and making it this far.

I'd love to hear your thoughts on what you've read, what you've learned, and if you would recommend it!

IF YOU ENJOYED THE READ, PLEASE FEEL FREE TO LEAVE YOUR PRECIOUS REVIEW ON THE AMAZON PAGE!

Doing this is **very simple** and will allow other readers like you to make the best choice. Consider including a video or photos to your review, making it even more vivid and informative!

THANKS IN ADVANCE FOR YOUR VALUABLE FEEDBACK - As a self-publisher it will allow me to improve my writing and reach more and more people!

Max Maverick

Made in the USA
Middletown, DE
30 January 2025